The
HIDDEN INNS
of the
SOUTH OF ENGLAND

including
Buckinghamshire, Berkshire, Oxfordshire, Wiltshire, Hampshire and the Isle of Wight

Edited by
Barbara Vesey

© Travel Publishing Ltd.

Published by:
Travel Publishing Ltd
7a Apollo House, Calleva Park
Aldermaston, Berks, RG7 8TN
ISBN 1-902-00756-5
© Travel Publishing Ltd

First Published: *2000*

Regional Titles in the Hidden Inns Series:

West Country	Southeast England
South of England	Wales

Regional Titles in the Hidden Places Series:

Cambridgeshire & Lincolnshire	Channel Islands
Cheshire	Chilterns
Cornwall	Derbyshire
Devon	Dorset, Hants & Isle of Wight
Essex	Gloucestershire & Wiltshire
Heart of England	Hereford, Worcs & Shropshire
Highlands & Islands	Kent
Lake District & Cumbria	Lancashire
Norfolk	Northeast Yorkshire
Northumberland & Durham	North Wales
Nottinghamshire	Potteries
Somerset	South Wales
Suffolk	Surrey
Sussex	Thames Valley
Warwickshire & W Midlands	Yorkshire

National Titles in the Hidden Places Series:

England	Ireland
Scotland	Wales

Printing by: Ashford Colour Press, Gosport
Maps by: © MAPS IN MINUTES ™ (2000)
Line Drawings: Sarah Bird
Editor: Barbara Vesey
Cover Design: Lines & Words, Aldermaston
Cover Photographs: The Lampet Arms, Tadmarton, Oxon; George and Dragon, Townsend, Hampshire; The Butchers Arms, Fringford, Oxon

FOREWORD

The *Hidden Inns* series originates from the enthusiastic suggestions of readers of the popular *Hidden Places* guides. They want to be directed to traditional inns "off the beaten track" with atmosphere and character which are so much a part of our British heritage. But they also want information on the many places of interest and activities to be found in the vicinity of the inn.

The inns or pubs reviewed in the *Hidden Inns* may have been coaching inns but have invariably been a part of the history of the village or town in which they are located. All the inns included in this guide serve food and drink and many offer the visitor overnight accommodation. A full page is devoted to each inn which contains a line drawing of the inn, full name, address and telephone number, directions on how to get there, a full description of the inn and its facilities and a wide range of useful information such as opening hours, food served, accommodation provided, credit cards taken and details of entertainment. *Hidden Inns* guides however are not simply pub guides. They provide the reader with helpful information on the many places of interest to visit and activities to pursue in the area in which the inn is based. This ensures that your visit to the area will not only allow you to enjoy the atmosphere of the inn but also to take in the beautiful countryside which surrounds it.

The *Hidden Inns* guides have been expertly designed for ease of use. *The Hidden Inns of the South of England* is divided into 8 regionally based chapters, each of which is laid out in the same way. To identify your preferred geographical region refer to the contents page overleaf. To find a pub or inn simply use the index and locator map at the beginning of each chapter which refers you, via a page number reference, to a full page dedicated to the specific establishment. To find a place of interest again use the index and locator map found at the beginning of each chapter which will guide you to a descriptive summary of the area followed by details of each place of interest.

We do hope that you will get plenty of enjoyment from visiting the inns and places of interest contained in this guide. We are always interested in what our readers think of the inns or places covered (or not covered) in our guides so please do not hesitate to write to us. This is a vital way of helping us ensure that we maintain a high standard of entry and that we are providing the right sort of information for our readers. Finally if you are planning to visit any other corner of the British Isles we would like to refer you to the list of Hidden Inns and Hidden Places guides to be found at the rear of the book.

Travel Publishing

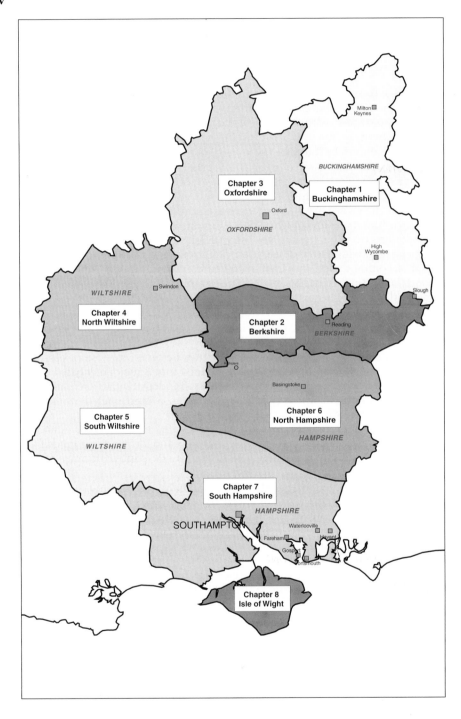

CONTENTS

1 Buckinghamshire

PLACES OF INTEREST:

PUBS AND INNS:

The Hidden Inns of the South of England

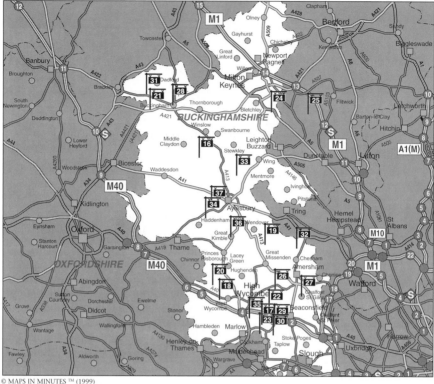

© MAPS IN MINUTES ™ (1999)

Please note all cross references refer to page numbers

Buckinghamshire

South Buckinghamshire, with the River Thames as its southern county border, lies almost entirely within the Chiltern Hills. This chalk range, most of which is classed as an Area of Outstanding Natural Beauty, is particularly noted for its beech woods and Burnham Beeches, with its abundance of deer and birdlife, is a fine example. However, the conservation of this beautiful area of wood and heathland as a place for wildlife and a recreation area for city residents, is an interesting story which has many parallels with today's struggle to keep the countryside away from the bulldozers.

In this charming and delightful area there are several places of interest. Many people have found inspiration amongst the rolling Chiltern range. Chalfont St Giles was the temporary home of the poet John Milton whilst he was escaping the plague in 17th century London. Other famous residents of this attractive region include Benjamin Disraeli and Sir Francis Dashwood, the infamous founder of the Hell Fire Club.

The region centred around Aylesbury, the county town since the 18th century and an ancient market place serving the Vale of Aylesbury, is still largely unspoilt vale, which runs from the Chilterns in the south to Buckingham in the north. This region offers visitors miles of secluded country walks and ridges. An attractive and rural landscape the area is littered with bustling market towns and charming villages and it has also inspired such writers as Shakespeare and Roald Dahl. This is also an area for those interested in architecture. Now the home of the University of Natural Law, Mentmore Towers, the first of the Rothschild mansions, was the backdrop, in the last century, of glittering society parties, while Waddesdon Manor, another Rothschild mansion, is a magnificent building in the style of a French chateau. This area of Buckinghamshire is also home to several windmills including Pitstone and Ford End.

The region centred around the county's ancient county town of Buckingham, which was granted its status in Saxon times though it has now relinquished this role, is perhaps the county's most undiscovered. Not crossed by any of the country's major roads, it has long been a chiefly rural district and there is a wealth of attractive villages and old market towns to find. Naturally, the rich have found this an excellent place in which to settle and there are many fine houses including Ascott House in Wing, Stowe (now a school, with magnificent gardens which are open to the public) and Winslow Hall, designed by Sir Christopher Wren. However, perhaps the most famous house in the area, but not necessarily the grandest, is Claydon House, the home of the Verney family and where Florence Nightingale was a frequent visitor, particularly in the last years of her life. This area of Buckinghamshire also boasts two very notable churches: Wing's church is a fine example of a Saxon building, while at Stewkley is, probably, the country's finest Norman structure.

The northern region of Buckinghamshire is dominated by the new town of Milton Keynes. Developed in the 1960s when there was a general move to provide housing away from the ever sprawling mass of London, though the town itself is new there are numerous ancient villages that are close by. This too is the area in which the poet William Cowper lived. A visit to his museum at Olney tells the story of his life and times. This region is also home to a 20th century place of interest: Bletchley Park, the top secret codebreaking station of the Second World War, where men and women worked around the clock to decipher the enemy's messages to help bring an earlier end to the war.

4

PLACES OF INTEREST

AYLESBURY

Found in the heart of Buckinghamshire and the county town since the 18th century, this ancient town is sheltered by the Chiltern Hills and also gives its name to the broad vale over which it looks. A rich pastureland, where cows where fattened for the tables of London and the famous Aylesbury ducks were raised, this town has held a market here since the 13th century. Found in the centre of the old part of Aylesbury, the market square has, on one side, an 18th-century County Hall where the Great Train Robbers were tried.

Much of the character of Aylesbury has been lost in a wave of post war planning and development but parts of the old town, particularly around the market square are now a conservation area. Here, are sleepy lanes and cottages, the parish Church of St Mary that was almost completely rebuilt in the 19th century and the King's Head inn where Henry VIII is said to have wooed Anne Boleyn. There are also three large monuments here: to Lord Chesham; to Benjamin Disraeli; and to John Hampden. Hampden, who lived nearby, was famous for making a stand against Charles I in 1635 when he refused to pay Ship Money believing that the tax would go straight into the King's pocket and not to the navy. During the Civil War, the town a base for both Cromwell and the King, depending on how well the battle was progressing, and nearby, at Holman's Bridge, saw a bitter blow for the Royalist cause when Prince Rupert of the Rhine suffered a crushing defeat.

Housed in a splendid Georgian building is the **County Museum**, the ideal place to find out more about the history of the town and the surroundings. There is also an excellent section on Louis XVIII of France who lived nearby, at Hartwell House, during his years of exile, and those who are familiar with such children's stories as Charlie and the Chocolate Factory will enjoy the display on the life and works of Roald Dahl who lived and wrote in the Vale of Aylesbury.

BEACONSFIELD

This is very much a town in two parts: the old town, dating back to medieval times and, to the north, the new town which grew up following the construction of the Metropolitan line into central London and consisting chiefly of between the wars housing.

The old town, home to the **Church of St Mary and All Saints** which is considered by many to be one of the finest in the Chilterns, is best known for its literary connections. The poet Edmund Waller, born in the village of Coleshill, just to the north, was a resident. After getting involved in a Royalist plot in 1643, he was banished from Parliament and spent some time in exile before returning to Beaconsfield to concentrate on writing. Somewhat more wise than in his youth, Waller took care to write poems in favour of Cromwell and, after his restoration to the throne, the King. Beaconsfield was also the home of GK Chesterton, author of the popular Father Brown crime stories, poet Robert Frost and the much loved children's author Enid Blyton.

For a unique step back in time to the 1930s, visitors should seek out the charm of Bekonscot, a rural model village. The oldest model village in the world, **Bekonscot** was begun in the 1920s by Roland Callingham, a London accountant, who started by building models in his garden. As the number of buildings and models grew, Callingham purchased more land and, with the aid of a friend from Ascot who added a model railway, created the village seen today. When the village first opened, people started throwing coins into bucket for charity and, even today, all surplus profits go to charity.

BLETCHLEY

Now more a suburb of Milton Keynes, Bletchley is famous for **Bletchley Park**, the Victorian mansion which housed the wartime codebreakers. During World War II, 12,000 men and women worked here and in outstations, unable to tell family and friends what they were employed doing, but their work is thought have helped end the war two years early and to have saved countless lives. The park is now opened to the public where, in the **Cryptology Museum**, the famous and now rebuilt Colossus, the world's first electronic valve computer which helped to break Hitler's messages to his generals, can be seen.

5

Bletchley Park

town's old gaol, is another fine building which dates from the mid 18th century though it has been extensively restored. Today it houses the **Old Gaol Museum**, which not only reflects the building's

However, though this once thriving country town is now all but merged with its larger neighbour, it still retains a distinctive air. The original village here dates back to Roman times and it was first recorded as a town in 1108.

BUCKINGHAM

This pleasant town, the centre of which is contained in a loop of the River Ouse, dates back to Saxon times and was once granted a charter by Alfred the Great. Although it became the county town in AD 888, when King Alfred divided the shires, from an early date many of the functions of a county town were performed by the more centrally located Aylesbury. According to the Saxon Chronicle, it was Edward the Elder who fortified the town in AD 918 when he brought his army here during his advance on the Danish invaders. The stronghold he built, on which later stood a Norman castle, is now the site of the parish Church of St Peter and St Paul.

At the time of the Domesday Survey, the manor of Buckingham was held by Walter Gifford, later created the Duke of Buckinghamshire by William the Conqueror, and it remained with the same family until the time of Henry VIII. A prosperous medieval market town there have been several notable visitors to Buckingham including Catherine of Aragon, who stayed at Castle House in 1514, Edward VI, who founded the Latin School, and Elizabeth I, who dined at the manor house whilst on a journey to Bicester.

Unfortunately few buildings remain from those times as, in 1725, there was a disastrous fire which destroyed much of the town. Many buildings were replaced and, particularly in Castle Street, there are some fine Georgian houses of which Castle House (which is actually in West Street) is the best example. The

Old Gaol Museum, Buckingham

history but also has displays on the town's past and the county's military exploits.

One building that did survive the devastating fire in the 18th century is the **Buckingham Chantry Chapel**. Now owned by the National Trust, the chapel was constructed in 1475 on the site of a Norman building whose doorway has been retained. Well worth a visit, the chapel was restored by George Gilbert Scott in 1875.

A much more recent addition to this delightful country market town is the **University of Buckingham** which was granted its charter in 1983. Unlike other British universities this institution does not receive any direct funding from the Government and the academic year is divided into four, rather than the usual three, terms.

CHALFONT ST GILES

This excellent example of a typical English village dates from Roman times and there was a reference to Stonewells Farm in the Domesday Book. Of the various ancient buildings of interest here there is an Elizabethan mansion, The Vache, that was the home of friends of Captain Cook and, in the grounds, is a monument to the famous seafarer. Madame Tussaud, famous

6

for her fascinating exhibitions in London, started her waxworks here in the village.

However, by far the most famous building in Chalfont St Giles, with an equally famous resident, is **Milton's Cottage**. A grade I listed building, dating from the 16th century, John Milton moved to this cottage, found for him by fellow Quaker and former pupil Thomas Ellwood, in 1665 to escape the plague in London. Though the blind poet moved back to London in 1666, Milton wrote *Paradise Lost* and began work on its sequel, *Paradise Regained*, whilst taking refuge in the village. The only house lived in by the poet to have survived, the cottage and its garden have been preserved as they were at the time Milton was resident. The building is now home to a museum which includes collections of important first editions of Milton's works and a portrait of the poet by Sir Godfrey Kneller.

Another fascinating and unusual place to visit in the village is the **Chiltern Open Air Museum** which rescues buildings of historic or architectural importance from across the Chilterns region and re-erects them on its 45 acre site. Though offers of buildings come from many sources, the museum will only accept one that is to be demolished. Once the decision to move a building has been taken the painstaking task of dismantling the structure, piece by piece, is undertaken, followed, finally, by its reconstruction at the museum site. The buildings rescued by the museum are then used to house and display artefacts and implements that are appropriate to the building's original use and history. Also on the museum site are a series of fields farmed using medieval methods where, amongst the historic crops, organic woad is grow from which indigo dye is extracted for use in dyeing demonstrations.

CHALFONT ST PETER

Now a commuter town, Chalfont St Peter dates back to the 7th century and, as its name means 'the spring where the calves come to drink', there is a long history here of raising cattle in the surrounding lush meadows. First mentioned in 1133, the parish Church of St Peter was all but destroyed when its steeple collapsed in 1708. The building seen today dates from that time as it was rebuilt immediately after the disaster.

Housed in a barn at Skippings Farm is the **Hawk and Owl Trust's National Education and Exhibition Centre**. Dedicated to conserving wild birds of prey in their natural habitats, the Trust concerns itself with practical research, creative conservation and imaginative educational programmes.

CHENIES

This picturesque village, with a pretty green surrounded by an old school, a chapel and a 15th-century parish church, is also home to **Chenies Manor**, a fascinating 15th-century manor house. Originally the home of the Earls (later Dukes) of Bedford, before they moved to Woburn, this attractive buildings has stepped gables and elaborately patterned high brick chimneys. Built by the architect who enlarged Hampton Court for Henry VIII, the house has played host not only to the king but also his daughter Elizabeth I. Naturally, there is a ghost here, that of Henry VIII, whose footsteps can be heard as he drags his ulcerated leg around the manor house in an attempt to catch Catherine Howard in the act of adultery with one of his entourage.

Whilst the house has much to offer, not just from the exterior but also inside where there are tapestries, furniture and a collection of antique dolls, the gardens should not be overlooked. Among the delights are a Tudor style sunken garden and a physick garden with a variety of herbs that were used for both medicinal and culinary purposes.

CHESHAM

This pleasant town, situated among wooded hills, has traditionally been a rival to Amersham and, in 1454, the Bishop of Lincoln allowed the parishioners here to process around their Church of St Mary at Whitsun to avoid the fighting associated with their processions at St Mary's Church in Amersham. Standing on a prehistoric holy site, as indicated by the great pudding stone foundations, the parish Church of St Mary was begun in the mid 12th century and has a sanctuary bell that was cast in 1458.

A successful combination of a commuter town, industrial centre and country community, Chesham's growth from a sleepy market town was due to its Metropolitan underground railway link with central London. The Metropolitan Railway Company began operating the first urban underground railway in the world in 1863, running trains from Paddington to Farringdon Street, but was never content with being just an urban or suburban railway. So the company pursued its main line ambitions through a policy of acquiring other lines to link into its system as well as building its own. At its high point the company ran trains as far into Buckinghamshire as Aylesbury and Quainton Road. Today, Chesham still retains its Metropolitan links with central London.

Whilst the town has seen itself expand at the hands of the railway, it has also had some interesting inhabitants. Chesham was the birthplace of Arthur Liberty, the son of a haberdasher and draper, who went on to found the world famous Liberty's department store in London's Regent Street in 1875. Another resident was Roger Crabbe who, having suffered head injuries during the Civil War, was sentenced to death by Cromwell. After receiving a pardon, Crabbe opened a hat shop in the town where he is reputed to have worn sack-cloth, eaten turnip tops and given his income to the poor. Not surprisingly, Crabbe was used by Lewis Carroll as the model for the Mad Hatter in *Alice in Wonderland*.

CHICHELEY

This attractive village is home of **Chicheley Hall**, a beautiful baroque house that was built in the early 18th century for Sir John Chester and which remains today one of the finest such houses in the country. However, over the years the hall's history has been somewhat uncertain and, whilst it has been used by the military and as a school, in 1952 it was bought by the 2nd Earl Beatty who restored it to its former glory.

The Earl's father, the 1st Earl, was a particularly courageous naval commander and, as well as receiving the DSO at the age of just 25, he was also a commander in the decisive battle of Jutland in 1916. Mementoes of the 1st Earl's illustrious career at sea can be seen in the study when the hall is occasionally open to the public.

DADFORD

Just to the south of the village lies **Stowe School**, a leading public school which occupies an 18th-century mansion that was once the home of the Dukes of Buckingham. Worked upon by two wealthy owners who both had a

great sense of vision, the magnificent mansion house, which was finally completed in 1774, is open to the public during school holidays.

Between 1715 and 1749, the owner, Viscount Cobham hired various well known landscape designers to lay out the fantastic gardens that can still be seen around the house. Taking over the house in 1750, Earl Temple, along with his nephew, expanded the grounds and today they

Stowe Landscape Gardens

remain one of the most original and finest landscape gardens in Europe. Worked on by the best designers of the day, the gardens at Stowe contain temples, alcoves and rotundas scattered around the landscape that were placed to evoke in the onlooker a romantic and poetic frame of mind.

It is one of the more intriguing quirks of fate that Lancelot Brown, always known as Capability Brown supposedly because he told his clients that their parks had capabilities, was head gardener at Stowe for 10 years. He arrived here in 1741 and began to work out his own style, a more natural style of landscape gardening which was to take over where gardens like the ones at Stowe left off. Brown's concept was to ensure that the landscape element of the garden, the tree planting, lakes and lawns, should look as natural as possible. **Stowe Landscape Gardens** are now in the hands of the National Trust and are open to the public.

GAYHURST

Built during the reign of Elizabeth I, **Gayhurst House** was given to Sir Francis Drake in recognition of his circumnavigation of the world though the building seen today was not the one

The Hidden Inns of the South of England

8

that Drake would have lived in. It was later occupied by Sir Everard Digby, one of the conspirators behind the Gunpowder Plot of 1605. By the 18th century, the house was the home of the Wrighte family and William Cowper was a frequent visitor.

The house can be seen from the village Church which is a perfect Georgian building that was begun in 1728. Though it has retained many of its original fittings and furnishings, the real eye-catcher inside is a monument to Sir Nathan Wrighte, in his robes of Lord Keeper of the Privy Seal, and his son George which was erected in 1728.

GREAT KIMBLE

Though the village is home to a church with an interesting series of 14th-century wall paintings, its real claim to fame is the nearby 16th-century mansion, **Chequers**, the country residence of the British Prime Minister. Originally built by William Hawtrey in 1565, but much altered and enlarged in the 18th and 19th centuries, the house was restored to its original form by Arthur Lee in 1912. Later, in 1920, as Lord Lee of Fareham, he gave the house and estate to the nation to be used as the prime minister's country home.

The first Prime Minister to make use of Chequers was Lloyd George and many who have known the house have since moved, or stayed, in the area: Ramsay MacDonald's daughter lived at nearby Speen; Harold Wilson bought a house in Great Missenden; and Nye Bevan owned a farm in the Chilterns.

GREAT LINFORD

Situated on the banks of the Grand Union Canal, this village , which is now more a suburb of Milton Keynes, has a 13th-century church, a

Stone Circle, Great Linford

17th-century manor house, and a **Stone Circle**, one of only a few such prehistoric monuments in the county. Despite the encroachment of its much larger neighbour, the village has retained a distinctive air that is all its own.

The central block of the present manor house was built in 1678 by Sir William Pritchard, Lord Mayor of London. As well as making Great Linford his country seat, Pritchard also provided a boys' school and almshouses for six unmarried poor of the parish. The manor house was extended in the 18th century by the Uthwatt family, relatives of the Lord Mayor, and they used various tricks to give an impressive and elegant appearance to the building. The Grand Union Canal, constructed in the mid 19th century, cuts through the estate. Today, the grounds of the manor house are a public park.

GREAT MISSENDEN

Home to the only other court house in the Chiltern Hundreds (the other is at Long Crendon), Great Missenden's **Old Court House** dates from the early 1400s. Also in this attractive village is an attractive flint and stone church and Missenden Abbey, which was founded in 1133 by the Augustinian order. A daughter community of St Nicholas's Abbey in Normandy, the abbey has long since gone and in its place stands a fashionable Gothic mansion dating from 1810.

The village too has had its fair share of famous visitors and amongst them is Robert Louis Stevenson, the author of *Treasure Island* and the anti-slavery campaigner, William Wilberforce. However, Great Missenden is probably best known as being the home of the late Roald Dahl, the internationally recognised author of, particularly, children's books. He lived here for 30 years and the gardens of his home are open the public once a year.

HADDENHAM

This large village, with its 12th-century church, is full of character and charm and is famous for having been a breeding place for the original Aylesbury ducks. It was also once known as Silly Haddenham because, as local hearsay has it, the villagers thatched the village pond to protect the ducks from the rain.

Here too can be found St Tiggywinkles, the world's leading wildlife hospital, and its visitor centre. Those coming here can not only walk through the ground but they also get a chance to meet the hospital's permanent residents. The visitor centre is open every day except Sundays from Easter to Christmas.

HAMBLEDEN

This much filmed village was given to the National Trust by the family of the bookseller WH Smith - who later became Viscount Hambleden. He lived close by at Greenlands, on the banks of the River Thames and is buried in the village churchyard. The unusually large **Church of St Mary**, known as the cathedral of the Chilterns, dates from the 14th century and, though it has been altered over the years, its size and beauty still dominates the area. Inside the building's 18th-century tower is a fascinating 16th-century panel which is believed to have been the bedhead of Cardinal Wolsey - it certainly bears the cardinal's hat and the Wolsey arms.

The village's other building of interest can be found by the River Thames and it is reached by a road that was first used by the Romans. **Hambleden Mill** certainly dates from the 14th century as it was first mentioned in 1338.

HIGH WYCOMBE

The largest town in Buckinghamshire, High Wycombe is traditionally known for the manufacture of chairs and, in particular, the famous Windsor design. It is still a centre of furniture manufacture today as well as being a pleasant town in which to live for those commuting to London.

Originally an old Chilterns gap market town, High Wycombe is still home to several old buildings of note. The **Little Market House**

Little Market House

was designed by Robert Adams in 1761 and is of a rather curious octagonal shape, while the 18th-century Guildhall is the annual venue for a traditional ceremony showing a healthy scepticism for politicians when the mayor and councillors are publicly weighed - to see if they have become fat at the expense of the citizens.

Found in an 18th-century house, with a flint facade, the **Wycombe Local History and Chair Museum** has displays which give the visitor an excellent idea of the work and crafts of the local people over the years. There is, of course, a superb collection of chairs and other furniture here which are more suited to the houses of ordinary people rather than those of the wealthy. In the grounds of the museum is a medieval motte which would normally indicate that a castle once stood here but, in this case, the structure was probably little more than a wooden tower.

However, the oldest standing building in the town is All Saints' Church; a large, fine building dating from the 11th century. Enlarged in the 13th century, in the north chapel can be found a very classical memorial to the Earl of Shelbourne erected in 1754.

HUGHENDEN

This village is famous for being the home of the great Victorian Prime Minister Benjamin Disraeli, from 1847 to his death in 1881, and he is buried in the estate church. The son of a writer and literary critic, Isaac D'Israeli, who lived for a time in the village of Bradenham on the other side of High Wycombe, Disraeli was also a novelist. He bought **Hughenden Manor** shortly after the publication of his novel *Tancred*. Though not a wealthy man, Disraeli felt that a leading Conservative politician should have a stately home of his own and, in order to finance the purchase, his supporters lent him the money so that he could have this essential characteristic of an English gentleman.

The house seen today, which, along with the grounds, is now in the hands of the National Trust and open to the public, is a remodelled 18th-century house refaced with various coloured bricks. The interior is less controversial and is an excellent example of the Victorian Gothic style. Here can be found an interesting collection of memorabilia of Disraeli's life as well as his library and much of his furniture. A

10

great friend of Queen Victoria, she is said to have preferred Disraeli to the other great statesman of her reign, William Gladstone.

IVINGHOE

As the large village church would suggest, Ivinghoe was once a market town of some importance in the surrounding area. In this now quiet village can be found **Ford End Watermill**, a listed building that, though probably much older, was first recorded in 1767. The only working watermill, with its original machinery, left in Buckinghamshire, the farm in which it is set has also managed to retain the atmosphere of an 18th-century farm.

To the east lies **Ivinghoe Beacon**, owned by the National Trust, that is a wonderful viewpoint on the edge of the Chiltern Hills. The site of an Iron Age hill fort, the beacon was also the inspiration for Sir Walter Scott's Ivanhoe.

LACEY GREEN

Buckinghamshire seems to have more than its fair share of windmills and, here at Lacey Green, is another fine example, this time of a Smock Mill. Technologically more advanced than post mills, where the body of the mill which carries the sails and all the grinding machinery is mounted on an upright post which can turn through 360 degrees, with a smock mill only the cap carrying the sails rotates to met the wind. As a result the body of the mill, housing the milling machinery, can be bigger, heavier and stronger. Lacey Green's smock mill was first built in the mid 17th century but it was moved from Chesham to this site in 1821. The oldest smock mill in the country, it still retains its massive mid 17th-century wooden machinery.

This was also the village where the young poet Rupert Brooke used to spend his weekends in the company of his friends at the quaintly named local pub, the Pink and Lily. The son of a master at Rugby School and a student at Cambridge University, Brooke began writing poetry as a boy and, in the years before World War I he travelled widely. Whilst early on in the conflict, in which he fought, his poetry showed a boyish enthusiasm for patriotism, his later works were full of bitter disillusion. He died in 1915 whilst on his way to the attempted landings at the Dardenelles in Turkey.

Close to the village lies Speen farm and the Home of Rest for Horses. Run by a charitable organisation that was established in 1886 to care for horses, ponies and donkeys who had finished their working life, the most famous former resident of centre was Sefton, the cavalry horse that was so horribly injured in the Hyde Park bomb blast of the early 1980s.

MENTMORE

The village is home to the first of the Rothschild mansions, **Mentmore Towers**, which was built for Baron Meyer Amschel de Rothschild between 1852 and 1855. A splendid building in the Elizabethan style it was designed by Sir Joseph Paxton, the designer of Crystal Palace, and is a superb example of grandiose Victorian extravagance. However, the lavish decoration hides several technologically advanced details for those times, such as central heating, and, as might be expected from Paxton, there are large sheets of glass and a glass roof in the design.

In the late 19th century the house became the home of Lord Rosebery and the magnificent turreted building was the scene of many glittering parties and gatherings of the most wealthy and influential people in the country. However, in the 1970s the house was put up for auction and, whilst the furniture and works of art were sold to the four corners of the world, the building was bought by the Maharishi Mahesh Yogi and it is now the headquarters of his University of Natural Law. Mentmore Towers is occasionally open to the public.

MIDDLE CLAYDON

This village is home to **Claydon House**, an historic building that dates from the 17th century but has 19th century additions. The home of the Verney family and now owned by the National Trust, the house contains a number of state rooms with magnificent carved wood and plaster decorations. Particularly delightful are the Chinese rooms which reflect the 18th century enthusiasm for all things Oriental. However, what makes the house particularly interesting is its associations with Florence Nightingale.

Florence's sister married into the Verney family and the pioneer of modern hospital care spent long periods at the house, especially during her old age. Her bedroom in the house and

Claydon House

a museum of her life and experiences during the Crimean War can be seen here. Now that nursing has become one of the most respected professions, it is difficult to imagine the strength of character needed by a young Victorian woman of a good family to go abroad to train as a nurse, which Florence did in 1851. At that time nursing had a poor reputation and was thought to be a menial job done by women who had no other means of supporting themselves. Florence died in 1910 after a long career which embraced concerns of public health as well as the training of nurses and she was the first woman to be awarded the Order of Merit.

Milton Keynes

Most people's perception of this modern town is of a concrete jungle but the reality of Milton Keynes could not be more different. The development corporation that was charged, in 1967, with organising the new town has provided a place of tree-lined boulevards, uncongested roads, spacious surroundings, and acres of parkland. It is too, of course, a modern town, with new housing, high-tech industries, modern leisure facilities, and a large covered shopping centre. One of the town's most notable buildings is **Christ Church**, built in the style of Christopher Wren. The first purpose-built ecumenical city church in Britain it was opened in March 1992 by HM the Queen.

However, whilst Milton Keynes is certain a place of the late 20th century it has not altogether forgotten the rural past of the villages which are now incorporated into the suburbs of the town. The **Museum of Industry and**

Rural Life, with its large collection of industrial, domestic, and agricultural bygones, is devoted to the lives

11

of the people who lived in the area in the 200 years leading up to the creation of the new town. Meanwhile, exhibitions on art, crafts, local history, and social life can be seen at the **Exhibition Gallery**, next to the town's library.

Olney

This pretty town on the banks of the River Ouse is famous for its association with William Cowper, who came to the town to be under the ministry of the Rev. John Newton, curate of Olney. Newton was a reformed slave-trader as well as a fiery preacher However there is more here to discover than the rather sad life of the poet Cowper.

The earliest recorded evidence of the town dates back to a Saxon Charter of AD 979 although archaeological finds in the area have been dated at 1600 BC. The parish Church of St Peter and St Paul, where Newton was curate, is a spacious building dating from the mid 14th century and its spire rises some 185 feet to dominate the skyline of Olney.

For over 300 years, this was a centre of hand lace making using wooden or bone bobbins. At its most expensive, in the 1700s, only the well-to-do could afford the lace but the rise in machine made lace from Nottingham saw a sharp decline in Olney lace. A revival of the trade was tried by Harry Armstrong when, in 1928, he opened the Lace Factory but, although handmade lace is still produced locally, the factory only lasted until Armstrong's death in 1943.

The town's present day claim to fame is its annual Pancake Race held every Shrove Tuesday. Legend has it that the first 'race' was run in the 15th century when a local housewife heard the Shriving Service bell ringing and she ran to church complete with her frying pan and pancake. Today's re-enactment is open to any lady of Olney over 18 years and she must wear a skirt, an apron, and a scarf as well as carry a frying pan and pancake.

Nearby **Emberton Country Park**, found on the site of former gravel pits, is an ideal place to relax. Not only are there four lakes and a stretch of the River Ouse within the park's boundaries but facilities here include fishing, sailing, and nature trails.

12

The house in which Cowper lived from 1768 to 1786 is now the **Cowper and Newton Museum**, an interesting place that not only concentrates on Cowper's life and work but also has some exhibits and collections concerned with times in which he lived and the life of Olney. Each of the rooms of the large early 18th-century town house have been specially themed and there are numerous displays of Cowper's work, including the "Olney Hymns". Cowper wrote 67 of these and the remaining 281 were written by his friend Rev. John Newton whose most

Pitstone Windmill

William Cowper's Summer House

famous hymn is probably "Amazing Grace". William Cowper was also a keen gardener and the summer house, where he wrote many of his poems, can still be seen out in the rear garden where he also chose to experiment with plants that were new to 18th-century England.

Also at the Museum is the nationally important Lace Collection which reflects the fact that Olney was at the centre of the bobbin lace making for over 300 years. Other displays include the finds from local archaeological digs which have unearthed dinosaur bones, Roman coins, and medieval fishing weights, Civil War relics, and items particular to the shoe making industry which was another busy local trade in the 19th and early 20th century.

PITSTONE

Though the exact age of **Pitstone Windmill**, owned by the National Trust, is not known, it

is certainly one of the oldest post mills in Britain. The earliest documentary reference to its existence was made in 1624. It is open to the public on a limited basis. Also in the village is a **Farm Museum**, where all manner of farm and barn machinery, along with domestic bygones, are on display.

STEWKLEY

Renowned for being England's longest village, Stewkley is also home to one of the country's finest Norman churches. Dating from around 1150, the Church is a splendid example of Norman architecture and it is decorated with zigzag patterns, including a string course which runs all around the building. Easy to spot with its massive central tower, the tympanum over the west door is carved with dragons and surrounded by three layers of decorated arches.

STOKE POGES

It was in the churchyard in this surprisingly still rural village that Thomas Gray was inspired to write his famous *Elegy Written in a Country Churchyard*. Often visiting Stoke Poges to see his mother who was staying with her sister in a large late Georgian house that was built for the grandson of the famous Quaker, William Penn, Gray was obviously taken with the village and its surroundings. He lies buried, with his mother in the church, and, to the east, is the **Gray Monument**, designed by James Wyatt and erected in 1799.

The Church of St Giles itself is very handsome and dates from the 13th century but perhaps its most interesting feature is the unusual medieval bicycle depicted in one of the stained glass windows. Behind the church is an Elizabethan manor house where Elizabeth I was entertained and Charles I imprisoned.

SWANBOURNE

This attractive village in the Vale of Aylesbury is home to several brick and half timbered houses though the most interesting building here is **Swanbourne House**, which lies just to the south. An earlier house on this site was the home of Elizabeth Wynne, one of the contributors of the collection of diaries and letters known as the Wynne Diaries. She and her sisters spent many of their early years abroad and the diaries offer the reader a fascinating insight into the lives of young girls during the 18th century. Elizabeth married Captain Thomas Fremantle, a friend of Lord Nelson, at the home of Lady Hamilton in Naples in 1797.

TAPLOW

The name Taplow comes from Taeppa's hlaw (the Old English word for mound) and when the remains of Taeppa's mound, a Saxon burial ground high above the River Thames, were excavated in 1883, archaeologists discovered many artefacts including the arms of the buried hero. Though nothing is known of Taeppa, the items discovered in his grand burial site are now on show at the British Museum, London.

To the north of the village lies the country house of **Cliveden**, once the home of Lady Nancy Astor, the first woman to take her seat as a Member of Parliament. Women were first given the right to vote and also stand for Parliament in 1918 and, when, in 1919, Lady Astor's husband became a viscount and moved from the Commons to the Lords, she stood as candidate for his Plymouth seat. Subsequently elected, Lady Astor concerned herself with social issues of the time during her spell as a member of Parliament.

Cliveden, now a hotel that is owned by the National Trust, is a magnificent 19th-century mansion overlooking the River Thames. A glittering centre of the social and political scene, in the 1930s, the Cliveden set became associated with the appeasement of both Mussolini and Hitler.

Though the house is not open to the general public the splendid gardens are and they include a great formal parterre, a water garden, a secret rose garden and informal landscapes.

To the south of the village lies Wickenden Vineyards which are open to the public. Whilst vine growing is not a very common feature of England's country landscape, Wickenden, which was established in 1976, covers some four acres and there are over 5000 vines.

THORNBOROUGH

This lively and attractive village is home to Buckinghamshire's only surviving medieval bridge. Built in the 14th century, the six-arched structure spans Claydon Brook. Close by are two large mounds which were opened in 1839 and revealed a wealth of Roman objects. Though it was known that there was a Roman temple here its location has not been found.

WADDESON

The village is home to another of the county's magnificent country houses, in this case **Waddesdon Manor**. Built between 1874 and 1889 for Baron Ferdinand de Rothschild, in the style of a French Renaissance chateau, the house is set in rolling English countryside and makes a lasting impression. The Baron came from the Austrian branch of the great banking family, but he made his home in Britain from the age of 21. In 1874 he bought the Waddesdon and Winchenden estates from the Duke of Marlborough and set about creating his fantastic country house.

The manor's construction was an immense operation and a steam railway was specially built to move the materials. After 15 years of work what had been a bare hill was topped with a superb building which borrows elements from several different French chateaux, surrounded by formal gardens and landscaped grounds. The French influence even extended to the carthorses used on the site - powerful Percheron

Waddesdon Manor

14

mares that were imported from Normandy.

Now in the hands of the National Trust, the house is home to one of the best collections of 18th-century French decorative arts in the world, including Sèvres porcelain, Beauvais tapestries and fine furniture. There are also paintings by Gainsborough, Reynolds and 17th-century Dutch and Flemish masters on display.

WENDOVER

This delightful old market town, situated in a gap in the Chiltern Hills, has an attractive main street of half timbered, thatched houses and cottages of which the best examples are **Anne Boleyn's Cottages**. A picturesque place, often seen as the gateway to the Chilterns, Wendover also has a fine selection of antique shops, tea rooms and bookshops. Whilst it is a great place for visitors today, in the past there have been

Anne Boleyn's Cottages, Wendover

several famous guests here including Oliver Cromwell and Robert Louis Stevenson who both stayed at the Red Lion.

The town also offers visitors an opportunity of seeing the glorious countryside as, situated on the edge of the Chiltern escarpment, lies **Wendover Woods**. Created for recreational pursuits as well as for conservation and timber production, these Forestry Commission owned woods offer visitors numerous trails through the coniferous and broadleaved woodland.

WEST WYCOMBE

This charming estate village, where many of the houses are owned by the National Trust, has a main street displaying architecture from

the 15th through to the 19th century. Close by is **West Wycombe Park**, the home of the local landowners, the Dashwood family until the 1930s and now a National Trust property. Of the various members of the family, it was Sir Francis Dashwood who had most influence on both the house and the village. West Wycombe house was originally built in the early 18th century but Sir Francis boldly remodelled it several years later as well as having the grounds and park landscaped by Thomas Cook, a pupil of Capability Brown. Very much a clas-

West Wycombe Park

sical landscape, the grounds contain temples and an artificial lake shaped like a swan whilst the house has a good collection of tapestries, furniture and paintings.

Hewn out of a nearby hillside are **West Wycombe Caves**, that were created, possibly from some existing caverns, by Sir Francis as part of a programme of public works. After a series of failed harvests, which created great poverty and distress amongst the estate workers and tenant farmers, Sir Francis employed the men to extract chalk from the hillside to be used in the construction of the new road between the village and High Wycombe.

The village **Church of St Lawrence** is yet another example of Sir Francis' enthusiasm for remodelling old buildings. Situated on the remnants of an Iron Age fort, the church was originally constructed in the 13th century. Its isolated position, however, was not intentional as the church was originally the church of the village of Haveringdon which has long since disappeared. Dashwood remodelled the interior in the 18th century in the style of an Egyptian hall and also heightened the tower, adding a great golden ball to the top. There is room in the ball for six people and it was here that Sir Francis entertained his notorious friends.

15

Apart from this building, Sir Francis had a racier side to his character and, as well as being remembered as a great traveller and a successful politician, he was the founder of the Hell Fire Club. This groups of rakes, who were also known as the Brotherhood of Sir Francis or Dashwood's Apostles, met a couple of times a years to engage in highly colourful activities. Though their exploits were legendary and probably loosely based on fact, they no doubt consumed large quantities of alcohol and enjoyed the company of women. Traditionally, the group meetings were held in the caves, or possibly the church tower, though between 1750 and 1774, their meeting place was nearby Medmenham Abbey.

WILLEN

Whilst the village Church of St Mary Magdalene, built in the late 17th century, is an elegant building in the style of Sir Christopher Wren, Willen is also home to the **Peace Pagoda and Buddhist Temple**, opened in 1980. It was built by the monks and nuns of the Nipponsan Myohoji, and it was the first peace pagoda in the western hemisphere. A place of great tranquillity and beauty, a thousand cherry trees and cedars, donated by the ancient Japanese town of Yoshino, have been planted on the hill surrounding the pagoda, in memory of the victims of all wars.

WING

The village is famous for its fine Saxon **Church of All Saints** which, although it has undergone much alteration in the intervening centuries, still retains its rare Saxon apse and crypt. Dating from about AD 970, it is one of the most interesting churches of its period left in England. Inside there are numerous brasses and monuments, including one to Sir Robert Dormer, dated 1552, that is in a pure renaissance style and said to be the finest contemporary example in the country. Also in the village and founded in 1569, is the Dormer Hospital though, unfortunately, the building was almost totally remodelled in the 19th century.

Just to the east of the village lies **Ascott House**, another mansion that was owned by a member of the Rothschild dynasty. Bought by Leopold Rothschild in 1874, he had the original Jacobean farmhouse essentially rebuilt though the timber framed core was kept. Now in the hands of the National Trust, and remodelled again in the 1930s, the house is home to Arthur Rothschild's fine collection of paintings and there is also some excellent French furniture and Oriental porcelain on display. The gardens too are superb and, as well as the fountain sculpted by the American artist Waldo Story, there are many rare plants and trees here.

WINSLOW

This small country town is full of charm and character, with the houses, shops and inns grouped around the central market square. However, though most of the buildings date from the 18th and 19th centuries, this is an ancient place and it is believed that Offa, the King of Mercia, stayed here in AD 752.

By far the most prominent building in Winslow is **Winslow Hall**, a delightful William and Mary house that was designed by Sir Christopher Wren in the early 18th century. Unlike many houses, this hall has remained remarkably unchanged both inside and out and, though it is not often open to the public, there is a fine collection of 18th century furniture and Chinese art held here. The gardens too are beautiful and the rare specimen plants will be of great interest to keen gardeners.

16 The Bell

High Street,
North Marston,
Buckinghamshire
MK18 3PD

Tel: 01296 670635

Directions:

From Aylesbury, take the A413 towards Buckingham. About 5 miles along this road turn left on a minor road and follow the signs to North Marston (3 miles). The Bell is on the main street of the village.

In early Victorian times much of this attractive village and the srrounding land was owned by an egregious miser, John Camden Nield. He had inherited a large fortune from his equally curmudgeonly father, a goldsmith, but he chose to live in scruffy lodgings and dressed in shabby clothes. He would invite himself to his tenants' houses in order to get a free meal. When Nield died in 1852 he bequeathed his entire fortune, £250,000, to Queen Victoria "for her sole use and benefit". The queen awarded £100 a year to a woman who had once saved Nield's life; much of the rest she devoted to a generously funded restoration of the village's already well-endowed church.

Just along the road from the church stands **The Bell**, an inviting-looking hostelry of local warm red brick. Picnic tables stand on the lawned area to the front of the inn and inside it has the welcoming atmosphere of a traditional country pub, with beamed ceilings and an inglenook fireplace. Quality food is a prime concern here and proprietor Bob Petherick offers a wide choice of dishes that range from steaks, through chicken or fish dishes to bar snacks. Everything is freshly cooked and the specials board changes on a regular basis. There are regular guest real ales and a full range of wines, spirits and other beers. The Bell doesn't provide accommodation but Bob can recommend b&b establishments nearby.

Opening Hours: Mon-Sat: 11.00-23.00; Sun: 12.00-22.30

Food: Main meals & bar snacks every lunchtime & evening

Credit Cards: All major cards accepted

Facilities: Beer garden; off road parking

Entertainment: Large screen TV

Local Places of Interest/Activities: Claydon (NT), 5 miles; Buckinghamshire Railway Centre, 5 miles; Waddesdon Manor (NT), 7 miles

The Black Lion | 17

Marlow Road,
Well End,
Bourne End,
Buckinghamshire
SL8 5PL
Tel: 01628 520421

Directions:

From Exit 4 of the M40, take the A404 towards Marlow. At the first roundabout (2.5 miles), turn left on the A4155 towards Bourne End. About 3.5 miles along this road, turn left on a minor road to Well End. The Black Lion is on the edge of the village

Bourne End is a prosperous commuter town on the banks of the River Thames and it was the river that led to its expansion in the late 1800s as the Victorians indulged a new found passion for boating. Until then the village was best known for making the cardboard tops for silk hats. This stretch of the river is considered to be the best sailing reach on the Thames and is also very popular with anglers. There are some pleasant riverside walks and on the other bank of the river lies the village of Cookham, immortalised by the eccentric painter Stanley Spencer (1891-1959) who set his Biblical scenes here.

In Well End itself, **The Black Lion** is an attractive late-Victorian building in the half-timbered Jacobean style which is run by Patrick Ayre and Matthew O'Keeffe, aided by Matthew's wife Anna at weekends. "When we took over the pub was very run down" says Anna, "but we're hoping it will become a community place again". "We want to go back to an old-fashioned Georgian style" adds Patrick, "with open fires and no music or juke boxes". So the home-cooked menu, which includes kedgeree, rabbit pie and sausage & mash is designed for lovers of traditional pub food. Matthew points out that the Black Lion had been avoided by locals because it was aimed at the youth market. "We want to run it for the locals and let them decide what they want".

Opening Hours: Mon-Fri: 11.00-15.00; 17.00-23.00. Sat-Sun: Open all day

Food: Main meals & sandwiches every lunchtime & evening; food available all day Sat-Sun

Credit Cards: All the major credit cards except American Express and Diners

Facilities: Patio area; off road parking

Local Places of Interest/Activities: River Thames, 1 mile; Cliveden (NT), 4 miles; Stanley Spencer Gallery, Cookham, 4 miles; Burnham Beeches, 6 miles

18 The Brickmakers Arms

Wheeler End Common,
High Wycombe,
Buckinghamshire HP14 3ND
Tel/Fax: 01494 881526

Directions:

From Exit 5 of the M40, take the A40 towards High Wycombe. After about half a mile turn right on the B482. Stay on this road for about 5 miles to Lane End. In Lane End, turn left and follow the signs for Wheeler End Common (1 mile)

This pleasant hamlet in the heart of the countryside lies close to three of Buckinghamshire's top visitor attractions. Only a couple of miles away is West Wycombe Park, home of the local landowners, the Dashwood family until the 1930s and now in the care of the National Trust which also owns most of the estate village. It was a Dashwood, Sir Francis, who created the nearby Hell Fire Club Caves, possibly from existing caverns, as a make-work project for his estate workers after a series of failed harvests. A few miles further is Hughenden Manor, a grand 18th century mansion remodelled in the Victorian Gothic style by Prime Minister Benjamin Disraeli who lived here from 1847 until his death in 1881.

Back in Wheeler End Common, **The Brickmakers Arms** is an inviting looking tavern, with parasol-shaded tables set out in front. It looks deceptively small from outside but once you step inside it's very spacious with lots of character and style. Dating back to the 17th century the inn was formerly a coaching house and at one time a bakery. Landlord Gary Bishop knows the inn very well. He was wine buyer and Manager for 12 years before taking over in 1998 together with his business partner Clive and sister Julie. There are two upstairs restaurants, one smoking, one non-smoking, but both overlooking the attractive garden. The menu offers a choice of between 15 and 20 main course daily specials. Booking at weekends is strongly recommended. A full bar menu is also available every day and there are always at least 4 real ales on tap.

Opening Hours: Mon-Fri: Lunchtime & evening; Sat-Sun: open all day

Food: Available every lunchtime & evening

Credit Cards: All major cards accepted

Facilities: Large beer garden; children's play area; outside bar; barbecue area; smoking & non-smoking restaurants; tables at front; parking

Entertainment: Music Night, Tuesdays

Local Places of Interest/Activities: West Wycombe Park (NT), 2 miles; Hell Fire Club Caves, 4 miles; Hughenden Manor (NT), 8 miles

The Cock & Rabbit Inn 19

The Lee,
Great Missenden,
Buckinghamshire
HP16 9LZ
Tel: 01494 837540
Fax: 01494 837512

Directions:

The Lee is a small village just east of the A413 Aylesbury to Amersham road, about 8 miles southeast of Aylesbury. The Cock & Rabbit Inn is located in the centre of the village.

Set amidst beech woods in an Area of Outstanding Natural Beauty, this pretty, hidden away village featured in the television series *Midsummer Murders* starring John Nettles and Kevin Whately. It's an ancient place with an Anglo-Saxon earthwork, Grim's Dyke or Ditch, nearby. The hamlet's most famous resident was Sir Arthur Liberty, founder of the famous Regent's Street store, and his descendants still live in The Lee.

Surrounded by a lovely garden, **The Cock & Rabbit Inn** is an absolute delight, - a quintessential English country house but offering top-class Italian cuisine. The owner, Gianfranco Parola, was born in the Piedmont district of Italy, worked on a cruise liner for 10 years and then settled in England. In 1986 he took over and renovated the Cock & Rabbit and created a tempting menu drawn from the dishes of his native region. Giancarlo's outstanding cuisine has featured in several television programmes, most recently in Carlton TV's *Heart of the Country*. Naturally, the wines on offer are also predominantly from Italy. With its lovely grounds and the surrounding Chiltern Hills, the Cock & Rabbit provides an ideal setting for a wedding reception or party. The inn can cater for up to 68 guests in its restaurant, extensive lounge bar and sun terrace, or marquees are available for hire for up to 150 guests. An evening barbecue is also available on request.

Opening Hours: Mon-Sat: 12.00-14.30, 18.00-23.00; Sun: 12.00-15.00, 19.00-22.30

Food: Excellent Italian cuisine

Credit Cards: All major cards accepted

Facilities: Beautiful grounds; sun terrace; barbecues on request; conference room; large car park

Local Places of Interest/Activities: Ridgeway Path, 2 miles; Pulpit Hill, 5 miles; Old Court House, Great Missenden, 5 miles

Internet/Website:
www.gianfranco. demon.co.uk/c&r/c&r.htm
e-mail: info@gianfranco.demon.co.uk

20   The Crown

City Road,
Radnage,
Buckinghamshire
HP14 4DW
Tel: 01494 482301

Directions:

From Exit 5 of the M40, take the A40 towards High Wycombe. About 1 mile along this road, turn left on a minor road to The City and follow the signs for Radnage (2 miles)

You can't help wondering whose delusions of grandeur (or sense of humour) led to a handful of cottages in the heart of the Chilterns being named 'The City'. 'The City' is actually an 'End' of Radnage parish which, like several other Buckinghamshire communities, is comprised of scattered groups of houses, each known collectively as an 'End'. Radnage has five of them: in addition to The City, there's Bennett End, Sprig's Alley End, Town End and Church End. Church End, naturally, includes Radnage's ancient parish church which contains many features of absorbing interest to ecclesiastical historians but to a casual visitor is primarily attractive because of its simple lines and lovely setting.

    The Crown inn is attractive for rather different reasons. Built in the mid-1800s, The Crown looks very inviting with its whitewashed walls and its parasol-shaded tables on the front patio. Inside, the old ceiling beams are festooned with a fascinating collection of vintage jugs, - jugs specially designed for cream, for water, for milk, for whatever. Barry and Bridgett Scales own and personally run this appealing free house hostelry and also share the cooking between them. Their regular menu is supplemented by daily specials which, on one sample day, offered Scotch Rib-eye Steak, Rack of Lamb and Breast of Duck in addition to the wide choice of other dishes. In good weather, you can sup your pint in the peaceful beer garden at the rear of the inn where there's also a secure children's play area.

Opening Hours: Open every session

Food: Available every lunchtime & evening

Credit Cards: All major cards accepted

Facilities: Beer garden at rear with children's play area; patio at front; ample parking

Entertainment: Dominoes; cards; TV games

Local Places of Interest/Activities: Chinnor & Princes Risborough Railway, 4 miles; Hell Fire Club Caves, 5 miles; West Wycombe Park (NT), 6 miles

The Crown Inn

Main Street,
Tingewick,
nr Buckingham
Buckinghamshire
MK18 4NL
Tel: 01280 847249
Answerphone: 01280 848442

Directions:

From Buckingham take the A421 towards Bicester. After about 3 miles turn right into Tingewick. The Crown Inn is on the main street in the centre of the village

This sizeable village lies close to the Oxfordshire border with the meandering River Great Ouse forming part of the boundary. It has an attractively sited church, part of which dates back to Norman times, with massively thick walls and some characteristic zigzag carving. There's also a very fine brass of Erasmus Williams, a Rector here in Tudor times, which shows him kneeling on a tomb between two pillars, on one of which sits the owl of wisdom, on the other stands a globe.

Located in the centre of the village is **The Crown Inn**, a lively establishment despite the fact that the bar was at one time a funeral parlour! A pool table, two darts boards and a juke box all add to the jollity, outside in the beer garden there's an Aunt Sally, and the pub also has its own golf team. And to make absolutely certain his regulars don't get bored, mine host at this welcoming inn, Trevor Barnett, lays on the occasional live music, a barbecue, or a visit to the local greyhound races. In short, a thriving community pub. Food is available every lunchtime and evening (except Monday lunchtime and Sunday evening) and the menu offers a good selection of home cooked traditional 'pub grub'. There's also a wide choice of ales, wines and spirits, and should you overdo the wining and dining a little, there's a bed above the bar where you can recover!

Opening Hours: Mon: 19.00-23.00; Tue-Thu: 12.00-14.00; 19.00-23.00; Fri: 12.00-14.00; 17.30-23.00; Sat-Sun: Open all day

Food: Available every lunchtime except Monday; every evening except Sunday

Credit Cards: Not accepted

Facilities: Beer garden; patio; parking

Entertainment: Pool table; 2 darts boards; Aunt Sally; occasional barbecues; occasional live music

Local Places of Interest/Activities: Old Gaol Museum, Buckingham, 2.5 miles; Stowe Gardens (NT), 4 miles; Aynho Park House, 10 miles

22   The Derehams Inn

Derehams Lane,
Loudwater,
nr High Wycombe,
Buckinghanshire
HP10 9RH
Tel: 01494 530965
Fax: 01494 512616

Directions:

Loudwater is on the A40, about 2.5 miles west of Beaconsfield

Hidden away in the Buckinghamshire countryside, **The Derehams Inn** is well worth seeking out, - especially if the weather is fine so that you can take advantage of its delightful beer garden. As it is situated very much off the beaten track, this cosy inn is a well kept secret although it is very well known locally. Housed in a building that began life as two farm workers cottages in the 18th century, this attractive old village pub offers customers a warm and friendly welcome. Run by Graham and Margaret Sturgess with the help of their two children and Shannon, their black Labrador, the inn has several comfortable and intimate areas that provide customers with the ideal place for a quiet drink and a chance to catch up on all the local news.

Very much an old English pub, there are low ceilings, open fires in winter, and, hanging from the exposed ceiling beams, a collection of pewter jugs and some gleaming horse brasses. Though there is no juke box, fruit machine or pool table, there are always some interesting people since the local netball team meets here twice a week and each week there's a gathering of local motorcycle enthusiasts. As well as the superb selection of real ales on tap traditional pub food and basket meals are served here Monday to Saturday lunchtimes. No children although pets are welcome.

Opening Hours: Mon-Fri: 11.30-15.00; 17.30-23.00; Sat and Sun: All day

Food: Available every Monday to Saturday lunchtime

Credit Cards: All the major cards except Diners

Facilities: Lovely beer garden; parking

Entertainment: Darts, Quiz nights

Local Places of Interest/Activities: Odds Farm Park, 2 miles; Bekonscot Model Village, 4 miles; Cliveden, 4 miles

The Garibaldi
23

Hedsor Road,
Bourne End,
Buckinghamshire
SL8 5EE
Tel/Fax: 01628 522092

Directions:

From Exit 3 of the M40, take the A4094 towards Maidenhead. Bourne End is about 4 miles along this road. When you come to the T-junction (and roundabout) turn right along Station Road. Hedsor Road is the third street on the left and The Garibaldi is on the left

This riverside village takes its name from the spot where the Wye river (or bourne) enters the Thames. Keen walkers can join the Thames Path here, a long distance walk that extends 150 miles from Putney to the river's source near Cricklade in Wiltshire. A less strenuous outing can be made to Cliveden, once the home of Lady Nancy Astor, the first woman to be elected as a Member of Parliament. The stately old house is now a hotel but the splendid gardens are open to the public.

Dating back to the late 1700s, **The Garibaldi** is a delightful old tavern with beamed ceilings, real fire and lots of character. Fresh flowers on the tables and bygones displayed around the rooms all add to the inviting appearance. Moira MacMillan is your host and offers her customers an excellent choice of appetising dishes. They are listed on separate blackboards, - one for fish, one for vegetarian, and so on. The speciality of the house is pizzas, with a choice that includes, naturally, a Garibaldi (pepperoni, spicy beef, mushrooms, onion, peppers and spicy pork). Pizzas are available to take away and you can phone or fax your order in advance and it will be ready for you. Wines and beers are also available for takeaway. An attractive feature of the Garibaldi is its delightful beer garden at the rear, a great place to enjoy a drink on a sunny day.

Opening Hours: Mon-Fri: 12.00-14.30; 17.00-23.00; Sat: 12.00-23.00; Sun: 12.00-22.30

Food: Mon-Thu: 12.00-14.00; 18.30-21.00; Fri-Sat: 12.00-14.30; 18.30-22.00; Sun: 12.00-14.30; 19.00-21.00

Credit Cards: Visa, Mastercard

Facilities: Beer garden; tables at front; car park

Entertainment: Acoustic jamming night, Thursdays

Local Places of Interest/Activities: River Thames nearby; Stanley Spencer Gallery, Cookham, 2 miles; Cliveden (NT), 3 miles; Burnham Beeches, 5 miles

24   The George Inn

Watling Street,
Little Brickhill,
Milton Keynes,
Buckinghamshire
MK17 9NB
Tel: 01525 261298
Fax: 01525 261801

Directions:

Little Brickhill is just off the A5, about 6 miles south of Milton Keynes. The George Inn is on the main road in the centre of the village.

Situated astride the old Roman road, Watling Street, this village was once an important coaching centre as well as being an assize town where many executions took place. The most attractive building is the small Church of St Mary Magdalene with its battlemented 15th century tower from which there is a fine vista of the lush valley of the River Ouzel to the west and the pine-clad hills of Woburn to the north. A few miles to the east stands the Duke of Bedford's palatial home, Woburn Abbey, which boasts one of the most important private art collections in the world with major works by Cuyp, Gainsborough, Reynolds, Van Dyck and Velazquez.

At the heart of Little Brickhill village, **The George Inn** is an attractive 1930s building, very spacious inside and very well furnished and decorated. The inn is run by the Noble family who offer their guests a comprehensive à la carte menu in the restaurant as well as a good selection of bar meals and snacks. You can buy your steaks by the ounce, - just as large and small as you want, and there's a choice of more than 50 wines to complement your meal. Children are welcome and there's a pleasant family garden with a play area specially for them. The inn has 4 extremely well-equipped and beautifully furnished guest rooms, all en suite and with welcome extras such as trouser presses and hair dryers.

Opening Hours: Mon-Fri: 12.00-15.00; 17.00-23.00. Sat-Sun: All day

Food: A la carte restaurant & bar meals daily

Credit Cards: All major cards accepted

Accommodation: 4 luxury en suite rooms

Facilities: Family Garden with children's play area; air-conditioned conservatory;

large car park

Entertainment: Pool table

Local Places of Interest/Activities: Golf, 1 mile; Stockgrove Country Park, 2 miles; Woburn Abbey & Safari Park, 4 miles;

Internet/Website:
e-mail: thegeorgeinn@bun.com

Green Man

25

Church End,
Eversholt,
Bedfordshire
MK17 9DU
Tel: 01525 280293

Directions:
From Junction 13 of the M1 take the A4012 to Woburn (4 miles). In Woburn turn left on a minor road to Eversholt (4 miles)

Recorded in 1765 under the name "Go Further, Fare Worse", the **Green Man** is a substantial early Victorian building erected at a time when the whole of the village formed part of the Duke of Bedford's Woburn Estate. Eversholt is a village with ten 'Ends', or clusters of houses, and no obvious centre. 'Church End' is at the southern end of the village, a group of attractive buildings that includes St John's Church, notable for its 13th century font, 14th century piscina, 15th century porch and 19th century wall paintings by Edward Aveling Green (1842-1930) who lived in the village.

Charlie and Linda Owen are your hosts at the Green Man where you'll find a good choice of home cooked meals available every lunchtime and evening. In addition, bar snacks (Ham & Eggs, burgers, sandwiches and baguettes, for example) are served from 12 noon until 9pm. There's always a traditional Sunday lunch for which booking is definitely recommended. The Green Man's desserts are particularly appetising, - a mouth-watering range of sponges, sundaes, pies and cakes. Children have their own menu and vegetarians will find a selection of half a dozen options. The Owens are happy to cater for special parties and the inn is ideal for Club meetings and social events.

Opening Hours: Daily 12.00-23.00

Food: Home cooked meals served every lunchtime & evening

Credit Cards: Not accepted

Accommodation: 1 family room, also available as a single

Facilities: Beer Garden; children's play area; patio; aviary

Local Places of Interest/Activities: Woburn Abbey & Safari Park, 3 miles; Houghton House (English Heritage), 6 miles

26   The Hit or Miss

Penn Street Village,
Penn Street, Amersham,
Buckinghamshire
HP7 0PX
Tel: 01494 713109
Fax: 01494 718010

Directions:
From Exit 4 of the M40, take the A404 towards High Wycombe and Amersham. About 7 miles along this road, turn right on a minor road signposted to Penn Street (0.5 miles)

Hidden away on the edge of the tiny village of Penn Street, **The Hit or Miss** bills itself as a "country inn with dining". It's a charming old building whose mellow red brick walls are smothered with wistaria and hanging baskets of flowers. The inn's earliest deeds date back to 1730 and it's known that it opened as a pub on 1st June 1798. The unusual name is a cricketing term, inspired perhaps by players on the nearby village green which has its own cricket patch and a pond with ducks. The cricketing theme is continued with features such as autographed bats and framed caricatures of famous cricketers and commentators like John Arlott and Richie Benaud.

The inn's general manager, Richard Partington, is a very experienced restaurateur who has worked at Maxim's in Paris, for Sir Terence Conran in London and in Beverley Hills, California, where he managed the restaurant of a private members club.. So standards at the Hit or Miss are very high. In the separate restaurant the menu specialises in fresh fish and shellfish dishes and the Sri Lankan chef also offers a superb daily specials menu. Richard Partington is also a full member of the Academy of Food and Wine Service and has compiled an outstanding wine list which includes ten house wines available by the glass or bottle, and half a dozen wines available in half bottles. The inn also offers an extensive lunchtime menu of bar snacks which can be enjoyed either in the bar or in the lovely secluded garden at the rear. With its excellent food and superb service the Hit or Miss is definitely a hit!

Opening Hours: Mon-Fri: 11.00-15.00; 17.30-23.00; Sat: 11.00-15.00; 18.00-23.00; Sun: 12.00-15.00; 19.00-22.30

Food: Available every lunchtime & evening; fresh fish & shellfish a speciality

Credit Cards: All major cards accepted except Diners

Facilities: Secluded Beer Garden; cricket pitch

Entertainment: "Background music and stuff" - a quote from landlord Richard Partington

Local Places of Interest/Activities: Hughenden Manor (NT), 5 miles; Hell Fire Club Caves, 6 miles; Beckonscoe Model Village, Beaconsfield, 4 miles

Internet/Website: e-mail: richpartington@aol.com

Milton's Head

27

20 Dean Way,
Chalfont St Giles,
Buckinghamshire
HP8 4JL
Tel: 01494 875856

Directions:

From Exit 2 of the M40, take the A355 towards Amersham. After about 3.5 miles turn right to Chalfont St Giles (1.5 miles). The Milton's Head is on the main street, 300 yards from the village green

The most famous building in this typical English village is the 16th century cottage in which John Milton lived during 1665-66 while the plague raged in London. Here he completed Paradise Lost and began work on its sequel, Paradise Regained. A Grade I listed building, Milton's Cottage is the only house he lived in to have survived and the house and garden have been preserved as they were at the time the poet was resident. The building is now home to a museum which includes collections of important first editions of Milton's works and a portrait of him by Sir Godfrey Kneller.

Another picture of the poet hangs outside the **Milton's Head** pub on the main street of the village. The pub is a totally unspoilt traditional village inn where you suspect that little has changed in half a century or more. However, some things are changing. At the time of writing, Landlords Kevin and Alison Bonnas offer only a basic menu of typical pub snacks, complemented by real ales and all the popular brews, ut by the time you read this a small restaurant area will be in place offering home cooked and freshly prepared food. They are also developing a large beer garden and a sunny patio area, both of which again should be completed by our publication date.

Opening Hours: Mon-Sat: 11.00-23.00; Sun: 12.00-22.30

Food: Pub bar snacks

Credit Cards: Not accepted

Facilities: Large beer garden and patio area currently being developed

Local Places of Interest/Activities: Milton's Cottage, nearby; Chiltern Open Air Museum, 1 mile; Windsor Castle, 10 miles

28   The New Inn

18 Bridge Street,
Buckingham
Buckinghamshire
MK18 1AF
Tel: 01280 815713

Directions:

From Exit 13 of the M1, take the A421 to Buckingham (19 miles). The New Inn is a short distance from the town centre

It was Alfred the Great who designated Buckingham as the county town when he divided his kingdom of Wessex into shires, way back in 888AD. It remained the most important town in the county for more than 700 years until Henry VIII executed its paramount lord, the Duke of Buckingham, and removed the Assizes to Aylesbury. A disastrous fire in 1725 marked the town's lowest point. But the rebuilding that followed furnished the town with some fine Georgian buildings, notably in Castle Street, which add dignity and elegance to this pleasing little town set around the River Ouse.

Families with children visiting Buckingham will really appreciate **The New Inn**. Not only are children welcome here, they have their very own play room. It's equipped with TV, video games, books, toys and even its own bar area selling pop and sweets. Adults can relax in the main bar or the dining area knowing that their offspring are always being supervised. Deirdre and Michael Hall run this child-friendly hostelry where adults are also well looked after. There's a wholesome choice of appetising food, (with curries a speciality of the house), and always a choice of at least 3 real ales. If you appreciate Blues music, make sure you are here on a Friday evening and if your preference is jazz, the Halls lay on a live jazz band on the 1st Wednesday of every month. This lively and welcoming inn has come a long way since it was built as an alehouse in 1839 to serve workers at the local Gas Works!

Opening Hours: Mon-Sat: open all day; Sun: normal licensing hours

Food: Available every lunchtime & evening

Credit Cards: Not accepted

Facilities: Patio; very well-equipped children's room; on street parking

Entertainment: Darts; pin ball; live music, Fridays; live jazz, 1st Wednesday of the month

Local Places of Interest/Activities: Stowe Gardens (NT), 3 miles; Silverstone Racing Circuit, 7 miles; Claydon (NT), 8 miles

Internet/Website:
www.thenewinn.8.m.com

The Old Bell 29

Town Lane,
Wooburn Green,
Buckinghamshire
HP10 0PL
Tel/Fax:
01628 520406

Directions:

From the A40, about 2.5 miles west of Beaconsfield, turn left to Wooburn Green (0.5 miles). The Old Bell is near the centre of the village, a short distance from the church

Wooburn Green grew up on the banks of the River Wye, a tributary which flows into the River Thames a couple of miles downstream. It has an interesting old church but the best-known visitor attraction is Odds Farm Park which is home to a fine collection of rare breeds of domestic animals. It's especially popular with children who can try their hand at milking a goat, can pat-a-pet, or burn off some energy in the playbarn, conveniently provided with hay bales for climbing.

Adults might be a tad more interested in the attractions on offer at **The Old Bell**, a charming old inn some 200 years old, located just along the road from the village church. It boasts all the appurtenances of a traditional English inn, - ancient beams, wooden floors and many old bygones scattered around. But you'll also find an attractive collection of quality ceramics on display. These have been crafted by Kim Lim, a gifted ceramicist, who together with her husband Peter run this outstanding hostelry. The other thing you wouldn't expect to find in a traditional English inn is the cuisine on offer at the Old Bell. It's almost exclusively Oriental and the extensive menu includes appetising dishes from Malaysia, Thailand, Singapore and Szechuan, with plenty of options for vegetarians. The Old Bell provides a fascinating combination of traditional village pub atmosphere and top quality Eastern cooking. Not to be missed!

Opening Hours: Open every session

Food: Mostly Oriental food, available every lunchtime & evening

Credit Cards: All major cards accepted

Accommodation: 5 en suite rooms available late 2000

Facilities: Beer garden; ample parking

Entertainment: Fortnightly theme nights on Tuesdays with jazz & meal (bookings required)

Local Places of Interest/Activities: Odds Farm Park, 1 mile; Cliveden (NT), 4 miles; Stanley Spencer Gallery, Cookham, 4 miles

Internet/Website:
e-mail: peterlim@oldbell.co.uk

30   The Red Cow

14 The Green,
Wooburn Green,
Buckinghamshire
HP10 0EF
Tel: 01628 531344

Directions:

From the A40, about 2.5 miles west of Beaconsfield, turn left to Wooburn Green (0.5 miles). The Red Cow is in the centre of the village, over-looking the green

Wooburn lies in the valley of the River Wye, a commuter village now but with its oval village green still intact and this is where you'll find **The Red Cow**. The inn dates back some 400 years but long before that, the Bishops of Lincoln had a palace at Wooburn. Within its walls stood a room known as 'The Little Ease'. According to John Foxe's *Book of Martyrs* heretics were imprisoned here and tortured, amongst them a certain Thomas Chase of Amersham who was "barbarously butchered by strangling". Wooburn Palace was considered one of the finest houses in England but in 1750 it was demolished and no trace remains.

Fortunately, the new Inn has survived the centuries. It enjoys a picture postcard setting and inside is full of atmosphere with its old beams and wooden floors still in place. Food is available every lunchtime when the blackboard lists a wide choice of basket meals, salads, curries, jacket potatoes, baguettes and sandwiches. When the weather's good, you canenjoy your refreshments either in the lovely secluded beer garden at the rear, a safe place for children, or at the tables in front of the inn where you can watch the village life pass by. The 3 real ales on tap are constantly changing and jugs of ale are available with the special offer of 4 pints for the price of 3.

Opening Hours: Open all day, every day

Food: Available every lunchtime, noon until 15.00

Credit Cards: All major cards accepted

Facilities: Beer garden at rear; seating in front; parking

Entertainment: Live music every Friday evening

Local Places of Interest/Activities: Odds Farm Park, 1 mile; Cliveden (NT) 4 miles; Stanley Spencer Gallery, Cookham, 4 miles

The Robin Hood Inn   31

Bufflers Holt,
Buckingham
Buckinghamshire
MK18 5DN
Tel: 01280 813387

Directions:

From Buckingham take the A422 towards Brackley. The Robin Hood Inn is on this road, about 3 miles west of Buckingham

The hamlet of Bufflers Holt lies just to the south of the National Trust's Stowe Landscape Gardens, one of the first and finest landscape gardens in Europe. Worked on by the best designers of the Georgian era, the gardens at Stowe contain temples, alcoves and rotundas strategically placed to create romantic vistas. The celebrated landscape gardener, Lancelot 'Capability' Brown, was head gardener at Stowe for 10 years from 1741 and during that time he developed his own, more natural style of landscape gardening which was to take over from the more formal effects of gardens such as those at Stowe.

Conveniently located for visitors to the gardens, **The Robin Hood Inn** also offers its customers a good choice of wholesome home cooked food, well-maintained beers and a warm welcome from mine host, Paul Mercier. The interior has beamed ceilings and a collection of interesting agricultural photographs on display; outside there's a pleasant patio and beer garden to enjoy in good weather. Restaurant meals and bar snacks are available every lunchtime and evening, offering a choice that ranges from a hearty Steak & Chips to salads and baguettes. The main menu is supplemented by daily specials and there are also home made pizzas to take away if required.

Opening Hours: Mon-Fri: 11.00-15.00 & 17.00-23.00; Sat: 11.00-23.00; Sun: 12.00-22.30

Food: Main meals and bar snacks available every lunchtime & evening

Credit Cards: All major cards accepted

Facilities: Beer Garden; patio; off road parking

Entertainment: Darts

Local Places of Interest/Activities: Stowe Landscape Gardens (NT), 1 mile; Silverstone, 4 miles; Claydon House (NT), Middle Claydon, 8 miles

32   The Rose & Crown

Hawridge Common,
nr Chesham,
Buckinghamshire
HP5 2UQ
Tel: 01494 758386
Fax: 01494 758825

Directions:

From the centre of Chesham, take the A416 towards Berkhamsted. On the northern edge of Chesham the main road turns sharp right. Keep straight on along the minor road to Hawridge and Hawridge Common (2.5 miles)

Approached by way of Chesham Vale, Hawridge Common is a tiny hamlet located way off the beaten track. But it's well worth seeking out for the outstanding food on offer at **The Rose & Crown**. Hawridge lies in a particularly attractive part of the Chilterns and a couple of miles beyond the village is a stretch of Grim's Ditch. This prehistoric dyke runs intermittently for some 25 miles from Naphill near West Wycombe to Dunstable in Bedfordshire. Archaeologists can't agree whether it was built in Saxon times or much earlier, during the Iron Age.

Back at the Rose & Crown, which was definitely built in the mid-1700s, there's also no doubt at all about the quality of the cuisine. Nick Carter, who runs the inn with his wife Hayley, has been a professional chef for many years and his menu offers an excellent choice of varied dishes. Fresh fish and chef's specials are available every day, and game dishes are served in season. The restaurant overlooks the spacious garden and across the common to woodland and if you plan to eat here at weekends, booking is definitely recommended. Lighter meals are also served from the Bar Snack menu which offers an extensive selection of speciality jacket potatoes, ploughmans, salads and samosas. Children are welcome at the Rose & Crown and there's a special play area for them in the spacious beer garden.

Opening Hours: Mon-Sat: 12.00-15.00, 17.30-23.00; Sun: 12.00-15.00, 18.30-22.30

Food: Available every lunchtime & evening except Sunday evening & Mondays (unless it's a Bank Holiday)

Credit Cards: All major cards accepted

Facilities: Spacious beer garden; patio; children's play area; barbecue area

Local Places of Interest/Activities: Rothschild Zoological Museum, Tring, 5 miles; Ashridge Estate and Bridgewater Monument, 6 miles

The Royal Oak Inn | 33

Wingrave Road,
Aston Abbotts, Aylesbury
Buckinghamshire
HP22 4LT
Tel: 01296 681262

Directions:
From Aylesbury, take the A418 towards Leighton Buzzard. About 5 miles along this road, take a minor road to the left signposted to Aston Abbotts (0.5 miles). The Royal Oak Inn is located in the centre of the village

Aston Abbotts is a typical Home Counties village with timbered and thatched cottages nestling around the village green and a church whose oldest fabric dates back to the 1300s. In its graveyard is the burial place of Sir James Clark Ross (1800-62), the celebrated polar explorer. Between 1831 and 1835 Ross spent four years imprisoned in Arctic ice. He used the time well by discovering the north magnetic pole. A few years later he led an expedition to the Antarctic where Ross Island, Ross Barrier and Ross Sea still commemorate his pioneering explorations. Sir James eventually retired to Aston Abbotts, occupying an old house which had once belonged to the Abbots of St Albans from whom the village takes its name.

One of the most attractive buildings in Aston Abbotts is **The Royal Oak Inn**, a lovely thatched, whitewashed and half-timbered building whose origins go back some 600 years. The cosy interior looks very inviting with its low-beamed ceilings and open fire. Gary and Teri Moult are your hosts at this appealing hostelry. The food they offer here is much more appetising than the usual 'Pub Grub'. Amongst the starters for example is a Spicy Combo of jalpeno peppers stuffed with mozzarella cheese, mozza melts and Taxas toothpick strips of jalpeno peppers with a dip. If you are feeling really hungry, you could tackle the 16oz Rump Steak as a main course while for lighter appetites there's a good choice of vegetable dishes, jacket potatoes and sandwiches.

Opening Hours: Mon-Sat: 12.00-14.30; 18.00-23.00. Sun: 12.00-14.30; 19.00-22.30

Food: A wide choice of main meals, filled jacket potatoes and sandwiches

Credit Cards: All major cards accepted

Accommodation: 4 rooms (2 doubles, 2 twins, 1 en suite)

Facilities: Beer garden with aviary, children's playhouse and swing; rabbits

Entertainment: Darts; dominoes; Morris dancing 3 or 4 times a year

Local Places of Interest/Activities: Ascott House (NT), 5 miles; Buckinghamshire Railway Centre, 9 miles; Waddesdon Manor (NT), 11 miles

34   The Seven Stars

Stars Lane,
Dinton,
nr Aylesbury
Buckinghamshire
HP17 8UL
Tel: 01296 748241

Directions:

From Aylesbury, take the A418 towards Thame and Oxford. About 5 miles along this road, a minor road to the left leads directly into Dinton. The Seven Stars inn is located in the centre of the village

Small though it is, this charming village has some interesting buildings. To the northeast is Dinton Castle, actually a folly built in 1769 by Sir John Vanhatten to house his collection of fossils. Much of the castle itself is constructed of ammonites, trilobites and many other fossils. Dinton's parish church boasts the finest Norman doorway in the country, an elaborate piece of work with a tympanum showing grotesque monsters eating fruit from a tree. The church also contains some well-preserved brasses dating from around 1370 to 1617. Adjoining the church is Dinton Hall (private) where Cromwell came to stay following his victory at Naseby and left his sword of victory with the owner, Simon Mayne.

The Seven Stars looks very inviting with its lawn set with picnic tables and umbrellas. The interior is equally attractive, providing everything one hopes for in a traditional country pub. An additional bonus is the high standard of the cuisine on offer. Mine hosts, Sue and Raimer Eccard, provide both an à la carte menu and an extensive choice of bar snacks. Main meals range from steaks to vegetarian dishes while the bar menu presents an even more comprehensive choice. Real ale is available as well as a selection of wines and a full range of all the popular brews. Sunday lunch is understandably very popular here so booking is strongly recommended.

Opening Hours: Mon-Sat: 12.00-15.00; 18.00-23.00; (Closed on Tuesday evenings). Sun: 12.00-15.00, 19.00-22.30

Food: Extensive menu of main meals and bar snacks available every lunchtime and evening

Credit Cards: All major cards accepted

Facilities: Children welcome; beer garden; off road parking

Local Places of Interest/Activities: Long Crendon Courthouse (NT), 8 miles; Waddesdon Manor (NT), 10 miles

The Stag Inn 35

Heath End Road,
Flackwell Heath,
High Wycombe
Buckinghamshire
HP10 9ES
Tel: 01628 521277
Fax: 01628 530404

Directions:

From the centre of High Wycombe, take the A40 towards London. After about 1.5 miles, turn right on a minor road to Flackwell Heath

Half a mile or so away, a ceaseless stream of traffic is hurtling along the M40 but if you settle down in the spacious beer garden at **The Stag Inn** you'll find yourself looking out across an unspoilt view of meadows and woods. Flackwell Heath nowadays makes the curious claim that it's the 'largest village in England', its population boosted by an influx of London commuters. But in the early 1900s, the village was famous for its cherry orchards and although most of them have disappeared, this corner of the village still has a pastoral charm.

The oldest parts of The Stag date back to the 1700s and the interior has retained a delightful olde-worlde atmosphere with beamed ceilings, partly wooden floors and some interesting old memorabilia on display. Carol Walsh is your host, a cheerful and welcoming lady who is assisted by her son Simon. Food is available every lunchtime and evening, served either in the separate restaurant, in the lounge or, weather permitting, in that inviting beer garden. The regular menu is supplemented by daily specials and if you plan to enjoy Sunday lunch at The Stag, do book ahead.

Opening Hours: Mon-Sat: lunchtimes & evenings; Sat-Sun: all day

Food: Available every lunchtime & evening

Credit Cards: All major cards accepted

Facilities: Beer garden with children's play area; ample parking

Entertainment: Quiz Night every other Sunday

Local Places of Interest/Activities: Golf, 1 mile; Thames Path, 1.5 miles; Stanley Spencer Gallery, Cookham, 4 miles; Cliveden (NT), 5 miles

36 The Swan

Grove Lane,
Great Kimble,
nr Aylesbury
Buckinghamshire
HP17 9TR
Tel: 01844 275288

Directions:

Great Kimble is on the A4010 Aylesbury to High Wycombe road, about 9 miles south of Aylesbury. Take the A413 from Aylesbury, and turn right on the B4009. The Swan is just off the main road.

Though the village is home to a church with an interesting series of 14th century wall paintings, its real claim to fame is the nearby 16th century mansion, Chequers, the country residence of the British Prime Minister. The house was originally built in 1565 by William Hawtrey and much altered and enlarged in the 18th and 19th centuries. In 1920 its then owner, Lord Lee of Fareham, gave the house and estate to the nation to be used as a rural residence for the prime minister of the day. Lloyd George was the first to benefit from this generous benefaction.

At the heart of the small village of Great Kimble is **The Swan**, a mid-Victorian hostelry which has recently been extended to provide 4 guest rooms with en suite facilities and a spacious new dining area. The lunch menu offers a good range of appetising home-made main meals (chilli and lasgane, for example, or a smoked salmon salad), and a wide choice of filled jacket potatoes, omelettes, ploughman's and sandwiches. There is a more extensive evening menu and the blackboard lists details of daily specials, the chef's home made pie of the day and freshly made puddings. Devotees of real ales will find 3 of them on tap: Fuller's London Pride, Adnam's Bitter and a guest ale. In good weather, enjoy your refreshments in the peaceful beer garden to the rear.

Opening Hours: Mon-Fri: 12.00-15.00; 17.30-23.00. Sat: 12.00-23.00; Sun: 12.00-22.30

Food: Available every lunchtime and evening

Credit Cards: All major cards accepted

Accommodation: 4 guest rooms all en suite (1 family; 1 double; 2 twin)

Facilities: Beer garden; off road parking

Local Places of Interest/Activities: Ridgeway Path, 1 mile; Pulpit Hill, 2 miles; Golf, 3 miles; Chinnor and Princes Risborough Railway, 7 miles

The Waggon & Horses | **37**

39 Oxford Road,
Stone, Aylesbury
Buckinghamshire
HP17 8PD
Tel: 01296 748740

Directions:

From Aylesbury take the A418 towards Thame and Oxford. After about 3 miles you will come to Stone. The Waggon & Horses is on this main road, in the centre of the village.

This pleasant little village has a long history that stretches back to Roman times. Jewellery, weapons and tools crafted nearly 2000 years ago have been found nearby and are now in the museum in Aylesbury. The village also boasts a fine, partly-Norman church and amongst its treasures are a beautifully carved Norman font, some Tudor bench ends and some outstanding 15th century brasses.

At the heart of the village is **The Waggon & Horses**, a substantial building of local brick. Andrew and Victoria Ladyman took over here in the summer of 2000 and undertook a comprehensive programme of refurbishment, - enlarging the bar, updating the kitchen, and completely redecorating the whole pub. They have also introduced a completely new menu which offers a very wide choice of appetising meals and snacks. There are separate menus for vegetarians and children as well as a special deal for senior citizens available at lunchtimes only. The inn has an inviting beer garden which also includes a children's play area. Those who enjoy pub games will find a good selection on offer and the Ladymans also organise occasional Golf Days and live entertainment featuring music of the 60s and 70s.

Opening Hours: Mon-Thu: 11.30-15.30, 18.00-23.00; Fri-Sat: 11.30-23.00; Sun: 12.00-19.00

Food: Extensive menu of main meals and snacks; senior citizens' and children's menus

Credit Cards: Applied for

Facilities: Large beer garden; children's play area; small function room; off road parking

Entertainment: Pool; darts; dominoes; darts; Golf Day; live music of the 60s & 70s

Local Places of Interest/Activities: Waddesdon Manor (NT), 7 miles; Buckinghamshire Railway Centre, 8 miles; Long Crendon Courthouse (NT), 8 miles

The Hidden Inns of the South of England

This page is intentionally left blank

2 Berkshire

PLACES OF INTEREST:

PUBS AND INNS:

The Hidden Inns of the South of England

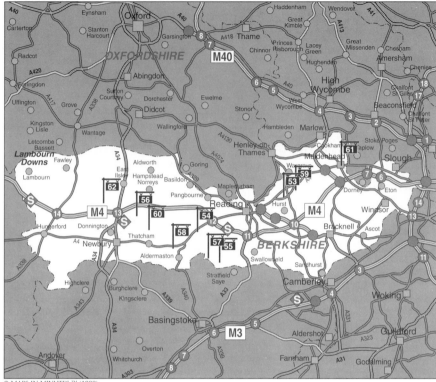

© MAPS IN MINUTES ™ (1999)

53 The Duke of Wellington, Twyford

54 The Fox & Hounds, Theale

55 Horse & Groom , Mortimer, nr Reading

56 Lamb Inn , Hermitage, nr Newbury

57 The Red Lion, Mortimer West End, nr Reading

58 The Rising Sun, Woolhampton, nr Reading

59 Royal Oak , Ruscombe

60 The Spotted Dog, Cold Ash, nr Newbury

61 The Stag & Hounds, Pinkneys Green, nr Maidenhead

62 Ye Olde Red Lion , Chieveley, nr Newbury

Please note all cross references refer to page numbers

Berkshire

The western area of Berkshire is dominated by the old Cloth Town of Newbury, which today is perhaps better known for its firstclass race course. The training of race horses is also a serious pursuit in the region, and the villages of Lambourn and East Ilsley are famous for the horses they have trained on the undulating downlands which run along the northern county border. Another feature of west Berkshire are the communication routes which flow across the region linking London with the West Country. Dominated today by the M4 motorway, the ancient Ridgeway path, England's oldest road, follows the county border with Oxfordshire. Thought to have become a route in the Bronze Age, over the centuries many different people have used the trackway as a thoroughfare for trade with the remoter parts of southwest England. Completed in 1810, the Kennet and Avon Canal crosses southern England from Bristol to join the River Thames at Reading. Entering the county at Hungerford, this major waterway passes through a charming rural landscape as it winds through villages and market towns. The canal prospered until the arrival of the Great Western Railway in 1841 and by the 1950s it was largely unnavigable. Fortunately, after a full clearing and restoration programme, the canal can once again by travelled its full length and it provides a wide variety of leisure activities for all.

Reading dominates the central region of Berkshire: a thriving commuter town with excellent links both to London and the west. However, although the town may, at first glance, seem to be very much a product of the 19th and 20th centuries, there has been a settlement here for many years and the remains of its Abbey can still be seen in Forbury Gardens. Perhaps, though, the town is best known for the imprisonment, in its gaol, of the playwright and poet Oscar Wilde.

Water dominates this area of Berkshire as the two main waterways, the River Thames and the Kennet and Avon Canal, join together at Reading. The Thames, forming the northern county border with Oxfordshire, has, along its southern banks, many delightful riverside villages where, naturally, boating has been a key feature for many years. The Victorian and Edwardian passion for the river has lead to the growth of many of the villages as fashionable places for a day trip or short holiday and they remain pleasurable places to visit today.

To the south, the Kennet and Avon Canal provides another insight into the days before road and rail travel became the norm for freight. Very much a working canal, linking London with the west, the visitor centre at Aldermaston Wharf offers visitors the chance to relive the lives of those working the waterway.

The eastern region of the Royal County of Berkshire is dominated by the 900 year presence of the Crown at Windsor. Building of the great castle was begun by William the Conqueror and, today, after the many additions and alterations over the centuries, it is a magnificent sight that provides a unique landmark for miles around. A major tourist attraction, whilst still being a royal residence, the castle is just one of the many places of interest which the small town of Windsor has to offer.

Across Windsor Great Park, the remains of the royal hunting forest, lies Ascot Racecourse. For one meeting each summer this is the place for the fashionable as people flock from all over the world to attend Royal Ascot but, for the rest of the year, this is an attractive and highly competitive course that was founded by Queen Anne in 1711.

42

The Thames also plays a great part in this area of Berkshire. There are numerous picturesque riverside towns and villages, several of which developed into fashionable riverside resorts during the Victorian era. Cookham, with its continuation of the ancient Swan Upping ceremony; Maidenhead, with the massive Boulter's Lock and Brunel's famous railway bridge; and Wraysbury, where King John signed the Magna Carta to appease the rebellious barons, are all places that not only exude history but provide pleasant walks along the river's banks. Places of Interest

PLACES OF INTEREST

ALDERMASTON

It was in this tranquil village, in 1840, that the William pear was first propagated by John Staid, the then village schoolmaster. First known as the Aldermaston pear, a cutting of the plant is believed to have been taken to Australia where is it now called the Bartlett pear. Still retaining much of its original 12th-century structure and with a splendid Norman door, the lovely **St Mary's Church** provides the setting for the York Mystery Cycle, nativity plays dating from the 14th century which are performed here each year. Using beautiful period costumes and contemporary music, including a piece written by William Byrd, the cycle lasts a week and the plays attract visitors from far and wide.

Another old custom still continued in the village is the auctioning of the grazing rights of Church Acres every three years. Using the ancient method of a candle auction, a pin, in this case a horseshoe nail, is inserted into the tallow of a candle one inch from the wick. The candle is lit while bidding takes place and the grazing rights go to the highest bidder as the pin drops out of the candle. Outside under a yew tree in the churchyard lies the grave of

Aldermaston Wharf

Maria Hale, formerly known as the Aldermaston witch. She was said to turn herself into a large brown hare and although the hare was never caught or killed, at one time a local keeper wounded it in the leg and from then on it was noticed that Maria Hale was lame!

Close to the village there is a delightful walk along the Kennet and Avon Canal to **Aldermaston Wharf**. A Grade II listed structure of beautifully restored 18th-century scalloped brickwork, the wharf is home to the **Kennet and Avon Canal Visitor Centre**, where the canalman's cottage houses an exhibition on the canal with information on its leisure facilities.

More recent history has seen the famous protest marches of the1950s outside the Atomic Research Establishment, which though situated in the grounds of Aldermaston Court, rather mysteriously, does not feature on Ordnance Survey Maps.

ALDWORTH

The parish **Church of St Mary** is famous for housing the **Aldworth Giants** - the larger than life effigies of the de la Beche family which date back to the 14th century. The head of the family, Sir Philip, who lies here with eight other members of his family, was the Sheriff of Berkshire and valet to Edward II. Though now somewhat defaced the effigies were so legendary that the church was visited by Elizabeth I. Outside, in the churchyard, are the remains of a once magnificent 1000 year old yew tree that was sadly damaged in a storm.

Nearby, at **Little Aldworth**, the grave of the poet Laurence Binyon, who wrote the famous lines "At the going down of the sun and in the morning, we shall remember them," can be

Church of St Mary, Aldworth

pavilion built in memory of his parents by the late Mr Childe-Beale which is, to-day, the focal point of **Beale Park**. Covering some 300 acres of ancient water meadow, the park is home to a wide range of birds and animals. There are carefully tendered small herds of unusual farm animals, including rare breeds of sheep and goats, Highland cattle, deer, and South American llama, over 120 species of birds living in their natural habitat, and a pets' corner for smaller children. However, the park's work is not confined to the keeping of animals and, as well as planting a **Community Woodland**, an ancient reed bed has been restored. The park's other main attraction housed in the pavilion is the **Model Boat Collection**, which is one of the finest of its kind.

However, the village's main feature is the National Trust owned **Basildon Park**, an elegant, classical house designed in the 18th century by Carr of York, which is undoubtedly Berkshire's foremost mansion. Built between 1776 and 1783 for Francis Sykes, an official of the East India Company, the house is almost text book in style though it does have the unusual addition of an Anglo-Indian room. The interior, finished by JB Papworth and restored to its original splendour after World War II, is rich in fine plaster work, pictures, and furniture and the rooms open to the public include the Octagon Room and a decorative Shell Room. If the name Basildon seems familiar it is probably as a result of the notepaper: the head of the papermaking firm of Dickinson visited the house and decided to use the name for the high quality paper.

seen in the churchyard and, opposite the Bell Inn, there is one of the deepest wells in the country. Topped by great beams, heavy cogs, and wheels, it is some 327 feet deep.

ASCOT

A small village until 1711 when Queen Anne moved the Windsor race meeting to here and founded the world famous **Ascot Racecourse**. Its future secured when the Duke of Cumberland established a stud at Windsor in the 1750s, by the end of the century the meetings were being attended by Royalty on a regular basis. Today, Royal Ascot, held every June, is an international occasion of fashion and style with pageantry and tradition that is followed by racing enthusiasts world wide.

To the west of the now small town lies **Englemere Pond**, a Site of Special Scientific Interest and also a local nature reserve. Once part of the royal hunting ground which surrounded Windsor Castle and still owned by the Crown Estate, the main feature is the shallow acidic lake which offers a wide range of habitats from open water to marsh, for the many species of plants, birds, and animals, and insects found here.

BASILDON

This small village is the last resting place of the inventor and agricultural engineer, Jethro Tull, and his grave can be seen in the churchyard. Here too is a monument which commemorates the tragic drowning of two brothers. Outside the churchyard is a further memorial, a classic

BRACKNELL

Designated a new town in 1948, Bracknell has developed quickly from a small place in poor sandy heathland into a large modern town with one of the first purpose built shopping centres in the country - opened in the 1960s. As well as being home to a number of high tech companies, Bracknell is also the home of the Meteorological Office.

However, the first mention of Bracknell has been traced back to a 10th-century Saxon document where, spelt as *Braccan Heal*, the name is thought to mean a piece of land belonging to Bracca. The community developed here at the junction of two major routes through Windsor Forest.

44

Seen from many parts of the town and a very prominent landmark is the centrally located **Bill Hill**. At the top of the hill can be found a circular mound of earth, hollowed out at the centre, which is all that remains of a Bronze Age round barrow. Used through out that period, these burial mounds, which may cover either individuals or groups, are the most common prehistoric monuments in the country even if this location, in the heart of a modern town, seems a little curious.

What remains of the great royal hunting ground, **Windsor Forest** (also called **Bracknell Forest**) lies to the south of the town and this vast area has over 30 parks and nature reserves and some 45 miles of footpaths and bridleways. Of particular interest in the area is The **Lookout Discovery Park**, an interactive science centre that brings to life the mysteries of both science and nature. Throughout the woodland surrounding the centre there are nature trails and walks to points of interest as well as the inappropriately named **Caesar's Camp**. Not a Roman fort, this camp is an Iron Age hill fort built over 2000 years ago but, close by, lies the

Eastern Gateway to Caeser's Camp, Bracknell

Roman link road between London and Silchester. Locally known as the **Devil's Highway**, it is said to have acquired the name as the local inhabitants, after the Romans had left, thought that only the Devil could undertake such a feat of engineering.

Also to the south of the town is the impressive Coral Reef, an indoor leisure pool with a tropical climate that provides family fun all year round.

COOKHAM

This pretty, small town, on the banks of the River Thames, was made famous by the artists Sir Stanley Spencer, who used Cookham as the setting for many of his paintings. Born here towards the end of the 19th century, the town's tribute to its most renowned resident is the **Stanley Spencer Gallery**, a permanent exhibition of his work which is housed in the converted Victorian chapel Stanley visited as a child.

DONNINGTON

Despite being so close to the town of Newbury, Donnington has managed to retain its village identity and atmosphere. To the west of the village, and visible from the road, is Donnington Grove House. Built in 1759 and designed by the architect John Chute, this was the home, in the late 18th century, of the Brummell family and Beau Brummell, the instigator of the Bath Society, lived here as a child.

However, most visitors to the village come to see the **Donnington Castle**, a late 14th-century defence that was built by Sir Richard Abberbury. Once a magnificent structure, only the twin towered gatehouse survives amidst the impressive earthworks. Owned by English Heritage, the castle had its most eventful period during the Civil War when it was the scene of one of the longest sieges of the conflict. Charles

Donnington Castle

I's troops were held here for 20 months and this was the time when most of the castle was destroyed. During the second of the two battles of Newbury, Charles I stayed at nearby Shaw House, whilst Sir John Boys defended the castle.

DORNEY

One of the finest Tudor manor houses in England, **Dorney Court**, just a short walk from the River Thames, has been the home of the Palmer family since 1530. Built in around 1440, it is an enchanting building which also houses some real treasures including early 15th and 16th century oak furniture, beautiful 17th century

Dorney Court

lacquer furniture, and 400 years of family portraits. It is also here that the first pineapple in England was grown in 1665. However, it is one owner who is perhaps remembered above all the others: Sir Roger Palmer was the husband of Charles II's most notorious mistress, Barbara, an intelligent and beautiful woman, Roger was given the title Earl of Castlemaine for his compliance with the affair.

Found on **Dorney Common** is the traditional English village of **Boveney**, which served as a wharf in the 13th century as timber was being transported from Windsor Forest. The flint and clapboard church of St Mary Magdalene, down by the riverside, was the setting for several scenes from Kevin Costner's film *Robin Hood Prince of Thieves*.

EAST ILSLEY

This attractive downland village has managed to retain several interesting features and, in particular, by the village pond can be seen the winding mechanism of the now long disused village well. However, it is on sheep that the village prospered and from the beginning of the 17th century East Ilsley held fortnightly sheep fairs that were second only in size to Smithfield, London. At their peak in the 19th century, permanent pens were erected in the main street to contain the animals and, on one

day, it was recorded that 80,000 sheep were penned.

There is an old jingle about the village which goes: "Far famed for sheep and wool, though not for spinners, for sportsmen, doctors, publi-

Village Green and Duck Pond, East Ilsley

cans, and sinners." Naturally, whilst the sheep fairs were flourishing, the publicans were also making good money but after the last fair, in 1934, the number of inns fell from as many as 26, at one time, to just three.

Today, along with its neighbour, West Ilsley, the village is associated with race horses which use the gallops on the downs as their training grounds. Though not as large as Lambourn, there are still successful stables in the area.

ETON

Found just across the River Thames from Windsor, this town has grown up around **Eton College**, the famous public school that was founded in 1440 by Henry VI. Originally intended for 70 poor and worthy scholars and to educate students for the newly created King's College, at Cambridge University, the college has been added to greatly over the years. Of the original school buildings, only the College Hall and the kitchen have survived; the great gatehouse and Lupton's Tower were added in the 16th century and the Upper School dates from around 1690. However, the school has kept many ancient traditions over the years including the black tail mourning coats that were originally worn on the death of George III in 1820 and which are still worn today.

For centuries the college has educated the great and the good, including 19 prime ministers, artists, poets, and authors including

46

William Pitt the Elder, Harold Macmillan, Thomas Gray (author of *Elegy Written in a Country Churchyard*), Henry Fielding, Shelley, George Orwell, and Ian Fleming. Eton has also been famous in the past

Eton College, Eton

for its strict discipline, personified in 1832 by a master who told the pupils when they rebelled: "Boys, you must be pure of heart, for if not, I will thrash you until you are."

FAWLEY

This small downlands village is known to many avid Thomas Hardy readers as the village of Marygreen in one of his most tragic novels, Jude the Obscure. The writer's grandmother, Mary Hardy, is known to have lived here with her aunt for the first 13 years of her life following the death of both her parents. Though Mary never spoke of her painful memories, her sad early life was known to Hardy and they certainly coloured his view of the village. The ill-fated hero of the book, Jude Fawley, is said to have been very much based on Hardy himself and, when the writer visited the village to trace his relatives, he wrote in his journal "I entered a ploughed field which might have been called the Valley of Brown Melancholy, where the silence was remarkable."

HAMPSTEAD NORREYS

Just to the north of the village lies **Wyld Court Rainforest**, a fascinating conservation centre that is owned by the World Land Trust. The Trust, a charitable organisation founded in 1989, not only purchases and protects areas of tropical forests all over the world but also concerns itself with education. Here, at the indoor

rainforest, where the temperature never falls below 70°C, visitors have the opportunity to walk through the humid and shadowy jungles of the Lowland Tropical Forests, the cool, orchid-festooned and ferny Cloudforests, and the Amazon with its amazing flowers and wonderful bromeliads. There is also a unique collection of spectacular and rare plants, tranquil pools, the sounds of the topics, and rainforest animals including a pair of time marmosets, tree frogs, iguanas, and Courtney, the dwarf crocodile.

HUNGERFORD

Although not mentioned in the Domesday Book, by the Middle Ages this old market town was well established and the manor of Hungerford had some distinguished lords including Simon de Montford and John of Gaunt. A quiet and peaceful place, Hungerford's heyday came in the 18th century when the turnpike road from London to Bath, which passes through the town, was built. By 1840, the town had eight coaching inns serving the needs of travellers and the prosperity continued with the opening of the **Kennet and Avon Canal** but the building of the railway took much of the trade away and the town reverted back, once more, to its early, gentle lifestyle. However, several of the old coaching inns have survived and, in particular, The Bear Hotel. Although it has an impressive Georgian frontage , the building actually dates back to 1494, making it one of the oldest in the town. It was here, in 1688, that a meeting took place between William of Orange and representatives of James II which culminated in the end of the House of Stuart and the flight of James II to France.

As well as still holding a weekly market, the town also continues the ancient tradition known as the Hocktide Festival or Tutti Day (tutti meaning a bunch of flowers). Held every year on the second Tuesday after Easter, the festival was originally used as a means of collecting an early form of council tax. During the colourful event, two men carrying a six foot pole decorated with ribbons and flowers go around each household collecting the tax. To ease the burden of their visit, the men share a drink with the man of the house, give him an orange, and kiss his wife before collecting their penny payment. Today, however, though the visits are made no money is collected.

HURST

This attractive, scattered village is home to a Norman church, well endowed with monuments, and facing which there are some 17th century almshouses. The village bowling green is said to have been made for Charles II though there is little evidence to support this claim.

Just to the south lies **Dinton Pastures Country Park**, a large area of lakes, rivers, hedgerows, and meadows rich in wildlife. Until the 1970s, this area was excavated for sand and gravel, but the former pits are now attractive lakes and ponds: one of which has been stocked for coarse fishing and the largest is set aside for canoeing and windsurfing.

LAMBOURN

Lying up on the Berkshire Downs, in the extreme west of the county, this village, which has the feel of a small town, is well known for the race horses that are trained here. Once known as Chipping - which means market - Lambourn, the village once had not only a weekly market but also three annual fairs.

Whether a horse racing fan or not, Lambourn has plenty to amuse and occupy the visitor. Its medieval **Church of St Michael** is one of the finest parish churches in Berkshire. Originally Norman and constructed on the cruciform plan, over the years the church has been greatly altered and extended though the west end still has its Norman doorway, complete with zigzag ornamentation. Close to the church can be found the pleasing **Isbury Almshouses**, built around a quadrangle, that were founded in 1502 though the present houses date from 1852.

The **Lambourn Trainers' Association** organise guided tours of the village's famous stables and also the trips up to the gallops to view the horses going through their paces. An informative and enjoyable way to spent a couple of hours, the visits, for obvious reasons, have to be by appointment only.

To the north of the village are **Lambourn Seven Barrows**, one of the most impressive Bronze Age burial sites in the country. However, the name is somewhat misleading as there are no fewer than 32 barrows up here but arguably the best group consists of six bowl barrows, two double bowl barrows, two saucer barrows, and a single disc barrow.

NEWBURY

This crossroads town has, for many years, dominated the rural area of West Berkshire. Prospering during the Middle Ages, and afterwards, on the importance of the woollen industry, the town became famous as **The Cloth Town**. Among the various characters who made their money out of the weaving of the wool the best known is Jack of Newbury (John Smallwood or Winchcombe), who died in 1519. Asked to raise two horsemen and two footmen for Henry VIII's campaign against the Scots, Jack raised 50 of each and led them himself. However, they only got as far as Stony Stratford in Buckinghamshire before news of the victory of Flodden reached them and they turned for home. In fact, Jack of Newbury was rather more than just a local merchant and his life story has become a local legend. Apprenticed to a rich Newbury clothmaker, when his master died, Jack married the widow and, upon her death, he inherited the wealthy business. Over the years he became one of the town's leading merchants employing as many as a thousand people. After displaying his loyalty to the king, Jack was offered a knighthood which he turned down on the grounds that he wanted to remain equal with his workers.

Evidence of the town's wealth can be seen in the splendid 'Wool' **Church of St Nicholas** which was constructed between 1500 and 1532. Built on the site of a Norman church, no expense was spared and Jack of Newbury gave the money for the magnificent five bayed nave. Unfortunately, the church has seen much restoration work, particularly during the Victorian age, but the fine pupil and elaborately decorated nave roof have survived.

During the Civil War there were two battles fought nearby, in 1643 and 1644, and following the war, the town's clothing industry declined. However, the 18th century saw the construction of turnpike roads and Newbury became a busy coaching stop on the road from London to Bath. The town further opened up to travellers and the needs of carriers with the completion of the **Kennet and Avon Canal** in 1810. **Newbury Lock**, built in 1796, was the first lock to be built along the canal and it is also the only one to have lever-operated ground paddles (the sluices that let in the water) which are known as 'Jack Cloughs'.

48

Back in the centre of the town, in the Market Square is the **Newbury Museum**, housed in the 17th-century cloth hall and the adjacent 18th-century granary, a store used by traders travelling the canal. As well as the archaeological section, the history of the town is fully explained, including the two battles of Newbury during the Civil War. Though much of the town centre dates from the Victorian age, there are some other interesting older buildings to be found. Aside from the Church of St Nicholas, visitors can see Lower Raymonds Buildings, a dignified row of almshouses dating from 1796, and the newer Upper Raymonds Buildings which were completed in 1826. Also in the area is St Bartholomew's Hospital, the town's oldest charitable institution, which was founded by King John though the building dates from the 17th century.

Just to the north of the town lies **Shaw House**, a splendid example of Elizabethan architecture and the finest in Berkshire, that dates from 1581. Built by a wealthy clothing merchant, Thomas Dolman, he chose to put his money into this elaborate house rather than his business, much to the displeasure of his workers. Though not open to the public, glimpses of the house can be seen from the road.

Those arriving in Newbury from the south will pass the Victorian **Falkland Memorial**, which should not be confused with the 1980s conflict in the South Atlantic. It is, in fact, a memorial to Lord Falkland who was killed at the first battle of Newbury in 1643. Finally, to the east of the town lies the first class **Newbury Racecourse** which offers both flat and National Hunt racing throughout the year.

PANGBOURNE

Situated at the confluence of the River Pang and the River Thames, the town grew up in the late 19th and early 20th centuries as a fashionable place to live. As a result there are several attractive Victorian and Edwardian villas to be seen including a row of ornate Victorian houses known as the Seven Deadly Sins. It was here that the author Kenneth Graham retired, living at **Church Cottage** beside the church. Graham married late in life and it was whilst living here that he wrote *The Wind in the Willows*, the original bedtime stories that he invented for his son which were based along the banks of the river between Pangbourne and Marlow.

Visitors to the town who cross the elegant iron bridge to neighbouring Whitchurch must still pay a toll, though now very small. The right to exact the toll has existed since 1792 and it is one of the very few surviving privately owned toll bridges. It was at **Whitchurch Lock** that the characters in Jerome K Jerome's *Three Men in a Boat* abandoned their craft, after a series of mishaps, and returned to London.

READING

This thriving commuter town is a delightful combination of over a thousand years of history and a vibrant and modern city. There are Victorian brick buildings nestling beside beautiful medieval churches, famous coaching inns opposite high tech offices and some of the best shopping in the area. However, Reading began as a Saxon settlement between the Rivers Thames and Kennet. A defensible site, it was used by the Danes as a base for their attack on Wessex in the 9th century.

The town grew up around its **Abbey**, which was founded in 1121 by Henry I, the youngest son of William the Conqueror, and it was consecrated by Thomas à Becket in 1164. The abbey went on to become one of the most important religious houses - its relics include a piece of Jesus' shoe, the tooth of St Luke, and a slice of Moses' rod - and parliament were known to meet here on occasions. As Henry I is also buried here, Reading is one of only a handful of towns where Kings of England have been laid to rest. Today, the abbey ruins can be found in **Forbury Gardens** on the banks of the River Kennet. Fortunately, some of the abbey's won-

St Mary's Church, Reading

derful architecture can still be seen and, in particular, there is St Laurence's Church and the abbey Gatehouse. The Gatehouse was, after the Reformation, turned into a school and, in 1785, Jane Austen was a pupil here. The gardens are also home to the **Maiwand Lion**, which commemorates the men of the Berkshire Regiment who died in the Afghan Campaign of 1879.

Another originally Norman building in the town is **St Mary's Church**, the south arcade of which dates from around 1200. The most attractive feature here is the church tower: erected in 1550 it is of a high distinguished chequerboard pattern which uses stone blocks and flint panels.

Adjacent to the abbey ruins is another of Reading's famous buildings - **Reading Prison**. Hardly a tourist attraction, it was here that Oscar Wilde was imprisoned and where he wrote *De Profundis*. His confinement here also inspired the writer to compose the epic *Ballad of Reading Gaol* whilst staying in Paris in 1898.

Though the town developed during the Middle Ages as a result of a flourishing woollen industry, it was during the 18th century with the coming of both the turnpike roads and the opening of the **Kennet and Avon Canal** which saw the town boom. By the 19th century, Reading was known for its three Bs: beer, bulbs, and biscuits. As the trade of the canal and River Thames increased, the movement of corn and malt explains the growth of the brewing trade here whilst bulbs is a reference to Sutton Seeds who were founded here in 1806. The world renowned biscuit-making firm of Huntley and Palmer began life here in 1826, when Joseph Huntley founded the firm, to be joined, in 1841, by George Palmer, inventor of the stamping machine.

The Story of Reading, a permanent exhibition at the **Reading Museum**, is the ideal place to gain a full understanding of the history of the town, from the earliest times to the present day. Here, too, can be seen the world's only full size replica of the Bayeux Tapestry, made in the 19th century and which features Edward the Confessor, once Lord of the Royal Manor in Reading, as a central figure. As a contrast to the museum's displays depicting the life of the town in the 20th century, The Silchester Gallery is devoted to the describing day to day life at Calleva Atrebatum, the Roman town of Silchester, using Roman artefacts unearthed there during early excavations.

Situated on the banks of the River Kennet and housed in a range of canal buildings, **Blake's Lock Museum** describes the life of the town in the 19th and early 20th centuries. Originally part of a pumping station built at Blake's Weir in the

Blake's Lock Museum, Reading

1870s, the buildings themselves are also of interest and are superb examples of Victorian industrial architecture combined with decorative Reading brickwork. As well as covering the town's close links with its waterways and the part they played in Reading's prosperity, visitors can wander around the reconstructed shops and workshops.

Finally, founded in 1892 Reading Extension College took the examinations of the University of London until 1925 when the college became a university in its own right. Lying to the south of the town centre, the university campus is home to the **Museum of English Rural Life**, where not only is there a splendid wagon collection but also displays covering farm tools, machinery, and equipment, as well as rural crafts.

SANDHURST

The town is famous as being the home of the **Royal Military Academy**, the training place for army officers since it was established in 1907. The academy's **Staff College Museum** tells the history of officer training from its inception to the present day. Long before the academy was founded, in Saxon times, this settlement, in the valley of the River Blackwater, was part of the Parish of Sonning. Although there are no written records of a church having been here, in 1220, William de Wanda, Dean of Salisbury, visited a new and beautiful chapel at Sandhurst. The present Church of St Michael and All Angels, situated high above the River

50

Blackwater, was built in 1853 to the designs of GE Street. However, it takes several old features from the previous church, including the Norman style doorway and an old beam supporting the wooden roof that is inscribed to Charles I and dated 1647.

Close by is **Trilakes**, a picturesque country park set in 18 acres and, naturally, there are lakes here. This is a wonderful place to visit with children as there are a wide assortment of pets and farm animals which they can get to know, including miniature horses, pygmy goats, donkeys, aviary birds, pot-bellied pigs and Soay sheep.

SWALLOWFIELD

This ancient settlement has been inhabited since prehistoric times and, by 1071, the manor was held by Roger de Breteuil, the originator of the Domesday Survey. Since then, the manor house, **Swallowfield Park**, has been associated with both royalty and notable personalities. The present house (unfortunately now all but a shell) was built in 1678 by Wren's assistant William Talman, for the 2nd Earl of Clarendon who acquired the estate upon marrying the heiress. In 1719, the park was purchased by Thomas Pitt, a former Governor of Madras, who used the proceeds of the sale of a large diamond he bought whilst out in India. The diamond can now be seen in the Louvre Museum, Paris, and Pitt's story was the basis of the novel, *The Moonstone*, by the author Wilkie Collins, who visited the house in 1860. The Italian Doorway, by Talman, is probably the house's most outstanding remaining feature and it marks the entrance to the walled garden. Here can be found a dog's graveyard where one of Charles Dickens' dogs, was bequeathed to his friend and owner of the house, Sir Charles Russell, by the novelist.

THATCHAM

Believed to be the oldest village in Britain, it is hard to imagine that this now large suburb of Newbury was once a small place. **Thatcham Moor** is one of the largest areas of inland freshwater reed beds in the country and, as well as the reeds which can grow up to six feet in height, the area supports numerous species of marshland and aquatic plants. Birds too abound here and it is an important breeding ground for reed and sedge warblers.

WARGRAVE

This charming village developed as a settlement in the 10th century at the confluence of the Rivers Thames and Loddon on an area of flat land in a wooded valley. Mentioned in the Domesday Book, when it was referred to as Weregrave, in 1218, the Bishop of Winchester was granted the rights to hold a market here by Henry III. However, this was obviously not a great success as there is no record of a market taking place after the 13th century.

Now an attractive riverside village, the peace was disturbed here in 1914 when suffragettes burnt down the church in protest at the vicar's refusal to remove the word 'obey' from the marriage service. In the churchyard however, undisturbed by the riot, lies the **Hannen Mausoleum**, a splendid monument that was designed for the family by Sir Edwin Lutyens in 1906.

Another interesting sight here can be found on the outskirts of the village, at Park Place. In 1788, the estate was owned by General Henry Conway, Governor of Jersey and, in recognition of his services, the people of the island gave the general a complete **Druids' Temple**. The massive stones were transported from St Helier to the estate and erected in a 25 foot circle in the gardens of his mansion. In 1870, Park Place was destroyed by fire and the estate broken up but today the temple stands in the garden of **Temple Combe**, close to a house designed by the famed American architect, Frank Lloyd Wright. The only house of his in this country, it was built, in 1958, on an elaborate U-shaped design and has suede panelled walls inside.

WINDSOR

This old town grew up beneath the walls of the castle in a compact group of streets leading from the main entrance. Charming and full of character, this is a place of delightful timber-framed and Georgian houses and shop fronts, with riverside walks beside the Thames, and a wonderful racecourse. The elegant **Guildhall**, partly built by Wren in the 17th century, has an open ground floor for market stalls whilst the council chambers are on the first floor. Concerned that they might fall through the floor onto the stalls below the council members requested that Wren put in supporting pillars in the middle of the market hall. As his reassurances that the building was sound fell on deaf ears, Wren complied with their wishes but the pillars he built did not quite meet the ceiling - there by proving his point!

The grand central station, in the heart of the town, was built in 1897 to commemorate Queen Victoria's Diamond Jubilee and it is now home to a fascinating exhibition, **Royalty and Empire**, which charts the life and times of the country's longest reigning monarch. Close by, in the High Street, is another exhibition well worth visiting, The **Town and Crown Exhibition**. Here the development of the town and the influences of the Crown are explained in an imaginative and visual manner.

Meanwhile a trip to The **Dungeons of Windsor** provides a step back in time and an investigation of the town's history with a special regard for stories of crime and punishment from the early days of 13th-century lawlessness through to the harsh Victorian era. The Household Cavalry also have their home in Windsor, at Combermere Barracks, and here there is the superb **Household Cavalry Museum**, which displays collections of their uniforms, weapons, and armour from 1600 through to the present day.

In a perfect setting beside the River Thames, **Royal Windsor Racecourse** is one of the most attractive in the country. Though less grand than neighbouring Ascot, the summer evening meetings here are particularly enjoyable.

However, it is **Windsor Castle**, situated on Castle Hill, which draws thousands of tourists

Windsor Castle

annually to this small town. The largest castle in the country and a royal residence for over 900 years, the castle was begun in the late 11th century by William the Conqueror as one in a chain of such defences which stood on the approaches to London. Over the years various

monarchs have added to the original typical Norman castle, the most notable additions being made by Henry VIII, Charles II, and George IV.

Various aspects of the castle are open to the public, in particular the sixteen state apartments which hold a remarkable collection of furniture, porcelain, and armour. Carvings by Grinling Gibbons are to be seen everywhere and the walls are adorned with a plethora of masterpieces, including paintings by Van Dyck and Rembrandt. On a somewhat smaller scale, but nonetheless impressive, is **Queen Mary's Dolls' House**. Designed by Sir Edwin Lutyens for Queen Mary, this is a perfect miniature palace, complete with working lifts and lights and also running water. Taking over three years to build, 1500 tradesmen were employed to ensure that every last detail was correct and the house was presented to the queen in 1924. In November 1992, a massive fire swept through the northeast corner of the castle and no-one in the country at the time will forget the incredible pictures of the great tower alight. After much restoration, the affected rooms, including the massive St George's Hall, the scene of many state banquets, have all been completed and are once again open to the public.

Windsor Castle is not just a defensive structure but it was also an ecclesiastical centre and, within its walls, is the magnificent **St George's Chapel**. Started by Edward IV in 1478, and taking some 50 years to finish, the chapel is not only one of the country's greatest religious buildings but also a wonderful example of the Perpendicular Gothic style. As well as being the last resting place of several monarchs, it is also the Chapel of the Most Noble Order of the Garter, Britain's highest order of chivalry.

Frogmore House, a modest manor house from the early 18th century, stands in Home

Frogmore House, Windsor

Park, and over the years it has acted as a second, more relaxed royal residence than nearby Windsor Castle. During Queen Victoria's reign it was the home of her mother, the Duchess of Kent and now, famously, it is also home to the magnificent **Royal Mausoleum** dedicated to Prince Albert and also where Queen Victoria herself is buried beside her beloved husband. Only open to the public on two days in May, the mausoleum, in the delightful gardens laid out in the 1790s, remains a sombre yet restful place.

To the south of the town lies **Windsor Great Park**, a remnant of the once extensive Royal Hunting Forest, and a unique area of open parkland, woodland, and impressive views. The **Long Walk** stretches from the castle to Snow Hill, some three miles away, on top of which stands a huge bronze of George III on horseback put there in 1831. Queen Anne added the three mile ride to nearby Ascot race course. On the park's southern side lies **Smith's Lawn**, where polo matches are played most summer weekends. Windsor Great Park is also the setting for the Cartier International competition, polo's highlight event held every July, and the National Driving Championships.

First laid in 1931, **The Savill Garden**, created by Sir Eric Savill, is one of the best and finest woodland gardens to be seen anywhere. A garden for all seasons, there are colourful flower gardens, secret glades, and alpine meadows.

Finally, to the southwest and in 150 acres of parkland, is **Legoland Windsor**, where there are a whole range of amazing lego models on display which have been made from over 20 million bricks, together with educational and fun rides and amusements for all ages.

The Duke of Wellington | **53**

27 High Street,
Twyford,
Berkshire
RG10 9AG
Tel: 0118 934 0456

Directions:

From the A4 Reading to
Maidenhead road, turn
right towards Twyford.
This will bring you into
Twyford High Street:
the Duke of Wellington
pub is on the left.

**The Duke of Welling-
ton** enjoys the distinc-
tion of being the old-
est pub in Twyford, with a history going back to the 1650s. It's a spacious, brick built
inn with a very large beer garden, complete with children's play area, and a patio with
tables and chairs for sunny days. Inside, there are 2 bars with ancient beams, a Victorian fireplace and vintage pictures.

Your hosts, Bill and Karen Suter, have been in the trade for some 8 years but only
recently took over here. They have already acquired a good reputation for the wholesome fare on offer. Every lunchtime except Sunday they serve a wide selection of bar
snacks and meals, - burgers, sandwiches, jacket potatoes, ploughman's, home-cooked
ham with eggs & chips, and main courses such as home-made Chilli with rice, as well
as daily specials. Real ale lovers will find a choice of five brews, one of which is regularly changed, and there's also a range of wines available.

The Duke of Wellington has been listed in the CAMRA Good Beer Guide every
year since 1982 giving an indication of the importance they attach to quality ales.

Opening Hours: Mon-Fri: 11.30-14.30;
17.00-23.00; Sat: 11.30-14.00, 18.00-23.00;
Sun: 12.00-22.30

Food: A full range of main meals and bar
snacks, lunchtime Mon-Sat

Credit Cards: None

Facilities: Large beer garden; children's
play area; functions for parties of 20-25

catered for in the Saloon Bar; small car
park but public car park nearby

Entertainment: On-line computer golf
game, Fruit machine

Local Places of Interest/Activities:
Courage Shire Horse Centre, 6 miles;
Thames Path, 2 miles; Henley-on-Thames,
5 miles

54 The Fox & Hounds

Sunnyside, Theale,
Berkshire, RG7 4BE
Tel/Fax: 01189 302295

Directions:

From Junction 12 of the M4 take the A4 towards Newbury and at the first roundabout turn left and follow the signs to the station. After crossing the bridge over the railway line by the station continue for 1 mile and the Fox and Hounds can be found on the left hand side.

Many hundreds of thousands of travellers speeding eastwards along the M4 must have wondered about the curious round tower that stands in a field on the left just before you reach Junction 12. Built of plain red brick, the hollow structure has pointed but bricked-up windows and an open arch at its foot. The favoured explanation for this purposeless building is that it was built a young Victorian gentleman who had fallen in love with a girl at nearby Sulhampstead House. He erected it to 'honour his forbidden love'.

The Fox and Hounds is a lively hostelry run by Don and Sue Guppy, a warm and sociable couple who have attracted a loyal clientele of locals and visitors alike to their welcoming inn. Both the food and the drink here are highly recommended. There's a comprehensive menu of main meals and bar snacks available at lunchtimes, Monday to Saturday, with a traditional roast lunch on Sunday. The evening menu again offers a wide choice of meat, fish and vegetarian options. The Fox and Hounds is a particular favourite with devotees of real ale. There are always half a dozen real ales on tap at any one time and during the pub's annual Beer festival no fewer than 18 different brews are available. Other appealing features of the inn include its family garden and the live jazz musicians who play during Sunday lunchtime and on regular jazz evenings.

Opening Hours: Mon-Fri: 11.00-15.00; 17.00-23.00. Sat: 12.00-15.00; 1800-23.00. Sun: 12.00-15.00; 19.00-22.30

Food: Main meals and bar snacks every lunchtime and evening, except Sunday lunchtime when there's a roast

Credit Cards: All major cards accepted

Facilities: Garden & patio to the front; function room; ample parking to the rear

Entertainment: Bar billiards; jazz quartet at Sunday lunchtimes; regular Jazz Nights; annual Beer Festival

Local Places of Interest/Activities: Kennet & Avon Canal nearby; Basildon Park (NT), 7 miles; Stratfield Saye House, 9 miles

Horse & Groom

The Street,
Mortimer, Reading,
Berkshire RG7 3RD
Tel: 0118 933 2813
Fax: 0118 933 1489

Directions:

From the M4 take Exit 11 on to the A33 towards Basingstoke. At the first roundabout, take the third exit, signposted to Mortimer Grazeley. Stay on this road until you come to a mini-roundabout. Turn right up the hill. The Horse & Groom is on the right, opposite the common.

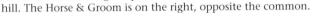

The **Horse & Groom** is rather unusual in having not just one, but two inn signs, - one for the horse and one for the groom. And instead of hanging out from the wall, they are placed flat against it as if in an Art Gallery. The village of Mortimer was well-established at the time of the Domesday Book and there's clear evidence that it was inhabited long before that. In the churchyard stands a rare Saxon tombstone marking the burial place of Aegalward, one of King Canute's most trusted ministers in the early 11th century. Also of interest in the village is its railway station, - one of the very few remaining to have been designed by the famed 19th century railway engineer, Isambard Kingdom Brunel.

During the summer, patrons of the Horse & Groom can enjoy its spacious beer garden, complete with a children's play area. All year round they can settle down in one of the two bars with their high Victorian ceilings, open fire and a decor that echoes the inn's equestrian name, - lots of brasses, horse tackle and sporting pictures. Mine hosts, Barrie and Pauline Ineson, offer an excellent choice of hearty, wholesome food that ranges from light meals (baguettes, burgers, jacket potatoes), to hearty main courses (home made pies, grills, curries and vegetarian choices). Add to that daily specials and a selection of tempting mini-dishes for children. For a drink to accompany your meal, choose between one of the 4 real ales on tap or a selection from the limited wine list.

Opening Hours: Mon-Thu: 11.30-15.00; 17.30-23.00; Fri-Sat: 11.30-23.00. Sun: 12.00-22.30

Food: Full meals and bar snacks

Credit Cards: All major cards accepted except Amex and Diners

Facilities: Large car park opposite

Entertainment: Quiz Night every other Sunday; darts, pool; cards; dominoes

Local Places of Interest/Activities: Roman Wall, 3 miles; Amphitheatre Museum, 3 miles; walking

Internet/Website: barrie.ineson@virginnet.co.uk

56 Lamb Inn

Long Lane
Hermitage
nr Newbury
Berkshire
RG18 9LY
Tel: 01635 200348
Fax: 01635 203153

Directions:

Take the B4009 from Newbury. About 5 miles along this road is the village of Hermitage. As you enter the village, the Lamb Inn is on the right.

Built in 1889 as a residence for the local gentry, the **Lamb Inn** was converted to a pub in the early 1900s. It's a pleasant looking building of warm red brick, colourful in summer with hanging baskets and window boxes of flowers. It boasts two gardens, one to the front, another at the rear. Inside, there are real fires and a panelled bar. A recently completed extension provides an additional seating area and a games room complete with darts, pool and fruit machines. Non-smokers will appreciate the designated non-smoking area. The Lamb Inn also has a function room which can accommodate up to 25 people.

Your hosts are Sally and Keith Giles who although they have not been here long have established a reputation for good, wholesome pub food which is served throughout the inn. They also offer 5 real ales, all of which are rotated, and a fairly extensive wine list based on a mini cellar.

Opening hours: Mon-Thu: 11.00-15.00; Fri-Sat: 11.00-23.00; Sun: 11.00-22.30

Food: Traditional "pub fayre"

Credit Cards: All major cards accepted

Facilities: Gardens to front and rear; Function Room accommodating up to 25, large car park

Entertainment: Darts, pool, and fruit machines in games room. Live music once a month

Local Places of Interest/Activities: Donnington Castle, Kennet & Avon Canal close by with horse-drawn barge tours

The Red Lion 57

Church Road,
Mortimer West End,
nr Reading,
Berkshire RG7 2HU
Tel: 0118 970 0169
Fax: 0118 970 1729

Directions:

From Exit 12 of the M4, take the A4 towards Newbury. After 4 miles, just before the roundabout, turn left on minor road towards Padworth. At the first crossroads (1.5 miles) turn left and follow the signs to Mortimer West End

The Red Lion is an appealing building of warm red brick and a history that has been traced back to 1700. It was then a farmhouse but by 1794 it was recorded as a pub when the landlady, Elizabeth Verry, was no doubt drawing beer straight from the barrel. Today, that tradition lives on, - the Red Lion has won the Cask Marque Award, an independent scheme to recognise excellence in the serving of cask ales. Qualified assessors regularly inspect the cask ale served for temperature, appearance, aroma and taste.

Landlord Joe Valentine takes just as much care with the food served here. A speciality of the house is fresh fish from Brixham but there's also a wide choice of other dishes, including local game in season, daily specials and a varied selection of bar snacks. Desserts include farmhouse dairy ice cream and there's an excellent choice of wines from around the world, 7 of them available by the glass. The inn has a welcoming, olde worlde atmosphere with an inglenook fireplace which has a roaring log fire in winter, and low-beamed ceilings. In good weather, enjoy your refreshments in the spacious garden at the rear or at the tables on the front patio. Incidentally, anyone interested in sailing will find a kindred spirit in Joe Valentine, an ex-sailing instructor who has made many sailing trips across the Atlantic.

Opening Hours: Mon-Sat: 11.00-23.00; Sun: 12.00-22.30

Food: Available every lunchtime and evening

Credit Cards: All major cards accepted

Facilities: 2 petanque courts; large garden; patio at front; children's play area; large car park

Entertainment: Annual beer festival

Local Places of Interest/Activities: Silchester Roman town, 1 mile; Stratfield Saye, 5 miles; Wellington Country Park, 6 miles

Internet/Website:
e-mail: joe_valentine@hotmail.com

58 The Rising Sun

Bath Road
Woolhampton
Reading
Berkshire
RG7 5RM
Tel: 0118 971 2717

Directions:

Take the A4 from Reading towards Newbury. Woolhampton is about 6 miles along this road. Just before you enter the village, The Rising Sun is on the left.

Woolhampton is a peaceful village set beside the Kennet & Avon Canal. It received an entry in the Domesday Book of 1086 at which time there was already a watermill here. The village is again noted in documents of 1351 when the manor and mill was owned by the Knights Hospitallers. The village still has a mill, one that was built in 1820 and further extended in 1875. Powered by a brook which runs into the Kennet, the mill was last used in 1930 and has recently been converted into offices. **The Rising Sun** pre-dates this mill by a century or more. It was built in the 1600s with brick walls and a slate roof and looks absolutely charming. Inside there are lots of old beams and brasses, open fires and a panelled bar, and walls decorated with pictures of canal boats and activities. Outside, there are two quiet gardens for fairweather days and a pets' corner for the children.

Mine hosts are Dave and Sue Clifton who have been here since 1998 but have worked in the licensed trade for more than 15 years. They offer a very varied menu of traditional pub food, all listed on the blackboard, and a choice of 4 real ales which are regularly rotated. There's also an extensive wine list. Separate dining areas are provided for both smokers and non-smokers.

Opening Hours: Mon-Sat: 11.00-15.00; 18.00-23.00. Sun: 12.00-22.30

Food: Traditional pub food

Credit Cards: All major cards except Amex and Diners

Facilities: Two beer gardens, large car park, pets' corner

Entertainment: Occasional live music

Local Places of Interest/Activities: Highclere Castle, Windsor Castle, Newbury race course

Royal Oak | 59

Ruscombe Lane,
Ruscombe,
Berkshire
RG10 9JN
Tel: 0118 934 5190

Directions:
Leave Twyford on the A3032 towards Maidenhead. Almost immediately take the B3024 towards Windsor and after half a mile enter the village of Ruscombe. The Royal Oak is opposite Ruscombe business park.

Tucked away in the village of Ruscombe, the **Royal Oak** is a welcoming traditional hostelry, built in 1860 and comprehensively refurbished over the last few years. It boasts an unusually large beer garden where there's a Wendy house for children, an aviary and live animals. Inside, the pub looks very inviting with its old beams, brasses and an interesting collection of vintage jugs. There's a spacious non-smoking dining area, part of which is a conservatory seating 30.

Dave the chef offers a good choice of traditional British food, all freshly cooked using top quality ingredients from local suppliers. The blackboard menu changes daily and Dave always likes to include a couple of unusual dishes. On Sundays he prepares a traditional Roast Dinner, complete with all the trimmings. To accompany your meal, there's a choice of 4 real ales, one of them a guest brew, and an extensive wine list.

Opening Hours: Mon-Thu: 10.00-15.00; 17.00-23.00. Fri-Sat: 12.00-23.00. Sun: 12.00-22.30

Food: Traditional British food, lunchtime & evening

Credit Cards: All major cards except Diners

Facilities: Very large beer garden with Wendy house, live animals and aviary; large car park

Entertainment: Live entertainment once a month

Local Places of Interest/Activities: Thames Path, 4 miles; Courage Shire Horse Centre, 6 miles; Legoland, 12 miles; Windsor Castle, 14 miles

Internet/Website: theroyaloak@ruscombelane.gonet.co.uk

60   The Spotted Dog

Gladstone Lane
Cold Ash
Newbury
Berkshire
RG18 9PR
Tel: 01635 862458

Directions:

From Newbury take the A4 towards Reading. At Thatcham, turn left to Cold Ash. In the village, The Spotted Dog is halfway up the hill, on the right.

With parts of the building dating back to the 1700s, **The Spotted Dog** is a traditional hostelry with lots of beams and brasses adding to the appeal of its large open-plan, panelled bar. The village of Cold Ash is within easy reach of some of Berkshire's leading visitor attractions. At Thatcham, there's the Nature Discovery Centre; a little further afield is the Wyld Court Rain Forest at Hampstead Norrey's, and a short spin along the M4 brings you to Windsor Castle and Windsor Great Park. Also near Thatcham is a restored stretch of the Kennet & Avon Canal, providing some gentle towpath walks, and if you prefer urban amusements, Newbury with its shops and racecourse is just 5 miles away.

Lisa Snow has been in the hospitality business since 1994 but took over at the Spotted Dog late in 1999. Her appetising menu offers a wide choice of dishes, supplemented by daily specials. There's an extensive wine list and also 3 real ales, one of them a local brew. The restaurant, which seats 30, is available for weddings, parties and other special functions.

Opening hours: Mon-Sat 11.30-14.30; 18.30-23.00. Sun 12.00-15.00; 19.00-22.30

Food: Extensive menu and daily specials

Credit Cards: All major debit and credit cards (except Amex; Diners)

Facilities: Large car park

Entertainment: Darts, occasional live music

Local places of interest/Activities: Nature Discovery Centre, Thatcham, 3 miles; Kennet & Avon Canal, 3 miles; Wyld Court Rain Forest, Hampstead Norrey's, 5 miles.

The Stag & Hounds   **61**

1 Lee Lane
Pinkneys Green
Maidenhead
Berkshire
SL6 6NU
Tel: 01628 630268

Directions:

From the M4, Exit 8/9, take the A404(M). At the second exit (A4) turn right to Maidenhead then left to Pinkneys Green. Take the next right turn and the pub is on the left.

An attractive black-and-white half-timbered building with latticed windows, **The Stag & Hounds** was built in the 19th century. It boasts a spacious beer garden with a small playarea for children. The pub stands at the heart of this small village on the outskirts of Maidenhead and close to the National Trust woodland known as Maidenhead Thicket.

The interior of the pub is really inviting with its two open fires, panelled walls and welcoming atmosphere. Sally and Steve Hart took over this Free House in 1997 but they have been in the hospitality business for some 20 years. They offer a wide-ranging menu, all listed on blackboards and including some tasty home cooked specials. There are 6 real ales on offer, four of which are regularly rotated, and also a limited wine list. There's no specific dining room, -just settle down anywhere in the two bars. Also available is a function room which can cater for 30 seated guests, 50 for buffet style catering. A popular feature at The Stag & Hounds is its skittles alley, -why not try your hand?

Opening hours: Mon-Fri: 12.00-15.00; 18.00-23.00. Sat: 12.00-23.00. Sun: 12.00-22.30

Food: Wide-ranging menu with home cooked specials

Credit cards: All major cards except Amex and Diners

Facilities: Large garden with small play area Entertainment: Skittles

Local places of Interest/ Activities: Windsor Castle, Shire Horse Centre, Legoland Park

62   Ye Olde Red Lion

Green Lane
Chieveley
Newbury
Berkshire RG20 8XB
Tel: 01635 248379

Directions:

From the M4, Exit 13, take the A34 north towards Oxford and after 500 yards turn left to Chieveley. As you enter the village, Ye Olde Red Lion is on the left.

With its cream-painted walls, latticed windows and attractive front patio, **Ye Olde Red Lion** has a very inviting appearance. It was built in the 1700s as a coaching inn and the old beams, brasses and many collectables scattered around the walls evoke a more leisurely age. Just moments from the M4 and the A34, Chieveley is a pleasant little village set on the edge of the Berkshire Downs. The Royal County of Berkshire Agricultural Showground is just a couple of miles away and the prosperous town of Newbury with its racecourse and extensive shopping opportunities lies a few miles to the south.

Your hosts at Ye Olde Red Lion are Lance and Jackie Headley who took over here in the summer of 1999 and have quickly established a reputation for providing excellent cuisine, fine ales and wines, and a warm welcome. They offer a surprisingly extensive menu, with lots of variety. You'll always find a good old traditional home made pie, but also Steak Fajitas, served with tortilla pancakes, along with succulent steaks that range from an 8oz Rump, Sirloin or Fillet to a mighty 16oz Rump or T-bone. Amongst the poultry dishes there's a Chicken Envortino (breast of chicken stuffed with asparagus & Parma ham), or, if you really enjoy spicy dishes, you should definitely try one of Marco's home made Madras curries. In addition, there are delicious seafood or pasta dishes as well as vegetarian options.

Opening hours: Mon-Sat 11.00-15.00, 18.00-23.00. Sun 12.00-15.00, 19.00-22.30

Food: Restaurant & bar meals

Credit Cards: All major credit cards and debit cards. Cash back facility

Entertainment: Darts, pool, occasional live entertainment

Parking: Two large car parks

Local Places of Interest/Activities: Newbury town and racecourse, 4 miles; good walking country

Internet/Website: lance.headley@virgin.net

3 Oxfordshire

PLACES OF INTEREST:

PUBS AND INNS:

The Hidden Inns of the South of England

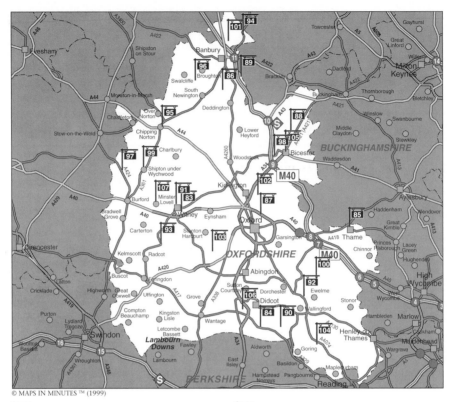

© MAPS IN MINUTES ™ (1999)

83 The Angel, Witney

84 The Barley Mow, Blewbury

85 The Bird Cage, Thame

86 The Black Boy Inn, Milton, nr Banbury

87 The Bricklayers Arms, Old Marston

88 The Butchers Arms, Fringford,
  nr Bicester

89 The Butchers Arms, Kings Sutton,
  nr Banbury

90 The Chequers Inn, Aston Tirrold

91 Court Inn Hotel, Witney

92 The Crown Inn, Benson, nr Wallingford

93 The Elephant & Castle, Bampton

94 The Griffin, Chipping Warden 94

95 The Kings Arms, Chipping Norton

96 The Lampet Arms, Tadmarton,
  nr Banbury

97 Merrymouth Inn, Fifield, nr Burford

98 The Red Cow, Chesterton, nr Bicester

99 The Red Horse Inn,
  Shipton-under-Wychwood

100 The Red Lion, Chalgrove

101 The Red Lion Inn, Cropredy,
  nr Banbury

102 The Red Lion, Islip

103 The Red Lion, Northmoor

104 The Red Lion, Woodcote

105 The Swan, Bicester

106 The White Hart, Harwell

107 The White Hart, Minster Lovell,
  nr Witney

Please note all cross references refer to page numbers

Oxfordshire

The southeastern corner of Oxfordshire is a place of ancient towns and villages which were well established settlements by the time of the Norman Conquest in 1066. There is the Roman town of Dorchester, the 7th-century abbey town of Abingdon, Henley-on-Thames - famous for its annual Regatta - and a mass of tiny villages and hamlets that are well worth exploring.

West Oxfordshire is a region of several different landscapes. There are the Berkshire Downs marking the southern border, with the Vale of the White Horse, the River Thames cuts the area in two, and to the north are the beginnings of the Cotswolds. A rural region, of ancient towns and villages, this is an excellent place that well deserves exploring. The region's most famous feature, the White Horse, lies away to the west, to the south of Uffington. Here, the edge of the downlands are littered with Iron Age hill forts and other relics and it is also the line of the famous Ridgeway footpath, over 80 miles in length.

Oxford is of course the county town of Oxfordshire, has dominated the surrounding area for centuries. The city of "dreaming spires", it was the influx of students and scholars in the 12th century which saw this walled Saxon town develop into the magnificent place it is today. Home to some of the finest buildings in the country, the city deserves exploration and there is a wealth of beauty and interest to be discovered. Many of the rural villages around the city have been the homes of the city's famous intellectuals and, in particular, there is Elsfield to the north where both John Buchan and RD Blackmore had homes. During the 1920s at Garsington Manor, the socialite Lady Ottoline Morrell entertained the great artists, writers, and thinkers of the day including DH Lawrence, Bertrand Russell, and Aldous Huxley.

The northwestern region of the county lies almost wholly in the Cotswold area, a place of honey coloured stone buildings and quaint old market towns. Burford, the Gateway to the Cotswolds, and Chipping Norton are typical of the towns found further west, in Gloucestershire, and they both owe their early prosperity to the wool gleaned from the Cotswold sheep.

To the east lies Woodstock, an ancient place which was once home to a medieval royal palace that was used as a hunting lodge for trips into Wychwood Forest, the royal hunting ground which stood to the west of the town and extended as far as Burford. Today, the town, a wealth of antique and tea shops, is best known for the magnificent Blenheim Palace, the thank you from a grateful Queen Anne to her loyal subject the Duke of Marlborough. The vast Blenheim estate dominates the area around Woodstock and many of the villages have connections with the family and the house. One, in particular, is worthy of a visit: on a bleak November day in 1965, Sir Winston Churchill was laid to rest in a simple grave in Bladon church. The River Evenlode divides this region into two and along this stretch the riverbanks are followed by the Oxfordshire Way. Some 65 miles long, this marked footpath passes through some of the most rural and scenic parts of the county from its start at Bourton-on-the-Water to its end at Henley-on-Thames.

North Oxfordshire, from Oxford to the Midlands, is one of rich farm land based on the clay soil. There are numerous rural villages, with ancient cottages and old stone farmhouses, that give an impression of not having changed for centuries - only the farm machinery and the television aerials give away the march of time. By far the largest town in the area is Banbury, that ancient place of the nursery rhyme and the cross. A fine blend of the old with the new, none of the town's rural heritage has been lost and today it is home to Europe's largest livestock market. Bicester too is another ancient settlement - the Romans had a town nearby - and the settlement was first home to the Saxons. There are some fine houses to visit here also, including Rousham, home to one of the few complete William Kent gardens in the country. However, lovers of rural architecture will delight in seeing Swalcliffe Barn, a magnificent 15th-century structure that is also home to a range of agricultural vehicles.

Across Windsor Great Park, the remains of the royal hunting forest, lies Ascot Racecourse. For one meeting each summer this is the place for the fashionable as people flock from all over the world to attend Royal Ascot but, for the rest of the year, this is an attractive and highly competitive course that was founded by Queen Anne in 1711.

The Thames also plays a great part in this area of Berkshire. There are numerous picturesque riverside towns and villages, several of which developed into fashionable riverside resorts during the Victorian era. Cookham, with its continuation of the ancient Swan Upping ceremony; Maidenhead, with the massive Boulter's Lock and Brunel's famous railway bridge; and Wraysbury, where King John signed the Magna Carta to appease the rebellious barons, are all places that not only exude history but provide pleasant walks along the river's banks.Places of Interest

PLACES OF INTEREST

ABINGDON

This is an attractive town and it is also one of the country's oldest as it grew up around a 7th-century **Benedictine Abbey** that was founded here in 675. Sacked twice for its gold and silver when the town was attacked by Danes, the abbey was practically derelict by the 10th century but, under the guidance of Abbot Ethwold, the architect of the great Benedictine reform, it once again prospered and was, in its heyday, larger than Westminster Abbey. Unfortunately little remains today of this great religious house, but the **Gatehouse**, built in the late 15th century, is a splendid reminder. Built on to the abbey gateway is the **Church of St Nicholas**, a much altered building but one which also has managed to retain some of its original Norman features.

The largest town in the Vale of the White Horse, Abingdon was also the county town of Berkshire between 1556 and 1869, in deed, at one time the Abbot here was the second largest landowner in Berkshire after the Crown. This prosperity and importance has given the town

an interesting history which can be discovered at the **Abingdon Museum**. Housed in the old County Hall, which was originally built as the County Assize Court and Market Hall in 1678, there is plenty to see inside as well as out.

Another of the town's pleasing buildings is the **Church of St Helen**, whose steeple domi-

Abbey Gatehouse, Abingdon

Abingdon Museum

nates the view southwards along the street. Originally built in the 14th century, the church was remodelled in the 15th and 16th centuries, when the town prospered from a thriving wool trade, to provide an altogether larger and more elaborate building. However, the main glory of the church, the painted ceiling of the Lady Chapel, has been retained from the 14th century.

Beside the churchyard, which contains a curious small building that was the blowing chamber for the church organ, are three sets of almshouses. The oldest, Christ's Hospital, was founded in 1446 whilst the other two, Twitty's Almshouses and Brick Alley Almshouses, date from the early 18th century.

BANBURY

Famous for its cross, cakes, and the nursery rhyme, this historic and thriving market town has managed to hang on to many of its old buildings as well as become home to Europe's largest livestock market. The famous **Banbury Cross** can be found in Horsefair where it was erected, in 1859, and replaced the previous one which had been demolished by the Parliamentarians during the Civil War. Built to commemorate the marriage of Queen Victoria's oldest daughter to the Prussian Crown Prince, the figures around the bottom of the cross, of Queen Victoria, Edward VII, and George V, were added in 1914. This, obviously, is not the cross referred to in the old nursery rhyme and that cross's whereabouts is now unknown.

The town's other legendary claim to fame is its cakes, made of spicy fruit pastry, which can still be bought. Banbury was also, at one time, famous for its cheeses, which were only about an inch thick. This gave rise to the expression 'thin as a Banbury cheese'.

On the east side of the Horsefair stands **St Mary's Church**, a classical building of warm-coloured stone and hefty pillars which are pleasantly eccentric touches. The original architect was SP Cockerell, though the tower and portico were completed between 1818 and 1822 by his son, CR Cockerell. The style reflects the strong influence on English architecture of Piranesi's Views of Rome, using massive shapes and giving stone the deliberately roughened appearance which comes from the technique known as rustication.

The **Banbury Museum** also lies nearby and here can be found the story of the town's development, from the days when it came under the influence of the bishops of Lincoln, through the woollen trade of the 16th century, to the present day. The affects of the Civil War on the town were also great; the Royalists held Banbury Castle and there were two sieges here. The completion of the Coventry to Oxford Canal in 1778, the coming of the railway in 1850, and the opening of the M40 in 1991, have all played their part in making Banbury a large and successful commercial town.

BICESTER

Though the name (which is pronounced Bister) suggests that this was a Roman settlement, the town was not, in fact, established until Saxon times and the Roman name comes as a result of the nearby and long since vanished Roman town of **Alchester**. By the time of the 12th century, the town was the home of both an Augustinian priory and also a Benedictine nunnery. Growing up around these religious houses and its market, the town suffered a disastrous fire in the early 18th century and most of the buildings seen here today date from that time onwards. Hunting and horse-racing played as much a part of the prosperity of Bicester as agriculture though industrialisation has been sporadic. The founding here of the Army's ordnance depot in 1941 has brought much new development which continued until the 1960s.

68

The **Church of St Eadburg** still has traces of the original 12th-century building, though over the following centuries much work on enlarging the church was undertaken. Fortunately, it is one of the few buildings which escaped the fire that wrecked the town.

BRADWELL GROVE

The 120 acres of park and garden which make up The **Cotswold Wild Life Park** are home to a whole host of animals, many of whom roam free in the wooded estate. Rhinos, zebras, ostriches, and tigers are just some of the animals in the spacious enclosures whilst tropical birds, monkeys, reptiles, and butterflies are all given the chance to enjoy the warmth of their natural habitat by staying indoors. With an adventure playground and a narrow-gauge railway, the park has something to offer every member of the family.

BROUGHTON

The moated mansion, **Broughton Castle**, was built in 1300 by Sir John de Broughton as his manor on the site of the existing house. Extended and altered in the 16th century to turn it into a fine Tudor home, the house has been owned by the same family since 1451. Over the years, there have been several Royal visitors including Queen Anne of Denmark, wife

Broughton Castle, Broughton

of James I. Both James I and Edward VII have used the aptly named King's Chamber, with its handpainted Chinese wall paper. The house also played a part in the Civil War as it has a secret room where leaders of the Parliamentary forces laid their plans.

BURFORD

Often referred to as The Gateway to the Cotswolds, Burford is an attractive old market town of honey coloured Cotswold stone found on the banks of the River Windrush. The site of a battle between the armies of Wessex and Mercia in 752, after the Norman Conquest, Burford was given to William I's brother, Bishop Odo of Bayeux. Lying on important trade routes, both north-south and east-west, the town prospered and its first market charter was granted in 1087. By the 16th century, the town was an important centre of the woollen trade and it was used as the setting for The Woolpack, in which the author, Celia Harknett, describes the medieval wool trade in Europe. After the decline in the wool, Burford became an important coaching centre and many of the old inns can still be seen today.

The **Church of St John the Baptist** was built on the wealth of the wool trade and this grand building has the atmosphere of a small cathedral. Originally Norman, the church has been added to over the centuries and there are several interesting monuments and plaques to be found. In the south wall of the tower stair is a caring, dated around AD 100, which shows the goddess Epona, with two male supporters whilst, the monument erected to Edmund Harman, the barber-surgeon to Henry VIII, shows North American natives - possibly the first representation of Red Indians in the country. Finally, in the south porch, is a small plaque which commemorates three Levellers who were shot in the churchyard in 1649.

The Levellers were troops from Cromwell's army who mutinied against what they saw as the drift towards the authoritarian rule they had been fighting against. While they were encamped at Burford, the Levellers were taken by surprise by Cromwell's forces. After a brief fight, some 340 prisoners were taken and placed under guard in the church. The next day there was a court martial and three of the rebels were shot as an example to the rest, who were made to watch the executions.

The town's old court house, built in the 16th century with an open ground floor and a half-timbered first floor, is now home to the **Tolsey Museum**. An interesting building in its own right, the collection on display here covers the history of the town and the surrounding area. Other buildings worth seeking out also include the 16th-century **Falkland Hall**, the home of Edmund Sylvester a local wool and cloth merchant, and **Symon Wysdom's Cottages**, which were built in 1572 by another of the town's important merchants.

Burford also has more recent literary associations as the writer Compton Mackenzie lived here before World War I. In his novel, *Guy and Pauline*, which was published in 1915, the town featured as 'Wychford'.

Buscot

This small village, in the valley of the upper Thames, is home to two National Trust properties: **Buscot Old Parsonage** and **Buscot Park**. The parsonage is a lovely house, with a small garden on the banks of the River Thames, that was built of Cotswold stone in 1703. However, Buscot Park is a much grander affair, as its name might suggest, and this classic example of a late Georgian house was built in 1780. Home of the Faringdon Art Collection, which includes paintings by Rembrandt, Murillo, and Reynolds, there is one room here that is decorated with a series of pictures painted by Edward Burne-Jones, the pre-Raphaelite artist who was a close friend of William Morris. Painted in 1890, they reflect Burne-Jones' interest in myths and legends and they tell the story of the Sleeping Beauty.

Anyone particularly interested in the work of Burne-Jones should also visit the village church, where a stained glass window showing the Good Shepherd was designed by him in 1891, when he was working with William Morris's firm, Morris and Co. The church itself is very nicely situated, by the river just outside the village.

Charlbury

Now very much a dormitory town for Oxford, Charlbury was once famous for its glovemaking as well as being a centre of the Quaker Movement - the simple Friends' Meeting House dates from 1779 and there is also a Friends' cemetery. **Charlbury Museum**, close to the Meeting House, has displays on the traditional crafts and industries of the town and the town's charters

given by Henry III and King Stephen can also be seen. Well known for its olde worlde **Railway Station**, built by Isambard Kingdom Brunel, complete with its fishpond and hanging baskets, the town has two interesting great houses.

On the other bank of the River Evenlode from the main town lies **Cornbury Park**, a large estate that was given to Robert Dudley by Elizabeth I. Although most of the house now dates from the 17th century, this was originally a hunting lodge in Wychwood Forest that has been used since the days of Henry I. Glimpses of the house can be seen from the walk around the estate.

Lying just to the west of the town is **Ditchley Park**, a restrained and classical house built in the 1720s by James Gibbs. The interiors are splendid, having been designed by William Kent and Henry Flitcroft, and Italian craftsmen worked on the stucco decorations of the great hall and the saloon; the first treated to give an impression of rich solemnity, the second with a rather more exuberant effect.

The house has associations with Sir Winston Churchill, who used it as a weekend headquarters during World War II. Appropriately enough, given that Sir Winston had an American mother, Ditchley Park is now used as an Anglo-American conference centre.

Chastleton

Chastleton is home to one of the best examples of Jacobean architecture in the country. In 1602, Robert Castesby, one of the Gunpowder Plot conspirators, sold his estate here to a prosperous wool merchant from Witney, Walter Jones. A couple of years later, Jones pulled the house down and built **Chastleton House**, a splendid Jacobean manor house with a dramatic five-gabled front. Though the style suggests that the house was designed by Robert Smythson, the most famous architect of his day, there is no absolute proof of this.

Inside, the house has a wonderful collection of original panelling, furniture, tapestries, and embroideries. Of the rooms themselves, the Long Gallery, which runs the entire length of the top floor at the back of the house, is particularly impressive. This has a wonderful barrel-vaulted ceiling plastered in intricate patterns of interlacing ribbons and flowers.

Railway Station, Charlbury

70

CHIPPING NORTON

The highest town in Oxfordshire, at 650 feet above sea level, Chipping Norton was once an important centre of the wool trade and King John granted the town a charter to hold a fair to sell wool. Later changed to a **Mop Fair**, the tradition continues to this day when the fair is held every September.

The town's medieval prosperity can be seen in the fine and spacious **Church of St Mary** which was built in 1485 with money given by John Ashfield, a wool merchant. The splendid east window came from the Abbey of Bruern, a few miles to the southwest, which was demolished in 1535 during the Dissolution. As with many buildings in the town, there has been substantial 19th-century remodelling and the present church tower dates from 1823. However, in 1549, the minister here, the Rev Henry Joyce, was charged with high treason and hanged from the then tower because he refused to use the new prayer book introduced by Edward VI.

Still very much a market town today - the market is held on Wednesdays - Chipping Norton has been little affected by the influx of visitors who come to see this charming place. The **Chipping Norton Museum** is an excellent place to start any exploration and the permanent displays here cover local history from prehistoric and Roman times through to the present day.

Found just to the west of the town centre is **Bliss Tweed Mill**, an extraordinary sight in this area as it was designed by a Lancashire architect, George Woodhouse, in 1872 in the Versailles style. With a decorated parapet and a tall chimney which acts as a local landmark, this very northern looking mill only ceased operation in the 1980s.

COMPTON BEAUCHAMP

The pretty parish **Church of St Swithin** is built of chalk, presumably from the local downs, and its key features are the medieval glass and the Victorian wall paintings. St Swithin is an unusual dedication and it was perhaps made here as St Swithin was the Bishop of Winchester in the late 9th century and therefore something of a local boy.

DEDDINGTON

Visitors to this old market town may find that it is familiar as this was place that was demolished by a runaway crane in the television adaptation of Tom Sharpe's Blott on the Landscape. The damage was, of course, cleverly faked and Deddington, which hovers between a small town and a large village, still retains all its medieval character.

Surveyed in the Domesday Book as twice the value of Banbury, the town has never developed, as Banbury and Bicester have, and it remains a prosperous agricultural centre with a still bustling market place.

Little can now be seen of the 12th-century **Deddington Castle**. This was destroyed in the 14th century and most of the building materials were put to good use in other areas of the town. However, excavations have revealed the remains of a curtain wall, a hall, and a small rectangular keep.

Meanwhile, the **Church of St Peter and St Paul** is still very visible and can be found on the edge of the Market Place. In the 1630s, the church's steeple collapsed, taking part of the main building with it and, though rebuilding work begun soon afterwards, the intervention of the Civil War made this a long project. During this time, Charles I had the church bells melted down to provide his army with another cannon. Another steeple was not built and the tower was heavily buttressed to ensure that it would never collapse.

Close by is **Castle House**, where Pier Gaveston, Edward II's favourite, was held before his execution in 1312. The house's two towers were added later, in the 1650s, when the house was in the ownership of Thomas Appletree. A supporter of Cromwell, Appletree was ordered to destroy the property of royalists and it was material from two local houses that he used in his building work.

DIDCOT

The giant cooling towers of Didcot's power station dominate the skyline for miles around and there is little left to be found of the old town. However, the saving grace is the **Didcot Railway Centre**, a shrine to the days of the steam engine and the Great Western Railway. Isambard Kingdom Brunel designed the Great Western Railway and its route through Didcot, from London to Bristol, was completed in 1841.

Until 1892 its trains ran on their unique broad gauge tracks and the GWR retained its independence until the nationalisation of the railways in 1948. Based around the engine shed, where visitors can inspect the collection of steam locomotives, members of the Great Western Society have recreated the golden age of the railway at the centre which also includes a beautiful recreation of a country station, complete with level crossing. Steam days are held through out the year when locomotives once again take to the broad gauge track and visitors can also take in the Victorian signalling system and the centre's Relics Display.

DORCHESTER

This small town, situated on the River Thames and just a short walk from the River Thames, was once an important Roman station called Dorocina. The name comes from the Celtic word, Dor, and the Roman word, Chester and it was here that Christianity was established in the southwest of England by St Birinus. Known as the Apostle of the West Saxons, Birinus was consecrated in Genoa, landed in Wessex in 634, and converted King Cynegils of Wessex the following year. In gratitude, the king gave Dorchester to Birinus and it became a centre of missionary activity.

The **Abbey Church of St Peter and St Paul** is all that remains of the Augustinian Abbey which was built on the site of the original Saxon Church in 1170. Its chief glory is the 14th-century choir and the huge 'Jesse' window, showing the family tree of Jesus, which has retained its original glass. The story of the abbey, along with the history of settlement in the area going back to neolithic times, is told in the **Abbey Museum** which is housed in a former Grammar Schoolroom, built in 1652.

Abbey Museum, Dorchester

In the 18th-century the High Street would have been a busy thoroughfare but it has now been by-passed which has had the effect of turning the street into a peaceful backwater and the attractive houses can be viewed at leisure.

EWELME

At the centre of this pretty village is a magnificent group of medieval buildings, including the Church, almshouse, and school which were all founded in the 1430s by Alice Chaucer, granddaughter of the poet Geoffrey, and her husband, the Duke of Suffolk. There is a wonderfully elegant alabaster carving of Alice inside the church and under this effigy is another rather macabre carving of a shrivelled cadaver. In the churchyard is the grave of Jerome K Jerome, author of *Three Men in a Boat*, who moved to the village following the success of his book.

Founded in 1437, the **Almshouses** were built to house 13 poor men and two chaplains were provided to take care of them. They are one of the earliest examples of almshouses built around a quadrangle and they are also one of the earliest brick buildings in the county. The **School** was founded in the same year and it too is of brick though it was extensively altered in Georgian times.

EYNSHAM

This ancient market town probably began as a Roman settlement and it was first referred to as a town in documents dating from as early as AD 571 when the name was spelt *Egonesham*. The site of an important Benedictine Abbey, founded in 1005, the town's early markets were controlled by the religious house. The town prospered and expanded in the early Middle Ages and, after the Black Death, a grant allowing two weekly markets was made in 1440.

Elements of the town's original medieval plan can still be seen, particularly around the market place, where there are some fine 16th- and 17th-century buildings that were constructed using materials from the abbey which was dismantled at the time of the Dissolution.

FILKINS

This tiny Cotswold village is now the home of a flourishing community of craft workers and artists, many of whom work in restored 18th-

72

century barns. Wool has played a great part in the wealth of this area and, also found in a converted barn is the **Cotswold Woollen Weavers**, a working weaving museum with an exhibition gallery and a mill shop.

Also found in this attractive village is the **Swinford Museum**, which concentrates on 19th-century domestic and rural trade and craft tools.

GARSINGTON

The main reason for visiting this village, which is surprisingly rural considering it's so close to Oxford, is the 16th-century **Garsington Manor**. Between 1915 and 1927, this was the home of the socialite Lady Ottoline Morrell who, along with her husband Philip, were unflaggingly hospitable to a whole generation of writers, artists, and intellectuals including Katherine Mansfield, Lytton Strachey, Clive Bell, Siegfried Sassoon, DH Lawrence, TS Eliot, Rupert Brooke, Bertrand Russell, and Aldous Huxley. Huxley based an account of a country house party in his novel *Crome Yellow* on his experiences at Garsington, thereby causing a rift with his hostess. She found his description all too apt, and felt betrayed. Huxley insisted that he had not meant any harm, but she remained hurt and they were estranged for some time.

It seems that Lady Ottoline was not very lucky in the artists on whom she lavished her attention and hospitality. DH Lawrence also quarrelled with her after drawing a less than flattering, but clearly recognisable, portrait of life at her house in *Women in Love*.

Garsington's other claim to literary fame is that Rider Haggard was sent to the school run by the Rev HJ Graham at the rectory in 1866. The present house is later, built in 1872, but across the road from the Church is a 16th-century gateway from the rectory he would have known. While there Haggard became friendly with a local farmer named Quartermain whom he must have remembered with affection as he used the name for his hero, many years later, in his novel *King Solomon's Mines*.

The village **Church of St Mary** is a pleasant and cosy building with fine views to the south over the Chilterns from its hill top position, but it also looks over the industrial belt to the south of Oxford. Though the interior is chiefly Victorian, the church has retained its Norman

tower and inside there is an elegant memorial to Lady Ottoline.

GORING-ON-THAMES

This ancient small town lies across the River Thames from its equally ancient neighbour, Streatly, and, whilst today they are in different counties, they were once in different kingdoms. This is a particularly peaceful stretch of the river, with the bustle of Pangbourne and Henley-on-Thames lying down stream and it is some distance to the towns of Abingdon and Oxford

Goring Lock, Goring

further up stream. However, this has not always been the case as, at one time, the two settlements were often in conflict with each other and excavations in the area have found numerous weapons which date back as far as the Bronze Age.

In the 19th century, after Isambard Kingdom Brunel had laid the tracks for the Great Western Railway through Goring Gap, the village began to grow as it was now accessible to the Thames-loving Victorians. Though there are many Victorian and Edwardian villas and houses here, the original older buildings have survived and they add an air of antiquity to this attractive place.

GREAT COXWELL

This village is well known for its magnificent 13th-century **Tithe Barn** and its **Church of St Giles**, which also dates from that time. A simple and elegant building, the church is often overlooked in favour of the barn which was originally built to serve the needs of the Cistercian Abbey at Beaulieu in Hampshire who were granted the land here by King John. An impressive building that is some 152 feet long, with Cotswold stone walls of over four feet thick, this huge barn was used to store the tithe - or taxes - received from the tenants of the church land. At the Dissolution it passed into private ownership and, today, it is owned by the National Trust.

HENLEY-ON-THAMES

Reputed to be the oldest settlement in Oxfordshire, this attractive riverside market town has over 300 listed buildings covering several periods. But it is the fine Georgian and Victorian houses and villas fronting on to the River Thames which epitomises the style of Henley-on-Thames.

A quiet and gentle town in 1829 the first inter-varsity boat race, between Oxford and Cambridge, took place here on the river and, within a decade, the event was enjoying royal patronage. Today, **Henley's Regatta**, held every year in the first week of July, is a marvellous and colourful event with teams competing on the mile long course from all over the world. It is also a stylish occasion and is still seen as very much part of the season.

Opened in 1998, the **River and Rowing Museum** is a fascinating place to visit which traces the rowing heritage of Henley, the river's changing role in the town's history, and there is even the opportunity to 'walk' the length of the River Thames, from source to sea, taking in all the locks. Housed in a spacious, purpose-built building by the award-winning architect, David Chipperfield, visitors can also see the boat in which the British duo, Redgrave and Pinsent, won their gold medal at the 1996 Olympics.

Also situated on the riverbank, beside the town's famous 18th-century bridge, which is appropriately decorated with the faces of Father Thames and the goddess Isis, is the Leander Club, the headquarters of the equally famous rowing club. Whilst on the opposite bank is the attractive Church of St Mary which also acts as a local landmark.

Apart from the boating, which is available throughout the summer, and the pleasant walks along the riverbanks, there are lots of interesting shops, inns, and teashops in the town. Most of the inns are old coaching houses with yards that were once the scene of bull and bear fights.

Just down river from the town centre lies **Fawley Court**, a wonderful private house that was designed by Christopher Wren and built in 1684 for Col W Freeman. Now owned by the Marian Fathers, the **Museum** it contains includes a library, documents relating to the Polish Kings, and memorabilia of the Polish army. The house, gardens, and museum are open to the public from March to October.

To the northwest of Henley lies another interesting house, **Greys Court**, which was rebuilt in the 16th century though it has been added to since. However, it does stand within the walls of the original 14th-century manor house and various of the old outbuildings can still be seen. The property of the National Trust, the gardens of the court contain the **Archbishop's Maze**, which was inspired, in 1980, by Archbishop Runcie's enthronement speech.

KELMSCOTT

Found near the River Thames and dating from about 1570, **Kelmscott Manor House** was famously William Morris' country home from 1871 to 1896. Morris loved the house dearly and it is the scene of the end of his utopian novel News from Nowhere, in which he writes of a world where work has become a sought after pleasure.

The house, which is open to visitors during the summer, has examples of Morris's work and memorabilia of Dante Gabriel Rosetti, who also stayed there. Rosetti is reputed to have found the village boring, so presumably the fact that he was in love with Morris' wife, Jane, drew

Kelmscott Manor House

him here. Morris himself is buried in the Churchyard, under a tombstone designed by his associate Philip Webb.

The church itself is interesting, the oldest parts dating from the late 12th century, and the village includes some fine farmhouses from around the end of the 17th and beginning of the 18th centuries.

74

KINGSTON LISLE

Just to the southwest of Kingston Lisle's attractive Norman Church of St John lies the **Blowing Stone** (or **Sarsen Stone**), a piece of glacial debris that is perforated with holes. When blown, the stone emits a fog-horn like sound and tradition has it that the stone was blown by King Alfred.

LETCOMBE BASSETT

This tiny village has a notable place in literary history: it is called Cresscombe in *Jude the Obscure*, which Thomas Hardy wrote whilst staying here. Earlier, Jonathan Swift spent the summer of 1714 at the village's rectory where he was visited by the poet Alexander Pope.

Just to the east of the village lies **Segsbury Camp**, which is sometimes also referred to as **Letcombe Castle**. Set on the edge of the Berkshire Downs, this massive Iron Age hill fort encloses some 26 acres of land.

LOWER HEYFORD

Situated at a ford across the River Cherwell, which was replaced in the late 13th century by a stone bridge, the village lies on the opposite bank from its other half - Upper Heyford. To the south of the village lies **Rousham**, a fine house built in the mid-17th century for Sir

Rousham House, Nr Lower Heyford

Robert Dormer that is set in magnificent gardens. On the banks of the River Cherwell, the gardens were laid out by William Kent in 1738 and they represent the first phase of English landscape gardening. Fortunately little changed since it was first planted, Rousham is the only complete William Kent garden to have survived. The garden is open to the public all year round whilst the house has limited opening.

MAPLEDURHAM

Found down a small lane which leads to the River Thames, this tiny village is home to **Mapledurham House**, a Watermill, and a church. The late 16th-century home of the Blount family, Mapledurham House was built on the site of an older manor house and it has remained in the same family ever since. As well as viewing the great oak staircase and the fine collection of paintings housed here, visitors will find the house's literary connections are equally interesting: Alexander Pope was a frequent visitor in the 18th century; the final chapters of John Galsworthy's *The Forsythe Saga* were set here; and it was the fictional Toad Hall in The *Wind in the Willows*. However, others may find that the house is familiar as it has also featured in films, such as *The Eagle has Landed*, and television series, including *Inspector Morse*.

Another attraction on the estate is the old riverside **Watermill**, a handsome late 15th-century construction which stands on the site of an earlier building that was mentioned in the Domesday Book. The mill remained in operation until 1947 and it was then the longest surviving working mill on the river. Now fully restored, the traditional machinery can be seen in action grinding wholemeal flour which is then sold through the mill shop.

Whilst in the village the **Church** is also worth a visit as, during restoration work in 1863, the architect, William Butterfield, made great use of coloured brickwork and he also refaced the tower with an bold chequered pattern using flint and brick.

MINSTER LOVELL

One of the prettiest villages along the banks of the River Windrush, Minster Lovell is home to the ruins of a once impressive 15th-century manor house. **Minster Lovell Hall** was built about 1431-42 and was, in its day, one of the great aristocratic houses of Oxfordshire, the home of the Lovell family. However, one of the family was a prominent Yorkist during the Wars of the Roses and, after the defeat of Richard III at Bosworth Field, he lost his lands to the Crown.

The house was purchased by the Coke family in 1602, but around the middle of the 18th century the hall was dismantled by Thomas Coke, Earl of Leicester, and the ruins became lowly farm buildings. They were rescued from complete disintegration by the Ministry of Works in the 1930s and are now in the care of English Heritage. What is left of the house is extremely picturesque, and it is hard to imagine a better setting than here, beside the River Windrush.

One fascinating feature of the manor house which has survived is the medieval dovecote, complete with nesting boxes, which provided pigeons for the table in a way reminiscent of modern battery hen houses.

OVER NORTON

To the northwest of the village lie the **Rollright Stones** - among the most fascinating Bronze Age monuments in the country. These great gnarled slabs of stone stand on a ridge which offers fine views of the surrounding countryside. They also all have nicknames: the **King's Men** form a circle; the **King Stone** is to the north of the circle; and, a quarter of a miles to the west, stand the **Whispering Knights**, which

Rollright Stones, Nr Over Norton

are, in fact, the remnants of a megalithic tomb. Naturally, there are many local legends connected with the stones and some say that they are the petrified figures of a forgotten king and his men that were turned to stone by a witch.

OXFORD

The skyline of this wonderful city can be seen from many of the hilltops which surround it and the view is best described by the 19th-century poet, Matthew Arnold: "that sweet City with her dreaming spires." However, Oxford is not all beautiful, ancient buildings but a town of commerce and industry and, around the academic centre, there are suburbs and factories. A city which has been the centre of the country's intellectual, political, and architectural life for over 800 years, it is still an academic stronghold amidst fine architecture.

A walled town in Saxon times, which grew on a ford where the River Thames meets the River Cherwell, the first students came here in the 12th century when they were forced out of Europe's leading academic centre, Paris. Intellectual pursuits, then, were chiefly religious, and the town al-

Part of Oxford's Famous Skyline

ready had an Augustinian Abbey and, in a short space of time, Oxford became the country's seat of theological thinking. However, there was much tension between the townsfolk and the intellectuals and, in the 14th century, in a bid to protect their students, the university began to build colleges - enclosed quadrangles with large, sturdy front doors. The first colleges, Merton, Balliol, and University, where soon joined by others which still maintain their own individual style whilst also coming under the administration of the university.

Merton College was founded in 1264 by Walter de Merton, Lord Chancellor of England, as a small community of scholars from the income of his Surrey estates. Though the present buildings mostly date from the 15th to 17th centuries, Mob Quad is the university's oldest. The key feature of the college is its splendid medieval library where the ancient books are still chained to the desks. Once considered the poor relation to other, wealthier colleges, **Balliol College** was founded in 1263 as an act of penance by John Balliol and for many years it was reserved for only the poor students. Most of the college buildings now date from the 19th century when the college was instrumental in spearheading a move towards higher academic standards. Thought by some to have been founded by Alfred the Great, **University College** was endowed in 1249 although the present college buildings are mostly 17th century. The poet Shelley was the college's most famous scholar though he was expelled in 1811 for writing a pamphlet on atheism. Whilst in Italy, at the age of 30, Shelley drowned and his memorial can be seen in the Front Quad.

One of the most beautiful colleges in the city, **Christ Church College**, was founded in 1525 as Cardinal College by Thomas Wolsey and then refounded as Christ Church in 1546 by Henry VIII after Wolsey had fallen from royal favour. The main gateway into the college leads through the bottom of Tom Tower (designed by Christopher Wren and home of the Great Tom bell) and into Tom Quad, the largest of the city's quadrangles. From here there is access to the rest of the college and also to the college's chapel. The only college chapel in the world to be designated a cathedral, Christ Church Cathedral is also England's smallest: it was founded in 1546 on the remains of a 12th-century building.

Another splendid college well worth a visit is **Magdalen College** (pronounced "Maudlin" for reasons best known to itself), which has the most extensive grounds that include a riverside walk, a deer park, three quadrangles, and a series of glorious well manicured lawns. Founded in 1458 by William Waynflete, Bishop of Winchester, the colleges 15th-century bell tower is one of the city's most famous landmarks. During the 17th century, the college was at the centre of a revolt against James II's pro-Catholic policies and, a century later, academic standards here had slipped so far that Edward Gibbon, author of *The Decline and Fall of the Roman Empire*, called his time here as "the most idle and unprofitable" of his whole life.

As well as the college buildings, Oxford has many interesting and magnificent places to explore. At the city's central crossroads, unusually named **Carfax** and probably derived from the Latin for four-forked, is a tower, **Carfax Tower**, which is all that remains of the 14th-century Church of St Martin. A climb to

Radcliffe Camera

the top of the tower offers magnificent views across the city. One of the most interesting buildings, the **Radcliffe Camera**, was built between 1737 and 1749 to a design by James Gibb. England's earliest example of a round reading room (camera is a medieval word for room), this splendid building still serves this purpose for the **Bodleian Library**. Named after Sir Thomas Bodley, a diplomat and a fellow of Merton College, Sir Thomas refounded the University Library in 1602 on the site of an earlier building. With over 5½ million books it is one of the world's greatest libraries and one of only six entitled to a copy of every book published in Great Britain. The collection of early printed books and manuscripts is second only to the British Library in London and, though members of the University can request to see any book here, this is not a lending library and they must be read and studied on the premises.

Close by is the **Clarendon Building**, the former home of the Oxford University Press and now part of the Bodleian. Designed by Nicholas Hawksmoor, a pupil of Christopher Wren, and constructed in the early 18th century, two of the original nine lead muses on the roof have had to be replaced by fibreglass replicas. Also in this part of the city is the **Bridge of Sighs**, part of Hertford College and a 19th-century copy of the original bridge which can be found in Venice. Here the bridge crosses a street rather than a canal.

However, Oxford's most famous building is the magnificent **Sheldonian Theatre** which was designed and built in the style of a Roman theatre by Christopher Wren between 1664 and 1668 whilst he was Professor of Astronomy at the University. It is still used today for its intended purpose, as a place for University occa-

Bridge of Sighs, Hertford College

sions including metriculation, degree ceremonies, and the annual Encaenia, when honorary degrees are conferred on distinguished people. As well as the superb wooden interior, the ceiling has 32 canvas panels, depicting Truth descending on the Arts, which are the work of Robert Streeter, court painter to Charles II.

Naturally, the city has several museums and the best place to start is at the innovative **Oxford Story**, which presents a lively review of the last 800 years of university life, from the Middle Ages to the present day. The **Museum of Oxford**, with a different style, also covers the story of Oxford through a series of permanent displays showing various archaeological finds.

First opened in 1683 and the oldest museum in the country, the **Ashmolean Museum** was originally established to house the collection of the John Tradescants, father and son. On display in this internationally renowned museum are archaeological collections from Britain, Europe, Egypt, and the Middle East; Italian, Dutch, Flemish, French, and English old masters; far eastern art, ceramics, and lacquer work; and Chinese bronzes. Found in the Ashmolean's original building and built up this century is the **Museum of the History of Sci-**

ence, a remarkable collection of early scientific instruments including Einstein's blackboard and a large silver microscope made for George III.

Found in a splendid high Victorian building, near the University Science Area, is the **University Museum** where the remains of a dodo, extinct since around 1680, and a mass of fossilised dinosaur remains are on display. Also here is the **Pitt Rivers Museum**, with its interesting collection taken from all over the world.

Musicians will enjoy the **Bate Collection of Historical Instruments**, whilst those captivated by old masters should take time to visit the **Christ Church Picture Gallery**, with its collection of works by Tintoretto, Van Dyck, Leonardo da Vinci, and Michaelangelo.

Another place worthy of a visit and a particularly peaceful haven in the city are the **Botanic Gardens**, down by the river. Founded in 1621, when plants were the only source of medicines, this was a teaching garden where the plants grown here were studied for their medicinal and scientific use. The rose garden here commemorates the work of Oxford's scientists in the discovery and use of penicillin.

Oxford is also the place where the River Thames changes its name to the poetic Isis and, at **Folly Bridge**, not only are there punts for hire but river trips can be taken, both up and down stream, throughout the day and evening.

RADCOT

This tiny hamlet boasts the oldest bridge across the River Thames. Built in 1154, **Radcot Bridge** represents an important crossing place and, as such, the hamlet has seen much conflict over the centuries. To the north of the bridge are the remains of a castle where, in 1141, King Stephen battled with the disenthroned Queen Matilda whilst, in the 13th century, King John

Radcot Bridge

78

fought his Barons before finally conceding and signing the Magna Carta.

SHIPTON-UNDER-WYCHWOOD

The suffix 'under-Wychwood' derives from the ancient royal hunting forest, **Wychwood Forest**, the remains of which lie to the east of the village. The name has nothing to do with witches - wych refers to the Hwicce, a Celtic tribe of whose territory the forest originally formed a part in the 7th century. Though cleared during the Middle Ages, it was still used as a royal hunting forest until the mid-17th century. By the late 18th century there was little good wood left and the clearing of the forest was rapid to provide arable land.

The forest was one of the alleged haunts of Matthew Arnold's scholar gypsy and, in the poem, published in 1853, Arnold tells the legend of the brilliant but poor Oxford scholar who, despairing of ever making his way in the world, went to live with the gypsies to learn from their way of life.

The village itself is centred around its large green, which is dominated by the tall spire of 11th-century **St Mary's Church**. Here too can be found **The Shaven Crown**, now a hotel, which was built in the 15th century as a guest house for visitors to the nearby (and now demolished) Bruern Abbey. Finally, there is the superb **Shipton Court**, built around 1603, which is one of the country's largest Jacobean houses.

SOUTH NEWINGTON

This small village, built almost entirely of ironstone, is home to the fine **Church of St Peter Ad Vincula**. Inside can be found some of the county's best medieval wall paintings which were created around 1330. What makes these paintings so special is the detail of the figures: Thomas à Becket, the martyrdom of Thomas of Lancaster, and St Margaret slaying a dragon.

STANTON HARCOURT

This beautiful village is noted for its historic manor house, **Stanton Harcourt Manor** which dates back to the 14th century. Famed for its well preserved medieval kitchen, one of the most complete to survive in this country, the house is also visited for its fine collection of antiques and the tranquil gardens. It was whilst

staying here, from 1717 to 1718, that Alexander Pope translated Homer's great work, Iliad. Working in the 15th-century tower, a remainder of the original manor house, this is now referred to as **Pope's Tower**.

However, whilst the manor house draws people to the village, the splendid Norman **Church of St Michael** is also worthy of a visit. Naturally the Harcourt chapel dominates but there are other features of interest, including an intricate 14th century shrine to St Edburg.

STONOR

The village is the home of Lord and Lady Camoys and their house, **Stonor**, has been in the family for over 800 years. Set in the a wooded valley in the Chilterns and surrounded by a deer park, this attractive house dates from the 12th century though the beautiful, uniform facade is Tudor and hides much of the earlier work. The interior of the house contains many rare items, including a mass of family portraits,

Stonor House

and there is also a medieval Catholic Chapel here that was in continuous use right through the Reformation. In 1581, St Edmund Campion sought refuge at the house and there is an exhibition featuring his life and work. The gardens too are well worth a visit and they offer splendid views over the rolling parkland.

SUTTON COURTENAY

A pretty village that was mentioned in the Domesday Book, the abbey here, first founded in 1350, is now a small community of both men and women who concentrate on personal and spiritual growth.

The village **Church of All Saints**, which dates back to Norman times, houses some fine stone carvings and woodwork but the real interest lies in the churchyard. Here can be found the grave of Herbert Asquith, the last Liberal Prime Minister (from 1908 to 1916) and also the grave of Eric Blair. Better known as novelist George Orwell, there are several yew trees planted here in his memory.

SWALCLIFFE

The village is dominated by the large **Church of St Peter and St Paul** which towers over all the other buildings here. Founded in Saxon times, the bulk of the building dates from the 12th, 13th, and 14th centuries and it is the trac-

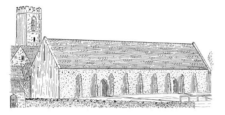

Swalcliffe Church

ery in the east window which makes the church noteworthy.

However, by far the most impressive building in Swalcliffe is the **Barn**, which has been acknowledged as one of the finest 15th-century half-cruck barns in the country. Built as the manorial barn by New College, Oxford, in 1400-1409, it was used to store produce from the manor and never to store tithes. Today, it is home to a collection of agricultural and trade vehicles.

To the northeast of the village, on **Madmarston Hill**, are the remains of an Iron Age hill fort which was occupied from the 2nd century BC to the 1st century AD.

THAME

Founded in 635 as an administrative centre for the Bishop of Dorchester, Thame first became a market town in the 13th century and its importance as a commercial centre is evident by the wide main street it still has today. Lined with old inns and houses, some of which go back to the 15th century, this is a delightful place to visit.

The imposing **Church of St Mary**, tucked away at one end of the High Street, was built in the 13th century though the aisles were widened in the 14th century and the tower was heightened in the 15th century. In the centre of the chancel is a monument to Lord John Williams, and his wife, who was notorious for

having helped burn Archbishop Thomas Cranmer in the 16th century.

To the west of the church lies the **Prebendal House** which, in its oldest parts, dates from the 13th century. A prebend was an income granted to a priest by a Cathedral or Collegiate Church and, at Thame, the prebend was established in around 1140 by Lincoln Cathedral. A special residence for the holders of the office was first mentioned in 1234.

The town also has a famous **Grammar School**, housed in a Tudor building in Church Lane. The schoolmaster's house faces the road and over the doorway are the arms of Lord Williams, who founded the school in 1558. John Hampden, one of the Parliamentary leaders during the Civil War, was at school here and he also died at Thame. An MP from 1621, Hampden sat in Parliament whenever it had not been dissolved by the King. He denied the right of the King to raise taxes without the sanction of Parliament and in 1636 refused to pay the 'ship tax' the King was demanding. As a result he was successfully prosecuted and, at the same time, became a popular leader in the country. When the Civil War broke out he raised a regiment of infantry for the Parliamentary Army and fought with great bravery at Edgehill and Reading. However, he was wounded at the battle of Chalgrove Field in June 1643 and was carried back to Thame, where he died some days later in an inn which stood on the High Street.

A little to the south of the town is **Thame Park**, a house built on the site of a Cistercian Abbey founded in 1138 and which, after the Dissolution, became the home of Lord Williams. The present, privately owned house incorporates some of the former monastic buildings to which has been added a gracious Georgian house.

UFFINGTON

This large village was, in 1822, the birthplace of Thomas Hughes, the son of the vicar. The author of *Tom Brown's Schooldays*, Hughes incorporates many local landmarks, including the White Horse and Uffington Castle, in his well known work. The **Tom Brown's School Museum** tells the story of Hughes' life and works.

However, the village is perhaps best known for the **Uffington White Horse**, where on the hillside a mysteriously abstract and very beautiful figure of a horse, some 400 feet long, has been created by removing the turf to expose the gleaming white chalk beneath. It is a startling sight which can be seen from far and wide, and many a tantalising glimpse of it has been caught through

Tom Brown's School Museum, Uffington

the window of a train travelling through the valley below. Popular tradition links it with the victory of King Alfred over the Danes at the battle of Ashdown, which was fought somewhere on these downs in 871, but modern thinking now considers that it dates from about 100 BC.

Above the White Horse is the Iron Age camp known as **Uffington Castle**, and to one side is a knoll known as **Dragon's Hill** where legend has it that St George killed the dragon.

WANTAGE

This thriving market town was, in 849, the birthplace of Alfred the Great and Wantage remained a Royal Manor until end of the 12th century. In the central market place, around which there are some fine Georgian and Victorian buildings, is a huge statue of the King of the West Saxons, who spent much of his life (he died in 899) defending his kingdom from the Danes in the north before becoming the overlord of England. An educated man for his time, as a boy Alfred had visited Rome, he not only codified the laws of his kingdom bur also revived learning.

Unfortunately, only the **Church of St Peter and St Paul** has survived from medieval times and, though much restored in 1857 by GE Street, there are various features that have remained from the original 13th-century struc-

ture and visitors can also see a brass commemorating the life of Sir Ivo Fitzwarren, the father of Dick Whittington's wife, Alice.

Opposite the church is the **Vale and Downland Museum Centre**, which is found in another of the town's old buildings - a house dating from the 16th century - and a reconstructed barn. Dedicated to the geology, history, and archaeology of Wantage and the Vale of the White Horse, the displays cover the centuries from prehistoric times to the present day.

Built as the home of the Wantage Sisterhood, an Anglican Order, in the 19th century, three architects were involved in the construction of **St Mary's Convent**: GE Street; William Butterfield, architect of Keble College, Oxford; and John Pearson, architect of Truro Cathedral.

Just to the east of the town lies **Ardington House**, a beautifully symmetrical, early 18th-century building that is the home of the Baring family. Occasionally open to the public, the best feature here is the Imperial Staircase - where two flights come into one - of which this is a particularly fine example.

WITNEY

Situated at the bottom of the valley of the River Windrush, this old town's name is derived from Witta's Island and it was once of importance as the Wittan, the Council of the Saxon Kings, met here. Developed as a planned town in the early Middle Ages, under the guidance of the Bishop of Winchester, the site of the Bishop's Palace lies alongside **St Mary's Church**. With an attractive exterior, though the interior does not live up to the promise, the church provides a dramatic focus to the town's market place. By 1278, Witney had a weekly market and two annual fairs and in the centre of the market place still stands the **Buttercross**. Originally a shrine, the cross has a steep roof with rustic-

Witney Buttercross

looking stone columns and it was probably built in 1600.

Wool was the economic base of life here and Witney developed weaving and, in particular, the making of blankets. The Witney Blanket Company was incorporated in 1710 but before that there were over 150 looms here working in the blanket trade employing over 3000 people. The **Blanket Hall**, in the High Street, has on it the arms of the Witney Company of Weavers and it was built for the weighing and measuring of blankets in an age before rigid standardisation. The trade began in the 16th century and, even though there has been a great decline in the industry since World War I, there are sill a couple of blanket factories here.

Just outside the town is the **Cogges Manor Farm Museum**, which stands on the site of a now deserted medieval village of which only the church, priory, and manor house remain. A museum of farming and country life, the displays tell the story of the lives of those who have worked the surrounding land over the centuries.

WOODSTOCK

Situated in the Glyme Valley, in an area of land that was originally part of the Wychwood Forest, the name of this elegant Georgian market town means a 'place in the woods'. To the north of the River Glyme is the old Saxon settlement whilst, on the opposite bank, lies the new town which was developed by Henry II in the 13th century to serve the Royal Park of Woodstock. There had been hunting lodges for the Kings of England here long before the Norman Invasion and it was Henry I who established the deer park around the manor of Woodstock.

It was whilst at his palace here that Henry II first seduced Rosamund, who he is said to have housed in a bower in the park. One story tells how Henry's wife, Queen Eleanor, managed to uncover the couple by following an unravelled ball of silk that had become attached to her husband's spur. Rosamund, the daughter of a local nobleman, became a nun at the infamous Godstow Nunnery where she also bore him several children.

This long since disappeared medieval palace was also the birthplace of the Black Prince in 1330 and Princess Elizabeth was held prisoner here in 1558 during the reign of her sister, Queen Mary. On ascending the throne, a grateful Elizabeth I granted the town a second weekly market and two fairs for its loyalty. The palace was damaged during the Civil War, when it served as a

Royalist garrison and the last remains were demolished in 1710.

Whilst the new town became an important coaching centre, many of the old inns survive to this day, and prospered as a result of the construction of the Oxford Canal and, later the railway, in 1886. The old town's trade was glovemaking and traditionally a pair of new

Woodstock

gloves are presented to a visiting monarch. Today's visitors can look round both the factory and showroom of **Woodstock Gloves**.

The town is also home to the **Oxfordshire County Museum**, which is housed in the wonderful and imposing 16th-century **Fletcher's House**. As well as the permanent displays on the life of the county through the centuries, the museum has a peaceful garden open to the public and, at the entrance, can be seen the town's old stocks.

However, it is the magnificent **Blenheim Palace**, one of only four sites in the country to be included on the World Heritage List, which brings most people to Woodstock. The estate and cost of building the palace was a gift from

82

a grateful Queen Anne to the heroic John Churchill, 1st Duke of Marlborough, for his victory at the Battle of Blenheim during the Spanish War of Succession. However, the Queen's gratitude ran out before the building work was complete and the duke had to pay the remainder of the costs himself.

As his architect, Marlborough chose Sir John Vanbrugh whose life was even more colourful than that of his patron. He was at the same time both an architect (although at the time of his commission he was relatively unknown) and a playwright, and he also had the distinction of having been imprisoned in the Bastille, Paris. The result of his work was the Italianate palace (built between 1705 and 1722), which is now seen sitting in a very English park that was later landscaped by Capability Brown. Unfortunately, once completed, the new house did not meet with universal approval: it was ridiculed by Jonathan Swift and Alexander Pope whilst Marlborough's wife, Sarah, who seems to have held the family purse strings, delayed paying Vanbrugh as long as possible.

A marvellous, grand place with a mass of splendid paintings, furniture, porcelain, and silver on show, visitors will also be interested in the more intimate memorabilia of Sir Winston Churchill. Born here in 1874, Churchill was a cousin of the 9th Duke and the family name remains Churchill.

First grown by George Kempster, a tailor from Old Woodstock, the Blenheim Orange apple took its name from the palace. Though the exact date of the first apple is unknown, Kempster himself died in 1773 and the original tree blew down in 1853. So famous did the spot where the tree stood become that it is said London-bound coaches and horses used to slow down so that passengers might gaze upon it.

The Angel   83

42 Market Square,
Witney,
Oxfordshire
OX8 6AL
Tel: 01993 703238

Directions:

From the Oxford ring road, take the
A40 towards Cheltenham. After
about 6 miles, take the B4022 into
Witney. The Angel is in the centre
of the town.

It was the medieval Bishops of
Winchester who developed this
pleasant little town beside the
River Windrush. They built a palace here which has long since vanished, - St Mary's Church now occupies its site. The town was famous for its blankets, a prosperous
business as witnessed by the 18th
century Blanket Hall in the High
Street. Just outside the town is the Cogges Manor Farm Museum which stands on the
site of an abandoned medieval village. The museum celebrates the farming and rural
life of the area over several centuries. Also well worth visiting is Minster Lovell Hall,
the ruins of a 15th century mansion in a lovely setting beside the River Windrush.

Back in the centre of Witney, **The Angel** is a picturesque building of honey-coloured Cotswold stone with twin bow-fronted windows on the ground floor; dormer
windows on the second. Mine host here is Diana Rosh and she offers her customers an
extensive choice of full meals and bar snacks along with a full English breakfast which
is available all day. You'll find all the traditional pub favourites on the menu along
with a very popular 'Combo' of spicy chicken goujons, mini chicken fillets, garlic
mushrooms, onion rings, cheese melters, potato wedges and dip. It goes down a treat,
especially if accompanied by one of the 4 real ales served here.

Opening Hours: Mon-Sat: 10.00-23.00;
Sun: 12.00-22.30

Food: Main meals and bar snacks

Credit Cards: Not accepted

Entertainment: Pool; darts; Sky Sports TV;
occasional quiz nights

Local Places of Interest/Activities:
Minster Lovell Hall, 1 mile; Cotswold Wild
Life Park, 8 miles; Blenheim Palace, 8
miles; City of Oxford, 12 miles

84   The Barley Mow

London Road,
Blewbury,
Oxfordshire
OX11 9NU
Tel: 01235 850296
Directions:

Blewbury is on the A417 about 5 miles southwest of Didcot. The Barley Mow is on the main road through the village

Set in the foothills of the Berkshire Downs, this beautiful village is full of attractive thatched and timber-framed houses. During the 19th century, Blewbury was popular with artists and writers seeking peace, quiet and inspiration. One of them was Kenneth Grahame, author of *The Wind in the Willows,* and the Tudor-brick house in which he lived from 1910 to 1924 is still to be seen here.

A spacious building with a typical country pub atmosphere, **The Barley Mow** offers good quality food, drink and accommodation. All of the guest rooms are attractively decorated, with high quality furnishings, and three of them have en suite facilities. Other rooms, not en suite, are also available. Meals can be enjoyed in the pleasant dining room extension and there's a choice of real ales along with all the usual popular beers, wines and spirits.

Opening Hours: Mon-Sat: 11.00-23.00; Sun: 12.00-15.00, 19.00-22.30

Food: Good range of food, all home cooked

Credit Cards: All major cards accepted

Facilities: Parking

Accommodation: 2 doubles and 1 single en suite, other rooms not en suite

Entertainment: Pool, darts, cribbage, quiz

Local Places of Interest/ Activities: Wallinbgford, 5 miles; Didcot Railway Centre, 5 miles; Cholsey & Wallingford Railway, 5 miles; Milton Manor, 6 miles

The Bird Cage

4 The Cornmarket,
Thame,
Oxfordshire
OX9 3DX
Tel: 01844 260381

Directions:
From Exit 8 of the M40 take the A418 to Thame (6 miles). The Bird Cage is in the centre of the town.

A market town since the 1200s, Thame is a delightful place to visit with its broad main street lined with ancient inns and houses. The most historic and atmospheric of the town's hostelries is undoubtedly **The Bird Cage** which is the oldest inn in Thame, built around 1300 or even earlier. In medieval times the building was used to detain thieves and other petty criminals; lepers were segregated on the upper floor. During the Napoleonic wars, the Bird Cage housed French prisoners who incidentally founded the local Masons. With such a variety of troubled men and women passing through its rooms, it's not surprising to discover that the inn is reputed to be haunted.

Inside the inn, the ancient plaster has been removed to reveal the beautiful elm beams and the two oriel windows in their oaken frames. Landlord Paul (Kiwi) Campion is the custodian of this lovely old building and he offers his customers not just a wonderful atmosphere but also an appetising choice of good quality home cooked food. To complement your meal, there's a a large selection of imported wines, available by the glass, 3 real ales, and aromatic Costa coffee. If the weather's fine, enjoy your meal or drink on the pavement outside where you can watch the world go by. By the time you read this, accommodation should also be available in an annex to the inn.

Opening Hours: All day, every day

Food: Good quality bar snacks, all home cooked

Credit Cards: All major cards accepted

Facilities: Pavement dining/drinking area

Local Places of Interest/Activities: Golf, 1 mile; City of Oxford, 14 miles

Internet/Website:
e-mail: birdcagepub@hotmail.com

86 The Black Boy Inn

Milton, nr Banbury,
Oxfordshire
OX15 4HH
Tel: 01295 722111
Fax: 01295 722007

Directions:

From Banbury, take the A361 towards Chipping Norton. After 4 miles, in the village of Bloxham, turn left on minor road to Milton (2 miles). The Black Boy Inn is located in the centre of the village

The pleasant village of Milton is tucked away in the north Oxfordshire countryside about halfway between Adderbury, noted for its famous Morris Dancing team, and Bloxham which attracts many visitors to its imaginative Village Museum. A new exhibition is set up every 6 months reflecting different aspects of past life in the village. Life at the other end of the social scale can be experienced at Aynhoe Park House, a grand 17th century mansion which has been the home of the Cartwright family for many generations.

The Black Boy Inn is Hugh and Janette O'Byrne's welcoming hostelry - Hugh is from Ireland and Janette from Indonesia so what else is there to say! The Inn is 400 years old and has been sensitively maintained and expanded to include accommodation, parking and dining areas. This is a place that takes good food very seriously. The lunchtime menu offers an extensive choice of main dishes and lighter meals such as hot or cold filled baguettes. The dinner menu has both an international and British flavour with a strong emphasis on fresh foods with herbs from the Inns' own gardens. Specialities include lamb kleftiko, baked trout, 10oz steaks, pasta, sword-fish as well as many other interesting dishes. You can complement this superior cuisine with a wide choice of beverages, amongst them real ale and a selection of wines.

Opening Hours: Tue-Sat: 12.00-15.00; 18.00-23.00. Sun: 12.00-20.00

Food: Extensive menu of quality food available lunchtime and Tuesday to Sunday evenings

Credit Cards: Visa, Mastercard, Switch

Accommodation: 2 rooms with queen size beds and private bathroom

Facilities: Patio to the front; parking, ½ acre garden with childrens facilities

Local Places of Interest/Activities: Bloxham Village Museum, 2 miles; Waterfowl Sanctuary & Children's Farm, Wigginton Heath, 6 miles; Aynhoe Park House, 7 miles, Walks, Cycling

Internet/Website: blackboyinn@btinternet.com

The Bricklayers Arms | 87

39/43 Church Lane,
Old Marston,
Oxfordshire
OX3 0PT
Tel: 01865 250177

Directions:

Old Marston is just off the A40, northeast of Oxford. The inn is in the centre of the village next to the church.

Just minutes from the A40, **The Bricklayers Arms** is a pleasant old building of local brick and stone, set in the heart of this historic village. Generals Cromwell and Fairfax made Marston their headquarters during the siege of nearby Oxford and it was here that they received the surrender of the city, - one of the most decisive moments in the Civil War.

The Bricklayers is a lively hostelry where mine hosts, Stephen and Sharon Jones, always seem to have something on, - or planning for something. They even produce a regular newsletter, the Bricklayers Bulletin to keep everyone abreast of all the activities. A recent issue for example applauded the success of the pub's Bar Billiards team, ("They WON the Third Division"), noted the formation of a Ladies' Darts team, provided details of the pubs latest addition to its ales, and provided a schedule of the artistes performing at the regular Saturday night live entertainments. The Jones' also arrange a Summer Party and visits by teams of Morris Dancers for which this area is celebrated. They also offer their customers a wide choice of wholesome traditional food, along with daily specials, a children's menu and a daily selection of desserts. Meals can be enjoyed either in the bar, where there's a non-smoking section, or in good weather in the spacious garden where, at one end, an impressive children's play area has been installed.

Opening Hours: Mon-Fri: 11.00-14.30; 17.00-23.00. Sat-Sun: Open all day

Food: Available every lunchtime and evening; children's menu

Credit Cards: Most major cards accepted

Facilities: Non-smoking area; large garden; large car park, Childrens play area, Disabled facilities, Baby change facilities

Entertainment: Bar billiards; darts; large-screen Sky Sports TV; live music every Saturday

Local Places of Interest/Activities: Cutteslowe Park Gardens, 2 miles; City of Oxford, 2.5 miles; Shotover Country Park, 3 miles; Blenheim Palace, 8 miles

88 The Butchers Arms

Fringford, Nr Bicester,
Oxfordshire
OX27 8EB
Tel: 01869 277363

Directions:

From Exit 9 on the M40, take the A41 to Bicester (3 miles). At the second roundabout continue straight on along the A4421 towards Bucking-ham. About 3½ miles along this road, a minor road to the left is signposted to Fringford (0.5 miles). The Butchers Arms stands beside the village green.

With its old stone walls smothered in Virginia Creeper, **The Butchers Arms** looks absolutely delightful. It stands at the heart of the village, looking across to the spacious green and the village cricket pitch. Fringford is a peaceful little place with a handsome-looking church containing some Norman features and, nearby, some lovely riverside walks. The village is also in the heart of Flora Thompson country - The Butchers Arms is referred to in "Lark Rise to Candleford" as "the Inn near the Green"

Mine hosts at the Butchers Arms are Gillian Marchant and Gez Owens, a friendly and welcoming couple who have recently been upgrading the inn's amenities. Parts of the building date back to the 16th century. The old wooden beams are still in place though and there's a splendid atmosphere of a real traditional village inn, an impression strengthened by the real ale on tap along with all the usual beers, spirits and a selection of wines. Fittingly for a genuine village inn, there's a good selection of pub games provided, - darts, dominoes, cards, an Aunt Sally and hopefully, by the time you read this, a piano. In good weather, you can enjoy your refreshment at picnic tables on the spacious patio from where you can keep an eye on the village green and maybe even follow a cricket match in progress.

Opening Hours: Mon-Thu: 19.00-23.00. Fri: 18.00-23.00. Sat: 12.00-23.00. Sun: 12.00-22.30

Credit Cards: Not accepted

Facilities: Patio; Cricket Pitch adjacent; parking

Entertainment: Darts; dominoes; cards; chess; Aunt Sally; piano

Local Places of Interest/Activities: Claydon House (NT), 8 miles; Stowe Gardens (NT), 9 miles; Aynho Park House, 10 miles;

The Butchers Arms | 89

Whittall Street,
Kings Sutton,
Banbury,
Oxfordshire
OX14 3RD
Tel: 01295 810898

Directions:

From Banbury, take the A41 towards Buckingham. About 2 miles past Adderbury turn left on minor road to Kings Sutton (1½ miles) The inn is located in the centre of the village

Located to the east of the River Cherwell, Kings Sutton is actually in Northamptonshire despite its address. It's an ancient village which is recorded in the Domesday Book and already had its own market. The splendid church is one of three to feature in a local saying: *Bloxham for length, Adderbury for strength, Kings Sutton for beauty*. It's well worth seeking out this small village close to both the River Cherwell and the Oxford Canal to sample the outstanding food on offer at **The Butchers Arms**.

The attractive old building of mellow local brick has a patio area to the front and a spacious Beer Garden to the rear. Inside, customers find a warm welcome from Ian and Lynda Fessey who have acquired a fine reputation for their hospitality. Their menu has something for everyone. There's a good choice of salads, (Salmon Rolls in honey mustard & dill, for example, or Warm Goats Cheese); steaks or gammon & eggs; Chicken Kiev; other fish and meat dishes, and a selection of delicious "Doorstep Sandwiches" with fillings that include all the old favourites as well as a filling of Hot Thai Vegetable Steak. On Sundays between noon and 3pm, traditional Sunday lunches are served, - prior bookings are definitely advisable.

Opening Hours: Mon-Sat: 11.00-15.00; 18.00-23.00. Sun: 12.00-16.00; 19.00-22.30

Food: Main meals and bar snacks every lunchtime and evening; traditional Sunday lunches

Credit Cards: All major cards accepted

Facilities: Large Beer Garden; patio; parking

Local Places of Interest/Activities: Oxford Canal, 1 mile; Aynhoe Park House, 3 miles; Banbury, 7 miles; Broughton Castle, 9 miles

90   The Chequers Inn

Aston Tirrold,
Oxfordshire
OX11 9DD
Tel: 01235 851275

Directions:

Th village of Aston Tirrold lies 6 miles SE of Didcot just off the A417. The Chequers Inn lies in the centre of village.

Located in the heart of this small village, **The Chequers Inn** is a substantial old

building dating back to the 1500s, built of local brick and set in its own garden. When James and Pauline Randall took over the inn's fortunes were at a low ebb but he has restored its reputation and it is now a typical country pub with a welcoming atmosphere, beamed ceilings and open fires in winter. The pleasant beer garden is furnished with an "Aunt Sally" and provides the setting for barbecues every Sunday. There are attractive local walks and for more serious walkers the Ridgeway Path is just a short drive away.

    The food served at The Chequers is good old traditional 'pub grub' with Steak & Kidney Pie, steaks, and Cod and Chips amongst the main meals. A special sweet is Spotted Dick and bar snacks include tasty hot baps such as beef & mustard. All the food is listed on chalk boards and the menu is regularly changed. Sunday Roasts are served during the winter; during the summer the Randalls concentrate on barbecues. James is in charge of the kitchen, Pauline looks after the front of the house, and Ben the pub dog is the 'greeter', offering a friendly welcome to one and all.

Opening Hours: Mon-Fri: 12.00-15.00; 18.00-23.00. Sat-Sun (May-Sept): open all day

Food: Restaurant meals

Credit Cards: All major cards accepted

Facilities: Beer Garden; "Aunt Sally"; barbecue every Sunday

Entertainment: Darts

Local Places of Interest/Activities: local walks; Cholsey & Wallingford Railway, 4 miles; Ridgeway Path, 6 miles

Court Inn Hotel 91

Bridge Street,
Witney,
Oxfordshire
OX8 6DA
Tel: 01993 705228
Fax: 01993 700980

Directions:
From the Oxford ring road, take the A40 towards Cheltenham. After about 6 miles, take the B4022 into Witney. The Court Inn Hotel is at the eastern end of the town.

Witney is an attractive market town, located at the head of the lovely Windrush Valley. In the market place stands the 320-year-old Buttercross, a quaint little building with a steeply-pitched roof and rustic-looking stone columns. Witney prospered greatly in the middle ages from the wool trade and at one time there were more than 150 looms clattering away in the town. That industry is recalled by the Blanket Hall in the High Street which was built for the weighing and measuring of Witney's famous blankets.

Nearby, in Bridge Street, is the **Court Inn Hotel** which has been developed from a 17th century coaching inn and modernised to provide warm and comfortable accommodation at modest prices. The inn, which has been awarded a 3 Diamonds classification, is run by Nick and Allyson O'Brien who extend a warm welcome to all their guests. The hotel has 10 bedrooms and offers a choice of single, twin and double beds, with either standard or en suite facilities. The O'Briens take food seriously and their menu offers an excellent choice that ranges from steaks to vegetarian options, from fish dishes to jacket potatoes. Real ales are served, including a local brew. The lounge bar has considerable character, with a cheerful real fire in winter, and there's also a Sports Bar and games room offering pool, darts or crib. It also contains 4 television sets for watching sports events.

Opening Hours: Mon-Sat: 11.00-15.00; 18.30-23.00. Sun: 11.00-15.00; 18.30-22.30

Food: Wide choice of home cooked dishes

Credit Cards: All major cards accepted

Accommodation: 10 bedrooms, both en suite and standard

Facilities: Games room; 4 TV sets for sports events; parking

Entertainment: Darts; pool; live music on Saturdays

Local Places of Interest/Activities: Minster Lovell Hall, 1 mile; Cotswold Wild Life Park, 8 miles; Blenheim Palace, 8 miles; City of Oxford, 12 miles

Internet/Website: info@thecourtinn.co.uk

92 The Crown Inn

52 High Street,
Benson,
Wallingford
Oxfordshire
OX10 6RP
Tel: 01491 838247

Directions:

From the A4074, 12 miles south-east of Oxford, turn left on the B4009 to Benson. The Crown Inn is in the centre of the village.

Recently totally refurbished to a very high standard, **The Crown Inn** is an attractive former coaching inn with gleaming cream-coloured walls and brightly coloured hanging baskets of flowers. The friendly and efficient staff make customers feel particularly welcome and the freshly prepared food is served in very generous portions. If you are planning to stay in the area, The Crown has 6 guest rooms, - 4 doubles, 1 single and 1 twin.

Paul and Maureen Henderson are your hosts and they have recently introduced a new menu which retains some of the old favourites while adding lots of new dishes. How about an Oriental Platter as a starter, - crispy prawn balls, hoi sin duck spring rolls, chicken & ginger puffs, chicken and coconut potstickers, chicken saté and sesame prawn toast, served with 2 dips and prawn crackers. Main courses include The Crown Grill, a giant platter of meat with all the trimmings, Cajun Spiced Chicken, and vegetarian options such as Mediterranean Vegetable & Nut Wellington. Specialities of the house are the home made individual pies, the shortcrust pastry stuffed full of mouth-watering fillings. The "Half" Crown menu caters for the under 12s and for those with smaller appetites there's a good choice of sandwiches, baguettes and jacket potatoes.

Opening Hours: Mon-Thu: 12.00-15.00; 17.00-23.00. Fri-Sat: 12.00-23.00. Sun: 12.00-22.30

Food: Traditional main meals; bar snacks and sandwiches; children's menu

Credit Cards: All major cards accepted

Accommodation: 4 doubles, 1 single, 1 twin

Facilities: Beer Garden; patio; parking

Entertainment: Pool; darts; themed evenings

Local Places of Interest/Activities: The Thames Path, Ridgeway, Henley-on-Thames 10 miles, Oxford 14 miles, Cotswolds 20 miles

The Elephant & Castle

93

Bridge Street,
Bampton,
Oxfordshire
OX18 2HA
Tel: 01993 850316

Directions:

Bampton is on the A4095, about 6 miles north of Faringdon. The Elephant & Castle is located in the centre of the village.

The Elephant & Castle stands at the heart of this ancient market town which at the time of the Domesday Book was recorded as one of the largest settlements in Oxfordshire. Profits from the medieval wool trade enabled Bampton's citizens to build the splendid Church of St Mary the Virgin. Its spire soars 170ft high and inside there's a strikingly carved reredos more than 600 years old. Even older is the Saxon chancel arch carved with a herring-bone design. Another of the town's claims to fame is its team of Morris Dancers, - the oldest recorded Morris team in the country. Three local teams and invited guests traditionally dance in the village on Spring Bank Holiday Monday.

George and Patricia Blackwell are your hosts at this charming old inn with its beamed ceilings, inglenook and real log fire during the winter. Dating back to the 17th century, the building of mellow local stone is a Grade II listed building. A free house, the Elephant & Castle offers a good range of real ales and other popular brews and at lunchtime bar snacks are available. In fine weather these can also be enjoyed in the spacious garden. If you are planning to stay in the area, the inn has 3 guest rooms, (1 double, 1 twin, 1 single), in the converted dairy. All of them are en suite with colour TV and tea/coffee-making facilities.

Opening Hours: Mon 17.00-23.00, Tue-Fri 12.00-14.30, 17.00-23.00; Sat 12.00-23.00; Sun 12.00-17.00, 19.00-22.30

Food: Bar snacks at lunchtime

Credit Cards: All the major cards

Accommodation: 3 rooms (1 double, 1 twin, 1 single)

Facilities: Large Beer Garden; courtyard; parking

Entertainment: Darts, dominoes, shove ha'penny, Aunt Sally, Morris Dancing

Local Places of Interest/Activities: Thames Path, 2 miles; Cotswold Wildlife Park, 7 miles; Kingston Bagpuize House, 10 miles, Oxford 18 miles

94

The Griffin

Culworth Road,
Chipping Warden,
Oxfordshire
OX19 1LB
Tel: 01295 660230

Directions:

From the M40, Exit 11, take the A361 towards Daventry. After about 5 miles you will come to the village of Chipping Warden. The Griffin is located in the centre of the village

Any town or village with "Chipping" in its name reveals a very ancient heritage. *Ceaping* was the Saxon word for a market town where customers "cheaped", or bargained, for the goods on offer. Where the "Warden" part of its name came from has unfortunately been lost in the mists of time.

Located in the heart of this ancient village, **The Griffin** is a wonderfully unspoilt traditional pub where mine hostess Pauline Brick offers a warm welcome to locals and visitors alike. This is a hostelry that will definitely appeal to connoisseurs of real ales. Beneath its beamed ceilings you can sample a choice of real ales that range from a comparatively harmless home brewed beer with a strength of 3.3 to a sturdy Winter Ale XXX which is credited with a staggering rating of 6.0.

Opening Hours: Mon-Thu: 11.30-14.30; Fri-Sat: all day; Sun: 12.00-22.30

Food: All home cooked food

Credit Cards: Not accepted

Facilities: Parking

Entertainment: Pool, darts and other pub games; quiz nights

Local Places of Interest/Activities: Granary Museum, Claydon, 4 miles; Edgehill Country Park, 6 miles; Canons Ashby (NT), 8 miles

The Kings Arms | 95

18 West Street,
Chipping Norton,
Oxfordshire
OX7 5AA
Tel: 01608 642668
Fax: 01608 646673

Directions:
Chipping Norton is on the A44, about 20 miles north of Oxford. The Kings Arms is in the centre of the town, on the A361 to Burford.

The highest town in Oxfordshire, at 650ft above sea level, Chipping Norton was once an important centre of the wool trade, a fact reflected in the medieval magnificence of the Church of St Mary. It was a Vicar of St Mary's who in late-Victorian times investigated a local belief that juice from the bark of willow trees eased rheumatics and fevers. His tests confirmed the efficacy of the ancient country remedy and aspirin became the most widely-used product in pharmaceutical history. To the west of the town stands the extraordinary Bliss Tweed Mill, built by the Bliss family who instructed their architect to create a factory that could be mistaken for a great house in a park.

Located in the centre of this appealing market town, **The Kings Arms** is also an impressive building, constructed of honey-coloured Cotswold stone and smothered with hanging baskets and window boxes in summer. The landlord of this popular hostelry is Ken Bradshaw who offers his customers an extensive range of food, a selection of real ales and a choice of wines by the bottle or glass. The versatile menu includes traditional favourites such as Cheesy Cottage Pie or Liver & Onions, as well as a selection of 'Continental Classics', amongst them Vegetable Tikka Masala and New Orleans Cajun Chicken. In good weather, enjoy your refreshment in the beer garden at the rear.

Opening Hours: Mon-Sat: 11.00-23.00; Sun: 12.00-22.30

Food: Extensive choice of traditional favourites and 'Continental Classics'

Credit Cards: All major cards accepted

Facilities: Beer garden; patio; function room; limited parking

Local Places of Interest/Facilities: Bliss Tweed Mill, 1 mile; Rollright Standing Stones, 4 miles; Water Fowl Sanctuary & Children's Farm, Wigginton, 7 miles

96   The Lampet Arms

Main Street, Tadmarton,
nr Banbury, Oxfordshire
OX15 5TB
Tel: 01295 780070
Fax: 01295 780260

Directions:

From Banbury, take the B4035 towards Shipston-on-Stour. Tadmarton is about 5 miles along this road and The Lampet Arms is in the centre of the village.

Tadmarton is an attractive village with a church dating back to Norman times and boasting a very fine old font more than 600 years old, ornamented with grotesque heads and the Royal Arms of George IV. A nearby attraction is magnificent Broughton Castle which has been the home of the Saye and Sele family since it was built in 1300. Surrounded by a 3-acre moat, the house has a splendid medieval Great Hall, superb plaster ceilings and panelling, and contains a fascinating collection of arms and armour from the Civil War and other periods.

A free house, **The Lampet Arms** is owned and run by Tim and Jane Howard, a friendly and welcoming couple for whom "flexibility" is the key word! They offer good quality home cooked food every lunchtime and evening with a choice ranging from wholesome bar meals to main dishes such as Poached Chicken served with a leek and Stilton sauce, or a vegetarian Thai red vegetable curry. To complement your meal, there's a fine range of wines, cask ales and traditional beers. Tadmarton village is a peaceful and relaxing place to stay and the Howards have 4 guest bedrooms to let, all of them en suite and with remote control TV, direct dial telephone and tea/coffee-making facilities. Awarded 3 Diamonds by the AA, the attractive rooms occupy a beautifully converted coach house and if you stay for two or more nights there are special Short Break tariffs.

Opening Hours: Mon-Sat: 11.30-15.00; 17.00-23.00. Sun: 12.00-15.00; 19.00-22.30

Food: Full meals and bar snacks served every lunchtime and evening

Credit Cards: All major cards accepted

Accommodation: 4 bedrooms, all en suite

Facilities: Parking

Entertainment: Darts, dominoes, Aunt Sally, quiz nights, karaoke evenings

Local Places of Interest/Activities: Broughton Castle, 2 miles; Water Fowl Sanctuary & Children's Farm, Wigginton, 4 miles; Blenheim Palace, 15 miles; Stratford-upon-Avon, 20 miles

Internet/Website: www.banburycross.co.uk/lampetarms/index.htm
e-mail: lampet@compuserve.com

Merrymouth Inn

Stow Road,
Fifield,
nr Burford,
Oxfordshire
OX7 6HR
Tel: 01993 831652
Fax: 01993 830840

Directions:

The Merrymouth Inn is on the A424 Burford to Stow on the Wold road, about 3 miles north of Burford.

A beautifully restored and refurbished 13th century inn, the **Merrymouth Inn** derives its unusual name from the Murimuth family who acquired the nearby village of Fifield six centuries ago. At that time, the manor was owned by the monks of Bruern Abbey and the inn was undoubtedly a traveller's hospice. According to legend, there still exist underground passages from the inn's cellar to the abbey but these have yet to be discovered. The inn lies in a lovely part of the Cotswolds, not far from the picture postcard village of Bourton on the Water, famed for its model village and its Bird Garden.

Over the years the Merrymouth Inn has been a hunting lodge, a brewery-owned hostelry and is now a free house owned and run by the Flaherty family. Tim Flaherty is the chef and his deliciously sophisticated menu includes specialities such as Braden Rost (hot smoked salmon) with sour cream, and the inn's own Murimuth Chicken. A highly original range of fresh fish dishes is always available, - and make sure you allow room for Tim's wonderful puddings. This is a place where you will want to linger and the inn has quality accommodation to offer, - nine attractively furnished double rooms, all of them en suite, imaginatively created from converted stables around a pretty garden courtyard and overlooking the rolling Cotswold countryside.

Opening Hours: Open all year except Christmas and New Years Day

Food: Everything from a light snack to a full à la carte

Credit Cards: All major cards accepted except American Express or Diners

Accommodation: 9 double rooms, all en suite

Facilities: Patio; garden; parking

Local Places of Interest/Activities: Burford, 3 miles; Bourton on the Water, 6 miles; Snowshill Manor, 14 miles; Sudeley Castle, Winchcombe, 17 miles

98   The Red Cow

The Green,
Chesterton,
Bicester,
Oxfordshire
OX26 1UU
Tel: 01869 241339
Fax: 01869 240667

Directions:

From Bicester, take the A41 towards Oxford. After about 2 miles turn left on minor road to Chesterton (1 mile). The Red Cow is in the centre of the village.

The sizeable village of Chesterton stands on the old Roman thoroughfare Akeman Street and about a mile to the southeast are the remains of the Roman town of Alchester. A much more recent attraction is the Bicester Village Shopping Village which offers shoppers a choice of over 60 outlets for internationally known names. Designer clothes, china, perfume, sportswear and homewares are sold at up to 60% off the regular prices.

In Chesterton itself, **The Red Cow** is a delightful old inn built of mellow grey stone and with an unusual wooden porch. This welcoming hostelry is run by Colin Hale and Liz Aplin who spare no effort in ensuring quality food and ales, (including real ales), and in creating a hospitable atmosphere. This is very much a traditional village pub, very cosy and comfortable and offering first class food served in the small and intimate restaurant area. The menu is varied and interesting with fish dishes a speciality of the house. For fairweather days, there's a peaceful beer garden to the rear of the inn.

Opening Hours: Daily: 11.00-23.00

Food: Varied menu, fish dishes a speciality

Credit Cards: All major cards accepted

Facilities: Beer Garden; Parking, Childrens play area

Entertainment: Pool; darts; Aunt Sally

Local Places of Interest/Activities: Golf, 0.5 miles; Bicester Outlet Shopping Village, 1 mile; Blenheim Palace, 9 miles; City of Oxford, 11 miles

Internet/Website: www.redcow.com

The Red Horse Inn

99

High Street,
Shipton-under-Wychwood,
Oxfordshire OX7 6BA
Tel/Fax: 01993 830391

Directions:

From the A40, 8 miles west of Witney at Burford, turn right on the A361 towards Chipping Norton. Shipton-under-Wychwood is about 5 miles along this road. The Red Horse Inn is on the A361 at the northern end of the village.

Shipton-under-Wychwood is a charming village with a wealth of old houses. The most striking of them is Shipton Court (private), a fine Elizabethan house completed in 1603 and visible on the left as you enter the village from Burford. The 'Wychwood' part of the village name comes from the ancient royal hunting preserve, Wychwood Forest, remains of which lie to the east. The village is picturesquely set around a large green dominated by the tall spire of St Mary's Church, parts of which date back to Norman times. Close by is **The Red Horse Inn**, an outstanding hostelry run by Paul Sutcliffe and Mandy Large.

Beautifully furnished and appointed, the inn has a traditional inglenook fireplace in the lounge bar and a separate restaurant which is available for buffets and private parties. The enticing menu offers a good choice of home made pies, fresh fish, home cooked meats, vegetarian and vegan dishes. Real ales and fine wines are available to complement your meal. In good weather, enjoy your meal in the large garden and orchard where there's also a secure children's play area, fish pond and a pets corner with rabbits, dogs, guinea pigs, and parrots. By the time you read this, an elegant conservatory restaurant will have been added to the inn's excellent amenities. Located in 'the heart of the Wychwoods, on the fringe of the Cotswolds!', The Red Horse has 4 bedrooms, with en suite available, - an ideal base for exploring this lovely area.

Opening Hours: Mon: 18.30-23.00. Tue-Sat: 11.30-14.30; 18.30-23.00. Sun: 12.00-15.00; 19.00-22.30

Food: Tuesday to Sunday lunchtimes; Monday to Saturday evenings

Credit Cards: All major cards accepted

Accommodation: 4 bedrooms with en suite available

Facilities: Large beer garden with pond, pets and children's play area; games room; non-smoking restaurant

Entertainment: Barbecues, bouncy castles and other events throughout the summer; special 'Silly Nights' for charity

Local Places of Interest/Activities: Cotswold Wildlife Park, 5 miles; Bourton-on-the-Water (Model Village, Cotswold Motor Museum, Birdland Zoo), 8 miles; Blenheim Palace, 12 miles

Internet/Website:
www.red-horse.demon.co.uk
mandy&paul@red-horse.demon.co.uk

100   The Red Lion

115 High Street,
Chalgrove,
Oxfordshire
OX44 7SS
Tel: 01865 890625
Fax: 01865 890795

Directions:

From the M40, Exit 6, take the B4009 towards Watlington. After about 3 miles in Watlington, fork right on the B480. Stay on this road for about 4 miles and it will bring you to Chalgrove. The Red Lion is in the centre of the village, opposite the War Memorial

There can't be many pubs that are owned by the local parish church but **The Red Lion** has been the property of Chalgrove church since before the first known written record of 1637. In a village with many picturesque houses, The Red Lion is strikingly pretty and boasts one garden overlooking the village street and another, exceptionally lovely, to the rear. Parts of the building have been dated to the 11th century and a few hundred years ago the pub provided free dining and carousing facilities for the 'naughty' church wardens, much to the disapproval of a future Archbishop of Canterbury. Today, the Red Lion is run on a more conventional basis by Maggi and Jonathan Hewitt. The church wardens still come - but now as paying customers.

The regularly changing cuisine at the Red Lion is quite outstanding with imaginative dishes such as Escebesh of Cornish Mackerel with root vegetables featuring on the menu alongside traditional favourites like the Beef, Mushroom & Red Wine Pie. At lunchtime (noon until 2pm) hearty sandwiches and warm open baguettes are also available. There's a short menu for children or they can have smaller portions of the main menu dishes at reduced prices. Dinner is served from 7pm until 9.30pm (except Sundays) and there's an extremely well-chosen wine list offering wines from both Europe and the New World. This delightful pub makes a wonderful venue for special events and business meetings. It can provide a professional conference facility for up to 16 people in a relaxed pub atmosphere, cater for weddings with up to 200 guests, dinners for 26 and most things in between!

Opening Hours: 12.00-15.00, 18.00-23.00 every day

Food: Quality food served every lunchtime and evening except Sunday evening.

Credit Cards: All major cards accepted

Facilities: Excellent beer garden & patio; conference facilities

Local Places of Interest/Activities: Medieval wall painting, Chalgrove Church; Battle of Chalgrove field, 1 mile;Thames Path, 5 miles; Dorchester Abbey, 8 miles; City of Oxford, 12 miles

The Red Lion Inn   101

8 Red Lion Street,
Cropredy,
nr Banbury,
Oxfordshire
OX17 1PB
Tel: 01295 750224

Directions:

From the M40 at Exit 11, take the A361 towards Daventry. After just over a mile take the minor road to the left signposted to Cropredy (1 mile). The Red Lion Inn is in the centre of the village, next to the church

It would be difficult to imagine a more picturesque building than **The Red Lion Inn** with its walls of honey-coloured local stone and its roof of grey, beautifully crafted thatch. Even the porch has its own covering of thatch. Cropredy village sits beside the Oxford Canal, with towpath walks stretching for miles in either direction and the inn is right next to Cropredy lock. A few miles to the west of the village is the National Trust property of Upton House. This late-17th century building is notable for its outstanding collection of paintings which includes works by Pieter Brueghel and El Greco, and a porcelain collection that boasts many very fine English porcelain figures and a number of good Sèvres pieces.

The display of china plates at the Red Lion may not be quite so valuable but they certainly provide an interesting conversation subject at this lovely old inn with its low-slung beamed ceilings. Your hosts here are Ian Errington and Susan Linnell. Their menu offers a good choice of traditional pub meals such as steaks, home cooked ham and home-made desserts along with vegetarian options, salads, omelettes, ploughmans and baguettes. The regular menu is supplemented by a choice of daily specials . To accompany your meal, there's a good selection of beverages on offer, amongst them four real ales and a good selection of reasonably priced wines.

Opening Hours: Mon-Thu 12.00-15.00, 17.30-23.00, Fri-Sat 12.00-16.00, 17.30-23.00, Sun 12.00-16.00, 19.00-22.30

Food: Meals and bar snacks available every lunchtime and evening

Credit Cards: All the major cards

Facilities: Patio; Car park at rear

Entertainment: Pool, darts, dominoes, cribbage, quiz team

Local Places of Interest/Activities: Canalside walks, ½ mile; Banbury, 4 miles; Broughton Castle, 7 miles; Upton House (NT), 8 miles

102 The Red Lion

High Street,
Islip,
Oxfordshire
OX5 2RX
Tel: 01865 375367

Directions:

From the A34, about 7 miles north of Oxford, turn right on the B4027 to Islip (1 mile). The Red Lion is on the main street of the village

This pleasant little village with many stone-built thatched cottages stands beside the River Ray. Its major claim to fame is that it was birthplace of Edward the Confessor, Saxon king and founder of Westminster Abbey. He was born in 1004 in the royal palace at Islip but sadly all traces of the building have disappeared. About a mile south of the village there's a grand hilltop view across Otmoor, a rare tract of peat-covered bogland which has been jealously guarded by local people over the years. They resisted attempts to enclose and drain the land in the early 1800s and more recently proposals to route the M40 across the moor were successfully opposed.

Located in the heart of the village, **The Red Lion** is a former coaching inn and boasts lots of atmosphere. It has only recently been taken over by Hugh and Pam Curran who have maintained its traditional character while upgrading the facilities on offer. They offer a good choice of all the old favourites, home made Steak & Kidney Pie for example, along with filled crusty baguettes or jacket potatoes, and a children's menu. Beverages served include all the popular brews, a real ale, and a selection of wines. If you are considering staying in this attractive village, The Red Lion has 3 guest rooms, - 2 doubles and 1 single.

Opening Hours: Mon-Sat: 11.00-23.00; Sun: 10.30-22.30

Food: Traditional pub meals and bar snacks; children's menu

Credit Cards: All major cards accepted

Accommodation: 3 guest rooms (2 doubles, 1 single)

Facilities: Spacious garden; skittle alley; ample parking

Entertainment: Pool, darts, Aunt Sally, skittle alley

Local Places of Interest/Activities: Oxfordshire Way skirts the village; Oxford, 7 miles; Blenheim Palace, 9 miles

The Red Lion 103

Northmoor,
Oxfordshire
OX8 1SX
Tel: 01865 300301

Directions:

From the Oxford ring road take the A420 towards Swindon. After 8 miles, at Kingston Bagpuize, turn right on the A415 towards Witney. About 2 miles along this road it crosses the Thames. Turn right on minor road to

Northmoor (2 miles). You will see the Red Lion as you enter the village.

If you approach Northmoor by the route given above, you will pass through Newbridge which, ironically, has the oldest bridge over the Thames. During the Civil War the bridge was seized by Cromwell's troops, posing a threat to Charles I who had established himself in nearby Oxford. The King fled north. Northmoor itself sits surrounded by Thames-side pastures and there pleasant riverside walks extending for miles in both directions. The parish church is notable for two fine 14th century effigies of a knight and his lady. On the wall behind them are paintings showing their souls ascending into heaven.

In the heart of the village, **The Red Lion** is as pretty as a picture with its whitewashed walls, flower-filled tubs and hanging baskets, and steep roof with dormer windows. The interior is just as inviting, an archetypal English country pub. There's a separate dining area offering excellent home prepared and cooked food. Landlady Pauline Emery has made Wednesday and Thursday evenings 'Steak Nights' but you'll also a good choice of fish and other dishes with a traditional Roast Lunch served on Sundays. Real ale is available and in good weather you can enjoy your refreshments in the lovely garden

Opening Hours: Mon-Sat: 18.30-23.00. Sun: 12.00-15.30; 19.00-22.30

Food: Home cooked meals specialising in steaks and fish

Credit Cards: Not accepted

Accommodation: B&Bs nearby

Facilities: Parking

Entertainment: Darts; dominoes; chess; Aunt Sally; folk music or 60s, 70s, 80s music on Friday and Saturday evenings

Local Places of Interest/Activities: Riverside walks, 1 mile; Kingston Bagpuize House, 4 miles; City of Oxford, 8 miles

104   The Red Lion

Goring Road
Woodcote
Oxfordshire
RG8 0SD
Tel/Fax:
 01491 680483

Directions:

From Reading take the A4074 towards Wallingford. After about 7 miles turn left on the B471 to the village of Woodcote.

Located right in the heart of this picturesque village, overlooking the village green, **The Red Lion** is a handsome early-Victorian building dating back to 1845. Hanging baskets and tubs of flowers make it look particularly inviting during the summer months but there's a warm welcome throughout the year from Dennis and Jean Smith. They have been here since 1996 and altogether have some 15 years experience in the hospitality business. The Red Lion has one large L-shaped bar with old beams and an open fire, and a separate non-smoking restaurant with seating for 40. Outside, there's a small patio where you can watch the gentle pace of village life. And if you want to linger for a while in this pleasant spot, the inn has a family room to let for bed and breakfast.

Jean is the chef and her menu offers a tasty selection of home cooked traditional English dishes. Her Sunday lunches, when there's a choice of different roasts, have a particularly high reputation. You can complement your meal with one of the 4 real ales on tap or make a selection from the extensive wine list.

Opening Hours: Mon-Fri: 11.00-15.00; 17.00-23.00. Sat: 11.00-23.00. Sun: 12.00-22.30

Food: Home cooked traditional English fare. Selection of Sunday roasts

Facilities: Patio at the front

Accommodation: 1 family room

Credit Cards: All major cards except Amex and Diners

Entertainment: Pool, darts, weekly Quiz Night, Sky TV for sports events

Local Places of Interest/Activities: Wellplace Zoo, 4 miles; Beale Bird Park, 5 miles; Basildon Park (NT), 6 miles. Good walking and cycling country

The Swan | 105

13 Church Street,
Bicester,
Oxfordshire
OX6 7AY
Tel: 01869 369035

Directions:

From Exit 9 of the M40, take the A41 into Bicester (3 miles). The Swan is on the edge of the town centre

Though the name, (pronounced Bister), suggests that this was a Roman settlement, the town was not in fact established until Saxon times. The town stands on the Roman Akeman Street and it was from the nearby fort of Alchester, long since vanished, that the name derives. In medieval times there were 3 religious houses but a disastrous fire in the 1700s destroyed all the old buildings except for the Church of St Eadburg which still has traces of the original 12th century building. Bicester developed rapidly in the 1960s and one of the most recent additions to the town's amenities is the Bicester Outlet Shopping Village which offers designer goods at discounts of up to 60%.

A short walk from the town centre, **The Swan** is an attractive old building of mellow brick and stone. It's a free house so there's a good choice of well-maintained beers and real ales, a selection which has earned The Swan a mention in the *Good Pub Guide*. A blue and white plaque over the entrance promises another attraction, - good pub food. All the popular favourites are there and at very reasonable prices. If you're planning to stay in Bicester, The Swan's landlord, Keith Payne, has 7 standard rooms to let, again at very reasonable rates.

Opening Hours: All day, every day

Food: Bar food

Credit Cards: All major cards accepted

Accommodation: 7 standard rooms

Entertainment: Darts; dominoes; cribbage; live blues music at weekends

Local Places of Interest/Activities: Golf, 2 miles; Bicester Outlet Shopping Village, 2 miles; Blenheim Palace, 10 miles; City of Oxford, 13 miles

106   The White Hart

High Street,
Harwell,
Oxfordshire
OX11 0EH
Tel: 01235 831872

Directions:

Harwell village lies 3 miles west of Didcot just off the main A34. The White Hart lies in the centre of village

An ancient village of timber-framed cottages, with a Norman church and some fine almshouses, Harwell is best known for the Atomic Energy Research Establishment that was set up here in 1946. Lying to the south of the original village, this research centre almost forms a village in its own right. Located in the old village, **The White Hart** looks very inviting from the outside with its whitewashed and half-timbered walls. Inside, beamed ceilings add to the traditional atmosphere. Popular with local people, the inn also provides a warm welcome to all its customers.

Mark and Cindy Russell are the landlords here and they offer a good choice of home cooked and prepared food which is particularly in demand at Sunday lunchtimes. Complement your meal with one of the well-maintained real ales on tap.

Opening hours: Mon-Fri, Sun: 12.00-15.00; 18.00-23.00. Sat: 12.00-23.00

Food: All home cooked and reasonably priced

Credit Cards: All major cards accepted

Facilities: Beer Garden; children's climbing frame; "Aunt Sally"

Entertainment: Pool; Sky TV; live music; bell ringers

Local Places of Interest/Activities: Didcot Railway Museum, 4 miles; Ridgeway Path, 5 miles

The White Hart

Minster Lovell,
nr Witney,
Oxfordshire
OX8 5RA
Tel: 01993 775255

Directions:

The White Hart is on
the main A40 Oxford
to Cheltenham, road
about 4 miles west of
Witney.

One of the prettiest villages along the banks of the River Windrush, Minster Lovell is home to the picturesque ruins of the 15th century Minster Lovell Hall. It was the home of the Lovell family, one of whom was a close crony of Richard III. When the king was killed at Bosworth Field, the Lovell families estates were confiscated by the new monarch, Henry VII. What remains of the mansion occupy a lovely setting beside the River Windrush. One fascinating feature of the manor house which has survived is the medieval dovecote, complete with nesting boxes, which provided pigeons for the table in a way reminiscent of modern battery hen houses.

The White Hart is an attractive old building, dating in parts back to the 1500s and colourful in summer with its tubs and hanging baskets of flowers. The interior has a wonderful olde-worlde feeling with lots of old beams, flagstone floors and open fires. There's even a resident ghost. David Riddy is the landlord here and he offers an excellent choice of freshly-prepared, home cooked food with fish and steak dishes amongst the specialities of the house. Vegetarian options and daily specials add to the choice. Beverages include a real ale and you can complete your meal with an aromatic Coffee Floater, one of which is named after the White Hart Ghost!

Opening Hours: Daily: 12.30-14.30; 18.00-23.00

Food: Wide choice of meals; fish and steak dishes are specialities of the house

Credit Cards: Visa, Electron, HSBC, Solo, Switch

Facilities: Parking

Entertainment: Pool; darts; Aunt Sally; live entertainment wednesdays and occasional weekends, varying from folk to rock music

Local Places of Interest/Activities: Minster Lovell Hall, 1 mile; Oxfordshire Circular Walks, 1.5 miles; Windrush Valley Park, 2 miles; Cogges Farm Museum, Witney, 3 miles

The Hidden Inns of the South of England

This page is intentionally left blank

4 North Wiltshire

PLACES OF INTEREST:

PUBS AND INNS:

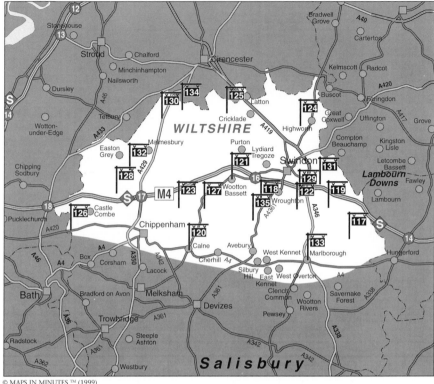

© MAPS IN MINUTES ™ (1999)

Please note all cross references refer to page numbers

North Wiltshire

Wiltshire is a county rich in the monuments of prehistoric man; it also has one of the highest concentrations of historic houses and gardens in the country. It's a great place for walking and cycling, with wide open spaces, woodland and downland and a number of chalk streams that are home to a huge variety of wetland wildlife. And, of course, the county has its very own surprises in the shape of the famous white horses, the intriguing crop circles and, above all, the great and ancient stone circles, rich in history and mystery and legend. Pretty villages abound, and the area in and around the distinguished town of Marlborough takes in some of the most renowned prehistoric sites in the country, as well as monutments to Wiltshire's industrial past.

PLACES OF INTEREST

AVEBURY

A 28-acre World Heritage Site is the centre of the **Avebury Stone Circles**, the most remarkable ritual megalithic monuments in Europe. A massive bank and ditch enclose an outer circle and two inner circles of stones. The outer circle of almost 100 sarsen stones (sand and silica) enclose two rings with about 40 stones still standing. Archaeologists working on the site have recently found the remains of a long-

Avebury Stones

vanished avenue of stones leading south towards Beckahmpton. This discovery seems to vindicate the theory of the 18th century antiquary William Stukeley, who made drawings of the stone circles with this avenue marked. The stones in the avenue had disappeared so completely (perhaps destroyed out of some superstition in the Middle Ages) that few believed Stukeley. The research team from Southamp-

ton, Leicester and Newport Universities uncovered a series of subterranean features which appear to be buried stones and the sockets in which they were set. Two large stones, known as Adam and Eve, had always been known about on this route, but there were no further traces until the team's discoveries in 1999. The **Avebury Stones** bear testimony to the enormous human effort that went into their construction: some of the individual stones weigh 40 tons and all had to dragged from Marlborough Downs. The Avebury stones are in two basic shapes, which have been equated with male and female and have led to the theory that the site was used for the observance of fertility rites. Many of the archaeological finds from the site are displayed in Avebury's **Alexander Keiller Museum**, which also describes the reconstruction of the site by Keiller in the 1930s.

Avebury Manor

112 Avebury has a gem from Elizabethan times in **Avebury Manor**, which stands on the site of a 12th century priory. The house and its four-acre walled garden, which features a wishing well, topiary, a rose graden and an Italian walk, are owned by the National Trust. Open daily except Monday and Thursday.

CALNE

A former weaving centre in the valley of the River Marden; the prominent wool church reflects the prosperity of earlier times. One of the memorials in the church is to Dr Ingenhousz, who is widely credited with creating a smallpox vaccination before Jenner.

A short distance from Calne, to the west, stands **Bowood House**, built in 1625 and now a treasury of Shelborne family heirlooms, paintings, books and furniture. In the Bowood Laboratory Dr Joseph Priestley, tutor to the 1st Marquess of Lansdowne's son, conducted experiments that resulted in the identification of oxygen. The house is set in lovely Capability Brown grounds with a lake and terraced garden. The mausoleum was commissioned in 1761 by the Dowager Countess of Shelborne as a memorial to her husband and was Robert Adam's first work for them. A separate woodland garden of 60 acres, with azaleas and rhododendrons, is open from late April to early June.

The **Atwell Motor Museum**, on the A4 east of Calne, has a collection of over 70 vintage and classic cars and motorcycles from the years 1924 to 1983.

CASTLE COMBE

The loveliest village in the region, and for some the loveliest in the country, Castle Combe was once a centre of the prosperous wool trade, famed for its red and white cloth, and many of the present-day buildings date from the 15th and 16th centuries, including the Perpendicular Church of St Andrew, the covered market cross and the manor house, which was built with stones from the Norman castle that gave the village its name. One of the Lords of the Manor in the 14th century was Sir John Fastolf, who was reputedly the inspiration for Shakespeare's Falstaff. A small museum dealing with the village's history is open on summer Sunday afternoons.

CHERHILL

Cherhill was another stop on the London-Bristol coaching route, and, for a time in the 18th century, one which caused passengers some trepidation. The Cherhill gang regularly held up and robbed the coaches, and the fact they carried out their crimes wearing nothing at all made identification more than a little tricky.

On the chalk ridge south of the village by the ancient earthwork of **Oldbury Castle** (National Trust) is another of Wiltshire's famous white horses. This one was built in 1790 under the instruction of Dr Christopher Alsop, known as "the mad doctor". For some years the horse's eye, four feet across, was filled with upturned bottles which sparkled in the sunlight.

CHIPPENHAM

This historic settlement on the banks of the Avon was founded around 600 by the Saxon king Cyppa. It became an important administrative centre in King Alfred's time and later gained further prominence from the wool trade. It was a major stop on the London-Bristol coaching run and is served by the railway between the same two cities. Buildings of note include the Church of St Andrew (mainly 15th century) and the half-timbered Hall, once used by the burgesses and bailiffs of the Chippenham Hundred and latterly a museum (as we went to press the museum was due to move into a Heritage Centre in the market place). At Hardenhuish Hall on the edge of town, John Wood the Younger of Bath fame built the Church of St Nicholas; completed in 1779, it is notable for its domed steeple and elegant Venetian windows.

In the flood plain to the east of Chippenham stands the 4½ mile footpath known as **Maud Heath's Causeway**. This remarkable and ingenious walkway consisting of 64 brick and stone arches was built at the end of the 15th century at the bequest of Maud Heath, who spent most of her life as a poor pedlar trudging her often muddy way between her village of Bremhill and Chippenham. She died a relatively wealthy woman, and the land and property she left in her will provided sufficient funds for the upkeep of the causeway, which is best seen near the hamlet of Kellaways. A statue of Maud, basket in hand, stands overlooking the flood plain at Wick Hill.

CRICKLADE

The only Wiltshire town on the Thames was an important post on the Roman Ermin Street and had its own mint in Saxon times. There are many buildings of interest, notably the Church of St Sampson, with its cathedral-like four-spired tower, where a festival of music takes place each September; the famous school founded by the London goldsmith Robert Jenner in 1651; and the fancy Victorian clock tower. Nearby **North Meadow** is a National Nature Reserve where the rare snakeshead fritillary grows. Cricklade is the centre of the Cricklade Corridor Trust set up to secure the maximum economic, heritage, leisure and environmental benefits from a number of projects between Swindon and Cricklade and beyond. These include railway and canal restoration, nature conservation and the development of a branch of the National Cycle Network. Tel: 01249 706111.

EAST AND WEST KENNET

West Kennet Long Barrow, one of Britain's largest neolithic burial tombs, is situated a gentle stroll away from the twin villages. The tomb is of impressive proportions - 330' long, 80' wide and 10' high - and is reached by squeezing past some massive stones in the semicircular forecourt.

EASTON GREY

Here the southern branch of the River Avon is spanned by a handsome 16th century bridge with five stone arches. A manor house has overlooked the village since the 13th century, and the present house, with a classical facade and an elegant covered portico, dates from the 18th century. It was used as a summer retreat by Herbert Asquith, British Prime Minister from 1908 to 1916, and in 1923 the Prince of Wales was in residence during the Duke of Beaufort's hunting season at Badminton.

HIGHWORTH

The name is appropriate, as the village stands at the top of a 400' incline, and the view from **Highworth Hill** takes in the counties of Wiltshire, Gloucestershire and Oxfordshire. There are some very fine 17th and 18th century buildings round the old square, and the parish church is of interest: built in the 15th century, it was fortified during the Civil War and was attacked soon after by Parliamentarian forces under Fairfax. One of the cannonballs which struck it is on display outside. The church contains a memorial to Lieutenant Warneford, who was awarded the VC for destroying the first enemy Zeppelin in 1915.

LATTON

A lovely old village with some delightful 17th century Cotswold-stone cottages and larger Victorian houses. It was once an important junction of the **Wiltshire & Berkshire and Thames & Severn Canals**. Work is being carried out to provide a connection between the former at Swindon and the latter, here. Note the impressive old wharf-owner's house.

LYDIARD TREGOZE

On the western outskirts of Swindon, **Lydiard Park** is the ancestral home of the Viscounts Bolingbroke. The park is a delightful place to explore, and the house, one of Wiltshire's smaller stately homes, is a real gem, described by Sir Hugh Casson as "a gentle Georgian house, sunning itself as serenely as an old grey cat". Chief attractions inside include the little blue Dressing Room devoted to the 18th century society artist Lady Diana Spencer, who became the 2nd Viscountess Bolingbroke.

Golden Cavalier, Lydiard Park

St Mary's Church, next to the house, contains many monuments to the St John family, who lived here from Elizabethan times. The most striking is the **Golden Cavalier**, a life-size gilded effigy of Edward St John in full battledress (he was killed at the 2nd Battle of Newbury in 1645).

114

MALMESBURY

England's oldest borough and one of its most attractive. The hilltop town is dominated by the impressive remains of the **Benedictine Malmesbury Abbey**, founded in the 7th century by St Aldhelm. In the 10th century, King Athelstan, Alfred's grandson and the first Saxon king to unite England, granted 500 acres of land to the townspeople in gratitude for their help in resisting a Norse invasion. Those acres are still known as King's Heath and are owned by 200 residents who are descended from those far-off heroes. Athelstan made Malmesbury his

Market Cross, Malmesbury

capital and is buried in the abbey, where several centuries later a monument was put up in his honour.

The abbey tower was the scene of an early attempt at human-powered flight when in the early part of the 11th century Brother Elmer strapped a pair of wings to his arms, flew for about 200 yards and crashed to earth, breaking both legs and becoming a cripple for the rest of his long life. The flight of this intrepid cleric, who reputedly forecast the Norman invasion following a sighting of Halley's Comet, is commemorated in a stained glass window. The octagonal **Market Cross** in the town square is one of many interesting buildings that also include the Old Stone House with its colonnade and gargoyles, and the arched Tolsey Gate,

whose two cells once served as the town jail.

In the **Athelstan Museum** are displays of lace-making, costume, rural life, coins, early bicycles and tricycles, a manually-operated fire engine, photographs and maps. Personalities include a local notable, the philosopher Thomas Hobbes.

A more recent piece of history concerns the **Tamworth Two**, the pigs who made the headlines with their dash for freedom. Their trail is one of many that can be followed in and around the town

MARLBOROUGH

Famous for its public school and its wide high street, Marlborough is situated in the rural eastern part of Wiltshire in the upland valley of the Kennet, which flows through the town. It was once an important staging post on the coaching run from London to Bath and Bristol, and the presence of the A4 means that it still has easy links both east and west. Its main street, one of the finest in the country, is dignified by many Tudor houses and handsome Georgian colonnaded shops, behind which are back alleys waiting to be explored. St Mary's Church, austere behind a 15th century frontage, stands in **Patten Alley**, so named because pedestrians had to wear pattens (an overshoe with a metal sole) to negotiate the mud on rainy days. The porch of the church has a ledge where churchgoers would leave their pattens before entering. Other buildings of interest include those clustered round The Green (originally a Saxon village and the working-class quarter in the 18th and 19th centuries); the turn-of-the-century Town Hall looking down the broad High Street; and the ornate 17th century Merchant's House, now restored as a museum.

Marlborough College was founded in 1843 primarily for sons of the clergy. The Seymour family built a mansion near the site of the Norman castle. This mansion was replaced in the early 18th century by a building which became the Castle Inn and is now C House, the oldest part of the College.

SILBURY HILL

The largest man-made prehistoric mound in Europe, built around 2800BC, standing 130' high and covering five acres. Excavation in the late 1960s revealed some details of how it was constructed but shed little light on its purpose. Theories include a burial place for King Sil and

Silbury Hill

his horse and a hiding place for a large gold statue built by the Devil on his way to Devizes. Scholarship generally favours the first.

SWINDON

Think Swindon, think the Great Western Railway. Think GWR, think Isambard Kingdom Brunel. The largest town in Wiltshire, lying in the northeast corner between the Cotswolds and the Marlborough Downs, was an insignificant agricultural community before the railway line between London and Bristol was completed in 1835. Swindon Station opened in that year, but it was some time later, in 1843, that Brunel, the GWR's principal engineer, decided that Swindon was the place to build his locomotive works. Within a few years it had grown to be one of the largest in the world, with as many as 12,000 on a 320-acre site that incorporated the Railway Village; this was a model development of 300 workmen's houses built of limestone extracted from the construction of Box Tunnel. This unique example of early-Victorian town planning is open to the public as the **Railway Village Museum**.

The **Great Western Railway Museum** moved from the same site in Faringdon Road in the autumn of 1999 to a new home in the former GWR works, with a new name, a great deal more space and a host of new interactive

Great Western Railway Museum, Swindon

exhibits. **STEAM** will keep the collection of locomotives (*6000 King George V* is the star), nameplates, signalling equipment and an exhibition of the life and achievements of Brunel; it will also focus on the human aspect of a hard industry, telling the story of the men and women who built and repaired the locomotives and carriages of God's Wonderful Railway for seven generations. The last locomotive to be built at the works was *92220 Evening Star*, a powerful 2-10-0 freight engine destined to have all too short a working life. Engineering work continued on the site until 1986, when the works finally closed. The site now also contains the **National Monuments Record Centre** - the public archive of the Royal Commission on the Historical Monuments of England, with 7 million photographs, documents and texts.

There's lots more to Swindon than the legacy of the GWR: it's a bustling and successful commercial town with excellent shopping and leisure facilities and plenty of open spaces. One such is **Coate Water Country Park** on the Marlborough road.

WEST OVERTON

The area between Marlborough and Avebury sees the biggest concentration of prehistoric remains in the country. The scattered community of West Overton stands at the foot of **Overton Hill**, the site of an early Bronze Age monument called **The Sanctuary**. These giant standing stones are at the southeastern end of West Kennet Avenue, an ancient pathway which once connected them to the main megalithic circles at Avebury (see below). Overton Hill is also the start point of the Ridgeway long-distance path, which runs for 80 miles to the Chilterns. Just off this path is **Fyfield Down**, now a nature reserve, where quarries once provided many of the great stones that are such a feature of the area. **Devil's Den** long barrow lies within the reserve. The local legend that Satan sometimes appears here at midnight attempting to pull down the stones with a team of white oxen has not in recent times been corroborated.

WOOTTON BASSETT

A small town with a big history. Records go back to the 7th century, and in 1219 King Henry lll granted a market charter (the market is still held

116

every Wednesday). The first known mayor of Wootton Bassett was John Woolmonger, appointed in 1408. A later mayor was acting as town magistrate when a drunk was brought before him after an overnight drinking spree. When asked by the mayor whether he pleaded guilty to drunkenness, the man said "You knows your worship was just as drunk as I was" (he was on the same spree). "Ah well", said the mayor. "That was different. Now I am the mayor and I am going to fine you five shillings."

The most remarkable building in Wootton is the **Old Town Hall**, which stands on a series of stone pillars, leaving an open-sided ground-floor area that once served as a covered market. The museum above, open on Saturday mornings, contains a rare ducking stool, silver maces and a mayoral sword of office.

A section of the **Wilts & Berks Canal** has been restored at **Templars Fir**. In May 1998 about 50 boats of all kinds were launched on the canal and a day of festivities was enjoyed by all. The railway station, alas, has not been revived after falling under the Beeching axe in 1966.

WROUGHTON

Wroughton Airfield, with its historic Second World War hangars, is home to the **National Museum of Science and Industry's** collection of large aircraft, and the road transport and agricultural collection. The museum is open on event days at the airfield. Tel: 01793 814466.

Nearby **Clouts Wood Nature Reserve** is a lovely place for a ramble, and a short drive south, by the Ridgeway, is the site of **Barbury Castle**, one of the most spectacular Iron Age forts in southern England. The open hillside was the scene of a bloody battle between the Britons and the Saxons in the 6th century; the Britons lost and the Saxon kingdom of Wessex was established under King Cealwin. The area around the castle is a country park.

The Bell @ Ramsbury | 117

The Square,
Ramsbury,
Marlborough,
Wiltshire SN8 2PE
Tel: 01672 520230
Fax: 01672 521476

Directions:

From the A4 at Hungerford take the B4192 northwards. After about 4 miles take the minor road to the left signposted to Ramsbury

In Saxon times the peaceful riverside village of Ramsbury was the seat of the Bishop of Wiltshire and its 13th century parish church stands on the foundations of a much earlier Saxon building. Present day Ramsbury contains a number of attractive Jacobean and Georgian houses, many of them with gardens running down to the River Kennet. The oak tree in the square was planted by a building society in 1986 to replace the one they had used as their logo but was now diseased. The removal of the old tree caused a certain amount of controversy however, since according to village legend it was the home of the local witch, Maud Toogood.

In the heart of the village is **The Bell**, a pleasing black and white building with a history stretching back some 300 years. The interior has been recently refurbished, very attractively, retaining traditional features such as the old church pews. The inn's name has been taken as the starting point for a whole range of items connected with bells, anything from a portrait of Alexander Bell to a photograph of a bell foundry. Rosemarie Derrick is mine host at this welcoming inn where food is taken very seriously. The outstanding à la carte menu offers a tempting range of dishes, - Fresh Scottish Lobster, for example, served with char-grilled vegetables and finished with a dressing of tomato and garlic, and to complement your meal there's a wide range of wines from all around the world.

Opening Hours: Mon-Sat: 12.00-15.00, 18.00-23.00; Sun: 12.00-15.00, 19.00-22.30

Food: Excellent à la carte food

Credit Cards: All major credit cards

Facilities: Beer garden, (picnic rugs made available); ample parking

Local Places of Interest/Activities: Riverside walks, 0.5 miles; Savernake Forest, 6 miles; Marlborough, 6 miles

Internet/Website: rosemarie@the-bell-inn.freeserve.co.uk

118 The Bell Inn

Devizes Road,
Broad Hinton,
Swindon,
Wiltshire SN4 9PF
Tel: 01793 731251

Directions:

The inn is on the A4361 Swindon to Devizes road, about 5 miles south of Swindon

Located in the northwestern corner of the Marlborough Downs, Broad Hinton village is a peaceful little place that provides a good base for exploring the great sights of Wiltshire. The prehistoric stone ring at Avebury is only 4 miles away and also within easy reach are the World Heritage site of Stonehenge, Lacock Abbey - one of the main locations for BBC-TV's Pride and Prejudice, and Cherhill White Horse. This distinctive hill carving lies beneath an ancient earthwork called Oldbury Castle but the horse itself is comparatively modern. It was created in 1780 at the instigation of a Dr Alsop of Calne. The 'mad doctor', as he was known, didn't actually help with the carving but remained on the main road and shouted instructions to his labourers through a megaphone.

The Bell Inn is a smart-looking whitewashed building, some 200 years old, that stands on the edge of Broad Hinton village. It's run by Sue Westcott-Clark, an enthusiastic and energetic lady with a love of lively company. She is aided and abetted by her children and this family arrangement creates a very friendly and welcoming atmosphere. Sue is the chef and her menu offers a choice of freshly-prepared food that ranges from sandwiches to hearty steaks. There's real ale on tap along with all the usual popular beverages and the coffee served here is quite outstanding. In good weather, you can relax outside in the peaceful garden which has a secure children's play area. If you are planning to stay in this attractive area, the Bell Inn has 3 comfortable and well-appointed guest rooms, all with quality furnishings, TV and refreshment tray.

Opening Hours: Mon-Fri 11.30-15.00, 18.00-23.00; Sat - Sun, all day

Food: Quality pub grub, from steaks to sandwiches

Credit Cards: All major cards accepted

Accommodation: 3 rooms (1 double, 1 twin, 1 family)

Facilities: Garden; children's play area; ample parking to the rear

Entertainment: Pool; darts (ladies & men's teams); raffles; quiz nights

Local Places of Interest/Activities: Avebury Stone Circle, Avebury Manor & Garden, both 4 miles; White Horse hill carving, Cherhill, 8 miles

The Blue Boar

The Green,
Aldbourne,
Wiltshire
SN8 2EW
Tel: 01672 540237
Fax: 01672 540557

Directions:

From the A346, to the southeast of Swindon, take the B4192 towards Hungerford. Aldbourne village is about 5 miles along this road. The Blue Boar is next to the church, overlooking the village green

Set 700ft up in the Marlborough Downs, Aldbourne has all the ingredients of a quintessential English village. There's a charming village green with a duck pond and weathered stone cross, a 15th century parish church containing a superbly-carved monument to a priest, a 16th century court house, and a square surrounded by ancient cottages and Georgian houses. During the 17th and 18th centuries Aldbourne was renowned for its bell founding, millinery and cloth weaving; today it is a quiet place which regularly wins the award for best-kept village in Wiltshire.

Naturally, such a typical village also has a traditional pub, **The Blue Boar**, although the two suits of Japanese armour guarding the entrance introduce an exotic note. They were brought back from the US by the inn's landlords, Janet and Michael Pattemore, who have worked in the pub and club business on both sides of the Atlantic. Once past the suits of armour, the interior of the Blue Boar is just as you would expect a country pub to be, - low, beamed ceilings, lots of brasses and copper pieces, an open fireplace and some vintage farming implements around the walls. The food here is much superior to the usual 'pub grub'. There are Japanese style Breaded Prawns amongst the starters, for example, a daily selection of home cooked specials, and a wide choice of bar meals and snacks.

Opening Hours: All day, every day

Food: Full à la carte to bar meals and snacks

Credit Cards: All major cards accepted

Facilities: Patio

Local Places of Interest/Activities: The Ridgeway path, 3.5 miles; Savernake Forest, 7 miles; Ashdown House (NT), 8 miles

120   The Bug & Spider

221 Oxford Road,
Calne,
Wiltshire
SN11 8AW
Tel: 01249 813318
Fax: 01249 813300

Directions:

The Bug & Spider is on the A3102 Calne to Lineham road

Lying in the sheltered valley of the River Marden, the former weaving centre of Calne boasts a fine medieval parish church and some attractive old almshouses in Kingsbury Street. About 3 miles to the west is Bowood House, an elegantly proportioned country mansion, partly designed by Robert Adam and set within grounds landscaped by 'Capability' Brown. Inside the house is the laboratory where Joseph Priestley first identified oxygen gas in 1774.

One of **The Bug and Spider's** most attractive features is its non-smoking conservatory restaurant, overlooking the garden and countryside. Here, chef-patron Quenton Harflett offers his customers a full à la carte menu from 19.00-22.00. The food is superb, - all freshly prepared and all home cooked. Amongst the starters you'll find Mushroom Chantel (mushrooms cooked in port, brandy, Stilton & cream) and Gambo Prawns in a garlic, Pernod & cream sauce. Main courses include Pork Normandy, Monkfish Roast and Tuna Bake. Consult the blackboard for details of the day's 'Market Specials'. A wide range of bar snacks and meals is also available, at lunchtime and in the evening, and if you are in a hurry you can ring ahead with your order. There's a choice of real ales and value for money wines to accompany your meal

Opening Hours: Mon-Thu: 12.00-14.30; 16.30-23.00. Fri-Sat: 12.00-23.00. Sun: 12.00-22.30

Food: Bar snacks lunchtime and evening; full à la carte restaurant menu in the evening

Credit Cards: All major cards accepted

Facilities: Beer garden with barbecue site; adventure playground; ample parking to side and rear

Entertainment: Darts, pool, quizzes, Sky TV, frequent live music and karaoke nights

Local Places of Interest/Activities: Bowood House, 3 miles; Lacock Abbey, 8 miles; Salisbury Plain, 15 miles

Internet/Website: qharflett@btclick.com

Crown Hotel 121

131 High Street,
Wootton Bassett,
Wiltshire SN4 7AY
Tel/Fax: 01793 852228

Directions:

From Exit 16 of the M4, take the A3102 to Wootton Bassett (1 mile). The Crown Hotel is in the High Street in the centre of the town.

The busy little town of Wootton Bassett contains a number of fine historic buildings, amongst them the Old Town Hall. It's an unusual structure standing on a series of tall stone piers. The open-sided ground floor area once served as a covered market and still provides shelter for the old stone stocks. On a much grander scale, just to the north of the town, is the imposing Georgian mansion of Lydiard Park, hereditary home of the Bolingbrokes. Set in 260 acres of rolling lawns and woodland, the house contains the family's ancestral portraits, some exceptionally fine plasterwork, and a room devoted to the 18th century society artist Lady Diana Spencer.

Back in the centre of Wootton Bassett, the **Crown Hotel** is an attractive white-washed grade II listed building dating back to the early 1600s, its interior decorated with a wealth of brass and copper items. There's a separate games room and a raised restaurant area at one end of the lounge bar. Here you'll find a good choice of steaks, fish dishes and vegetarian options. Also available is a very extensive selection of bar meals, - jacket potatoes, basket meals, sandwiches and baguettes. In good weather, you can take to the beer garden at the rear of the inn where there's also a children's play area. Devotees of real ales will be happy to find that these are on tap here, along with all the popular beers, lagers and spirits. Jackie and Paul Bowen who run the Crown also have 3 guest rooms to let, all with high quality furnishings and all en suite.

Opening Hours: Daily: 10.30-15.00; 17.30-23.00

Food: Extensive choice of main meals, basket meals and bar snacks

Credit Cards: All major cards accepted

Accommodation: 3 double or twin rooms

Facilities: Beer garden; children's play area; golf and car hire can be arranged; parking to the rear

Entertainment: Pool team; ladies' and men's darts' teams; cribbage; large-screen TV

Local Places of Interest/ Activities: Lydiard Park, 2 miles; "Steam" Museum, Swindon, 6 miles; Avebury Stone Circle, 9 miles

122

The Elm Tree

Stroud's Hill,
Chiseldon,
nr Swindon,
Wiltshire
SN4 0NH
Tel: 01793 740220

Directions:

From the M4, Exit 15, take the A346 towards Marlborough. After about half a mile, take the B4005 to Chiseldon. The Elm Tree is in the centre of the village.

The Elm Tree was a familiar watering-hole to British and US Army soldiers who were stationed at Chiseldon Camp in the days before the Normandy landings of World War II. The inn is rather unusual in having its own Pub Hall, a popular venue where Saturday night dances took place during the war years. It still has its original tin roof. Inside the Elm Tree, there's a wealth of old photographs depicting that period.

Alastair and Carol Kaye are the landlords of this spacious late-Victorian building. They describe their hostelry as a 'Pub with good food', rather than a restaurant. There's an extensive menu that offers a wide range of choice ranging from a hearty 12oz steak through pizzas, basket meals, jacket potatoes and sandwiches. Vegetarian options are always available, so too are children's portions and desserts. Complement your meal with one of the real ales on tap, other ales and lagers, wine, or just a cup of tea or coffee if you prefer. The inn has two bars, as well as a cosy snug, and in good weather customers can also take advantage of the peaceful beer garden and orchard to the rear.

Opening Hours: All day, every day

Food: Good pub food, from steaks to snacks

Credit Cards: All major cards accepted

Facilities: Beer garden at rear; function room; ample roadside parking

Entertainment: Darts; cribbage; dominoes

Local Places of Interest/Activities: The Ridgeway Path long distance walk passes close by; STEAM Great Western Railway Museum, Swindon, 5 miles; Lambourn Downs, 5 miles; Ashdown House (NT), 7 miles

The Foxham Inn 123

Foxham,
Chippenham,
Wiltshire
SN15 4NQ
Tel: 01249 740665
Fax: 01249 740665

Directions:
Just off the B4069
Chippenham   to
Lyneham road

Hidden away in this tiny village at the heart of a farming community, **The Foxham Inn** is a charming old building of warm red brick. The traditional character of the interior is enhanced by the wood-burning stove and the stained glass decorative panels that separate the seating areas at the front of the house. To the rear, there's a 24-cover non-smoking restaurant.

The inn is very much a family-run business, with Alison, Viv, Phil and Helen all involved in the enterprise. A Free House, The Foxham Inn offers a wide range of well-maintained ales, lagers and quality wines, along with a huge choice of fresh, wholesome food. The specials menu changes weekly and offers a selection of vegetarian dishes and other imaginative meals to suit every taste. A sample menu might have a warm smoked duck salad with a cherry dressing and prawns in filo pastry with a satay dip; braised beef in Guinness with pickled walnuts or parsnip and apple lasagne as main dishes. Among the sweets could be home-made crème brulée with shortbread thins or hot Belgium waffle with fresh bananas and butterscotch sauce. There's also a Little People's Menu with dishes "endorsed" by characters such as Obo-Wan Kenobi and the Beanie Babies!

Opening Hours: Closed all day Mondays and Tuesday lunch

Food: Extensive choice of restaurant main meals and bar snacks; children's menu, Party bookings taken

Credit Cards: All cards accepted

Facilities: Children welcome; Ample parking, Disabled access, Outside seating in an unspoilt rural setting

Local Places of Interest/Activities: RAF Lyneham, 5 miles; Castle Combe, 6 miles; Lacock Abbey, 7 miles; Corsham Court, 7 miles; Bowood House, 8 miles; Avebury, 13 miles; Royal City of Bath, 17 miles

124   The Freke Arms

Swanborough,
nr Highworth,
Swindon,
Wiltshire
SN6 7RN
Tel: 01793 762297
Fax: 01793 764460

Directions:

The Freke Arms is situated on the Hannington turning on the B4019, 1½ miles form Highworth and 3 miles from Blunsdon in the heart of the Wiltshire countryside.

The tiny hamlet of Swanborough is well worth seeking out in order to visit **The Freke Arms**. Ian and Liz Stuart have been running this 200-year-old pub since the early 1980s and they have a happy knack of making everyone feel really welcome. The inn takes its name from a 19th century local landowner.

The inn enjoys a lovely position with open countryside views and boasts not only a delightful beer garden, complete with a children's play area, but an apple orchard as well. Inside, the Freke Arms is all you could hope to find in a traditional country pub, - open fires, panelled walls, gleaming brasses, old prints, and every nook and cranny filled with something of interest. Toby jugs, for instance, and a fine collection of Bell's Whiskey Royal bottles. The fare here is quite outstanding. The comprehensive menu offers a wide choice that includes old-fashioned favourites such as home made Cottage Pie, basket meals, ploughman's, jacket potatoes, salads and sandwiches. And, naturally, for a traditional pub like this, there are real ales on tap. The Stuarts are also happy to cater for special events in the separate 20-seater restaurant, 'The Alcove'.

Opening Hours: Mon-Sat; 11.30-14.30, 17.30-23.00; Sun; 12.00-15.00, 19.00-20.30

Food: Extensive menu from à la carte to sandwiches

Credit Cards: All major cards accepted

Facilities: Beer garden; children's play area; ample parking

Local Places of Interest/Activities: Faringdon Great Barn (NT), 5 miles); Buscot Park (NT), 7 miles; Cotswold Water Park, 10 miles

The Horse & Jockey | **125**

15 Gosditch Street,
Ashton Keynes,
Wiltshire
SN6 6NZ
Tel/Fax:
01285 861270

Directions:

From Cirencester, take the A419 towards Swindon. About 5 miles along this road, at Cerney Wick, turn right on the B4696 to Ashton Keynes (4 miles). In the centre of the village, turn left on Gosditch and The Horse & Jockey is on the right.

The first community of any size on the infant River Thames, Ashton Keynes is a sprawling village dignified by some fine old Cotswold-stone residences. The river runs beside the main street and the houses are reached by a series of attractive small footbridges. The northeastern boundary of the village is formed by the Cotswold Water Park, a popular visitor attraction which was created by the extraction of gravel. In 1939, there were just 14 acres of water in the neighbourhood; today, after the removal of some 15 million tons of gravel, there are 150 acres of lakes.

Located in the heart of Ashton Keynes, **The Horse & Jockey** is an outstanding hostelry, the proud winner of the Pub of the Year title in 1998 and also the Millennium Award for Top Venue. The 400-year-old inn is famous for its food which uses only fresh seasonal produce and is always cooked to order. Your hosts, Melanie and Andrew Allen, offer exciting menus with strong Mediterranean influences along with traditional English dishes. So you'll find Pannini (Italian toastie) amongst the light meals as well as ploughman's and jacket potatoes, while the extensive main menu includes a Ratatouille Bake along with steaks and old favourites such as Steak & Ale Pie. Enjoy your meal in the spacious and sunny dining room or in the lounge bar, both of which overlook the garden. An additional attraction at this inviting old inn is the Skittle Alley in the converted stables.

Opening Hours: All day, every day

Food: Main meals & bar meals every lunchtime & evening; kids' menu

Credit Cards: All major cards accepted

Facilities: Ample off road parking

Entertainment: Skittle Alley

Local Places of Interest/Activities: Thames Path nearby; Cotswold Water Park, 1.5 miles; Lydiard Park, 10 miles

126 The Lord Nelson Inn

Marshfield,
nr Chippenham,
Wiltshire SN14 8LP
Tel: 01225 891820
Fax: 01225 891981

Directions:

From Exit 18 on the M4 take the A46 towards Bath. After 4 miles, turn left on the A420 towards Chippenham. Marshfield is about 3 miles along this road

Located in the centre of this small town, **The Lord Nelson Inn** is a striking Georgian building dating back to 1720 when it served the stage coaches plying between Bath and London. An interesting feature on the outside is the shell-shaped stone carving above the main entrance. Inside, there are low ceilings and old beams, a bar of Cotswold stone, and an ancient water well set into the top of the bar which is topped by an old ship's portal frame. In the bar, vintage barrels provide the tables and the separate restaurant is housed in the former stable.

David and Jennifer Short are your hosts here, with Jennifer in charge of the kitchen. Her menus offer a wide choice with lunches and lighter bites served between noon and 2.00pm and more substantial meals available in the restaurant. Something of a speciality amongst the bar snacks are the home made faggots, served with a rich onion gravy, while the restaurant menu offers such treats as Grilled Trout Cleopatra or Vegetable Pancakes containing a delicious white wine and cheese source. There are also special dishes for children. To complement your meal, the Lord Nelson serves a choice of real ales, wines, beers and spirits with tea and coffee also available all day.

Opening Hours: Mon-Fri: 12.00-14.30; 18.00-23.00. Sat-Sun: 12.00-15.00; 18.00-23.00

Food: Everything from sandwiches to à la carte restaurant menu

Credit Cards: All major cards except Amex

Accommodation: 2 rooms

Facilities: Garden to the rear; function room

Entertainment: Darts; shove ha'penny

Local Places of Interest/Activities: Dyrham Park (NT), 5 miles; City of Bath, 8 miles; Cotswolds to the north

The Mallard   127

2 Calne Road,
Lyneham,
Wiltshire
SN15 4PL
Tel: 01249 890522
Fax: 01249 890522

Directions:
From Exit 16 of the M4 take the A3102 through Wootton Bassett to Lyneham

Lyneham is perhaps best known for its RAF base but it's also worth visiting to enjoy the hospitality on offer at **The Mallard**, located in the centre of this expanding small town. The inn has a spacious modern extension, a patio for enjoying summer days' drinks, and a children's play area. Inside, there are two main bars, (a Lounge Bar and a newly refurbished Sports Bar), and the traditional part of the inn has lots of exposed timbers, brasses and copper items, small-paned windows and old style window seating. Another interesting feature is the collection of coins from around the world displayed over the bar.

Michael and Terry Clarke only took over here fairly recently although they have many years experience in the trade. They've already established a reputation for serving good, wholesome pub food, - fresh baguettes with a wide variety of fillings, ploughmans, beefburgers (including a Vegetarian Spicy Bean Burger), and other bar meals such as Chicken Goujons, salad and chips. There's a choice of real ales on tap along with a wide selections of beers, lagers, ciders, wines and spirits.

Opening Hours: Mon-Sat: 12.00-23.00; Sun: 12.00-22.30

Food: Bar meals available lunchtimes

Credit Cards: Not accepted

Facilities: Patio; children's play area; ample parking

Entertainment: Pool; darts; cribbage; dominoes; Sky TV; Quiz Nights (Tues); live music once a month; annual golf tournament

Local Places of Interest/Activities: Bowood House, 7 miles; Avebury Stone Circle, 9 miles

128   The Neeld Arms

Grittleton,
nr Chippenham,
Wiltshire SN14 6AP
Tel: 01249 782470
Fax: 01249 782358

Directions:

From the M4, Exit 17, take the Cirencester exit, (A429). Take the first turning on the left, signposted Stanton St Quintin and Grittleton. Go through Stanton St Quintin to a T junction. Turn left, signposted Grittleton. The Neeld Arms is on the right about 400 yards into the village.

Located in the heart of this unspoilt village and set in an Area of Outstanding Natural Beauty, **The Neeld Arms** is a charming 17th century country inn built in Cotswold stone and offering fine food, wines and comfortable, characterful accommodation. Although only minutes from the M4, Grittleton is a peaceful little place, tucked away in lovely countryside where the Cotswolds meet the Wiltshire Downs. The inn takes its name from Joseph Neeld, an 18th century entrepreneur who made his fortune during the French revolution from emigrés forced to sell their jewels cheaply. He made many improvements to the area around Grittleton, developing rides, avenues, woods and parklands, a legacy which endures to this day.

The Neeld Arms serves traditional and wholesome food, accompanied by fine wines and real ales, and the relaxed and friendly bar and dining areas retain their historic features. There are 6 guest bedrooms, all en suite and of a good size. They are individually furnished, with colour televisions, radio alarms and tea and coffee making facilities. The proprietors, Bill and Sara Clemence, make every effort to ensure that their guests enjoy a relaxing and comfortable stay. The picture postcard village of Castle Combe is just minutes away and also within easy reach are Lacock Abbey, which provided the romantic setting for the BBC's films of Jane Austen's *Pride and Prejudice* and *Emma*, the inspirational Arboretum at Westonbirt, and the historic City of Bath.

Opening Hours: Mon-Fri 17.30-23.00; Sat 11.00-15.00, 17.30-23.00; Sun 12.00-15.00, 18.00-22.30

Food: Traditional

Credit Cards: All major cards accepted

Accommodation: 6 rooms (1 four-poster, 2 doubles, 1 family, 2 twins), all en suite

Local Places of Interest/Activities: Castle Combe village, 4 miles; Westonbirt Arboretum, 8 miles; City of Bath, 11 miles; Lacock Abbey (NT), 11 miles.

Internet/Website: neeldarms@genie.co.uk

The Patriot's Arms | 129

6 New Road,
Chiseldon,
nr Swindon,
Wiltshire SN4 0LU
Tel: 01793 740331

Directions:

From the M4, Exit 15, take the A346 towards Marlborough. After about half a mile, turn right at the Esso garage onto the B4005 and the inn is at the end of the road on your left.

Dating back to 1846, **The Patriot's Arms** stands on the site of a "New Inn". It was renamed during World War I because of its association with the Armed Services at Chiseldon Camp and later at RAF Wroughton. This connection is emphasised further by the military insignia dotted around the walls. This is a lively pub where there always seems to be something going on. In addition to the pool table, darts and cribbage, there are frequent Quiz Nights, Murder Mystery Nights, and a bi-annual golf competition. More surprisingly, The Patriot's Arms also hosts regular French conversation classes. For fairweather days, there's a pleasant Beer Garden with a children's play area. And if you are planning to stay in the area, the inn has 3 guest rooms, (2 twins, 1 single), all attractively furnished and provided with TV and refreshment trays.

Before he took over here, Michael Brightman was a patron himself. Now he presides over a thriving business based on providing quality food and drink in a welcoming atmosphere. Virtually all the food served here is home made, - Tomato & Tarragon Soup, for example, amongst the starters; Beef, Ale & Mushroom Pie and Courgette, Mushroom & Tomato Pasta Bake as main courses; and some delicious desserts. There's a choice of 3 real ales and half a dozen wines available by the bottle or glass.

Opening Hours: Mon-Fri: 12.00-14.15; 17.30-23.00. Sat-Sun: Open all day

Food: Quality home made food and daily specials

Credit Cards: All major cards, including Switch and cash back

Accommodation: 3 rooms, (2 twins, 1 single)

Facilities: Garden; Children's play area; Function room; 37 dedicated parking spaces including some for disabled only

Entertainment: Quiz Nights; Murder Mystery Nights; pool; darts; cribbage; bi-annual Golf Competition

Local Places of Interest/Activities: The Ridgeway Path long distance walk passes close by; Barbury Castle; Avebury; STEAM Great Western Railway Museum, Swindon, 5 miles; Lambourn Downs, 5 miles; Ashdown House (NT), 7 miles

Internet/Website: www.patriotsarms.co.uk
e-mail: michael@patriotsarms.co.uk

130   The Plough Inn

Crudwell,
Malmesbury,
Wiltshire
SN16 9EW
Tel: 01666 577833

Directions:

On the A429 about 7 miles southwest of Cirencester on the right hand side

Conveniently located on the A429 Cirencester to Chippenham road, **The Plough Inn** is an inviting-looking whitewashed building with a history that goes back to the 1500s. The interior is full of nooks and crannies, with old beams supporting the low ceilings and gleaming brass and copper decorations everywhere. The separate restaurant, with seating for 24, stands on a raised platform, rather like a stage. Outside, there's a large garden with plenty of picnic tables for fine weather days. The inn has 3 guest rooms, (1 family, 1 double, 1 twin), all with TV, refreshment trays and furnished in cottage style to a very high standard.

Mine hosts, Terry and Pauline Hampson, came here from Devon in 1997. Both are very experienced in the hospitality business and they have created a very popular pub here. They offer an extensive à la carte menu that ranges from a mighty "Mixed Grill Challenge", (lamb chop, pork chop, steak, sausage, burger, bacon, mushrooms, tomato, egg), to lighter offerings such as Breaded Plaice stuffed with prawns, Chardonnay and mushroom filling, or freshly prepared sandwiches. Real ales and quality wines add to the pleasure of eating here.

Opening Hours: Mon-Fri: 11.00-15.00; 18.00-23.00. Sat-Sun: Open all day

Food: Restaurant à la carte and bar snacks

Credit Cards: All major cards accepted

Accommodation: 3 rooms (1 family, 1 double, 1 twin)

Facilities: Large garden; ample parking

Entertainment: Separate pool room; darts; Quiz Nights

Local Places of Interest/Activities: Westonbirt Arboretum, 8 miles; Cotswold Water Park, 8 miles; Badminton, 15 miles

The Shepherd's Rest **131**

Foxhill, nr Swindon,
Wiltshire SN4 0DR
Tel: 01793 790266
Fax: 01793 790353

Directions:

From junction 15 of the M4 turn right towards Swindon. At the first roundabout take the Liddington turn and continue for 1.8 miles. Turn left for about 1 mile and the Shepherds rest can be found at the junction of the Ridgeway and the Roman Ermine Street.

A traditional inn dating back more than 200 years, **The Shepherd's Rest** offers superb food and a huge range of different beverages. The inn has a welcoming olde-worlde atmosphere with low ceilings and ancient beams, lots of gleaming brasses and copper items, and prints of local scenes. Despite its age, the inn is disabled-friendly, with good wheelchair access and disabled toilets. Darts and pool are available and there's an attractive Beer Garden for fine days and a children's play area.

Henry and Shirley Kayne provide their customers with an outstanding choice of food. An à la carte menu is available in the stylish conservatory restaurant and offers a very extensive range of dishes which includes a wide selection of steaks, poultry & game, fish and vegetarian options. All the desserts are home made and the Kaynes are happy, where practical, to split an adult meal between two children or to make a smaller portion. The Bar Menu is equally extensive, - filled baguettes, omelettes, ploughmans, pasta and pizza, and much more. The choice of drinks at The Shepherd's Rest is exceptionally generous: 6 hand-pumped real ales, 42 different wines, (9 of them also available by the glass), and no fewer than 24 malt whiskeys.

Opening Hours: Mon-Sat: 11.00-15.00; 18.00-23.00. Sun: 12.00-15.00-19.00-22.30

Food: Full à la carte restaurant menu, and bar snacks

Credit Cards: All major cards except Diners

Facilities: Beer Garden; children's play area; ample parking

Entertainment: Pool, darts, theme evenings

Local Places of Interest/Activities: The Ridgeway Path long distance walk passes the door; Coate Water Country Park, 3 miles; STEAM Museum of the Great Western Railway, Swindon, 4 miles; Uffington White Horse, 6 miles; Cotswolds within easy reach

Internet/Website: henry@shepherdsrest.co.uk

132 The Star Inn

48 The Street,
Hullavington,
Chippenham,
Wiltshire
SN14 6DU
Tel: 01666 837561
Fax: 01666 837756

Directions:

From the M4, Exit 17, take the A429 towards Malmesbury. After about 1.5 miles turn left to Hullavington

During the era of the stage coach an old inn stood on this site but the present **Star Inn** is a handsome 1930s stone and brick building with double fronted windows made attractive by colourful window boxes in summer. Inside there's a spacious open plan bar and a function room which doubles as a skittle alley. Darts and pool are available and the Star is also the natural centre for Hullavington village's football team. The inn also hosts quiz nights, live music once a month, and occasional theme evenings. The Star has two guest rooms, (a double and a twin), both large and comfortable and equipped with TV and tea/coffee-making facilities.

Your hosts are Brian and Doreen Trevett who took over here in 1998 from Brian's parents who had run the Star for 18 years. They offer a superb range of wholesome pub food, - everything from sandwiches to steaks and including a hearty All Day Breakfast. There are real ales on tap and a wide selection of wines and spirits, with tea and coffee also available throughout the day.

Opening Hours: Mon-Thu: 11.00-14.00; 17.00-23.00. Fri-Sun: 11.00-23.00

Food: Superb pub food, from sandwiches to steaks

Credit Cards: All major cards accepted

Accommodation: 2 rooms, (1 twin, 1 double)

Facilities: Large garden; children's play area; DIY barbecue available; parking

Entertainment: Skittle alley; pool; darts; Quiz nights; live music monthly; theme nights

Local Places of Interest/Activities: Castle Combe, 6 miles; Badminton, 10 miles. Walking, fishing

The Wellington Arms 133

*46 High Street,
Marlborough,
Wiltshire SN8 1HQ
Tel: 01672 512954*

Directions:

From the M4, Exit 15, take the A346 to Marlborough. The Wellington Arms is in the centre of the town.

The historic market town of Marlborough lies in the valley of the River Kennet on the southern edge of the Marlborough Downs. An important former coaching centre, it stands at the intersection of 5 long-established trunk routes. William the Conqueror built a castle at Marlborough shortly after the Norman invasion and a number of early English monarchs are known to have come here to hunt in the nearby Savernake Forest. The town takes its name from 'Maerl's Barrow', an ancient burial chamber now within the grounds of the famous Marlborough College public school. Amongst the school's most distinguished alumni are Sir John Betjeman, William Morris and the spy Anthony Blunt.

Located in the heart of the town, **The Wellington Arms** is a traditional country town pub with oodles of atmosphere, - low ceilings, latticed windows, panelled walls and an open fire. The pub is run by Andrew and Maggie Jones with Maggie in charge of the kitchen. The choice of home made, freshly-prepared food is extensive, - from sandwiches to steaks with fish, poultry and vegetarian dishes, pastas and curries also available. Food is served in the restaurant at the rear, overlooking the garden which contains Maggie's herb garden. There's also a patio at the rear, a veritable sun trap and a peaceful place to enjoy a drink.

Opening Hours: All day, every day

Food: Home cooked, - from sandwiches to steaks

Credit Cards: Not accepted

Facilities: Patio at the rear

Local Places of Interest/Activities:
Savernake Forest, 1 mile; Kennet & Avon Canal and the Vale of Pewsey, 4 miles; Avebury Stone Circle, 6 miles

134 The Wheatsheaf at Oaksey

Oaksey,
nr Malmesbury,
Wiltshire SN16 9TB
Tel: 01666 577348/575067
Fax: 01666 575067

Directions:

From the A429 about 7 miles south of Cirencester turn left on a minor road to Oaksey (4 miles).

The Wheatsheaf at Oaksey stands at the heart of this attractive village which contains some fine 17th century cottages and a small 13th century church which is renowned for its rare medieval murals. The south wall, for example, features an unusual painting entitled *Christ of Trades* which shows Jesus surrounded by an array of hand tools. The church is also notable for its 'sheela-na-gig', a pre-Christian quasi-erotic stone carving embedded in the wall to the left of the porch. Most of these ancient images of women displaying their genitalia are to be found in Celtic countries, Ireland particularly, but they are few and far between in England.

The Wheatsheaf is also rather unique. With its cob walls, (a mixture of clay, gravel and straw), it's believed to date back some 600 years and has some astonishing features, like the stone cover of a Roman soldier's coffin which now provides a lintel over the open fire. Mine hosts at The Wheatsheaf, Mike and Sheila Scott, have also furnished their inn with a fascinating array of olde-worlde collectables, - items such as the leather shoes once worn by horses when mowing or rolling lawns and cricket pitches as well as providing an excellent selection of beers, wines and spirits. There are always three real ales on tap.

Sheila is the chef here and she offers comprehensive menus for both the stylish restaurant and the bar: anything from a Bacon & Mushroom sandwich to an 8oz sirloin steak is available. You may well want to linger a while longer in this appealing inn, - if so, there's a charming self-catering, 1 bedroom cottage attached to the pub which is available to rent all year round.

Opening Hours: Mon-Fri, 12.00-14.30, 18.00-23.00; Sat 12.00-15.00, 18.00-23.00; Sun 12.00-16.30, 19.00-22.30

Food: Full restaurant menu and bar meals and snacks

Credit Cards: All major cards accepted

Accommodation: Self-catering 1 bedroom cottage attached to the inn

Facilities: Beer terrace; ample parking at the rear

Entertainment: Quoits; darts; cribbage; shove ha'penny; shut the box; skittles

Local Places of Interest/Activities: Cotswold Water Park, 6 miles; walking in the Cotswolds, fishing, golf, cycling

The White Horse Inn   135

*Winterbourne
Bassett,
nr Swindon,
Wiltshire
SN4 9QB
Tel: 01793 731257*

Directions:

Winterbourne Bassett is just off the A4361 Swindon to Devizes road, about 6 miles south of Swindon.

For truly outstanding food the place to seek out is **The White Horse**. This is a family-run hostelry run by Christopher Stone, a professional chef, his wife Kathy, their daughter and son, and a very welcoming place it is. As the name suggests, it's located in the heart of 'White Horse Country'. The closest of these hill carvings is on Hackpen Hill, a couple of miles to the east. It's 27 metres long and was created in 1838 to commemorate the coronation of Queen Victoria. Also well worth visiting is Barbury Castle, an Iron Age stronghold which commands spectacular views over the downland landscape.

Winterbourne Bassett's own White Horse has been described as a 'diner's delight'. The à la carte menu is served in the delightful conservatory and amongst the starters are home made soup or pâté, Potato St Lucia (sautéed potatoes finished in a sauce of shallots, coconut milk, coriander, curry spices and cream), and prawn fritters. The main courses have something for everyone, - vegetarian choices, fish dishes, steaks of succulent grass fed Scottish beef, and a selection of international dishes that includes Tropical Jerk Chicken and Lamb Andalucia. Desserts range from a traditional 'Spotted Richard' to an aptly named 'Chocolate Corruption'. Definitely a dining experience not to be missed.

Opening Hours: Every day 11.00-15.00, 19.00-23.00

Food: À la carte restaurant and bar meals

Credit Cards: All major cards accepted

Facilities: Garden; conservatory restaurant; ample parking

Local Places of Interest/Activities:

Ridgeway Path, 2 miles; Avebury Stone Circle, 4 miles, Barbury Castle Country Park, 7 miles

Internet/Website:
www.whitehorsewinterbournebassett.co.uk
e-mail: ckstone@btinternet.com

The Hidden Inns of the South of England

This page is intentionally left blank

5 South Wiltshire

PLACES OF INTEREST:

PUBS AND INNS:

The Hidden Inns of the South of England

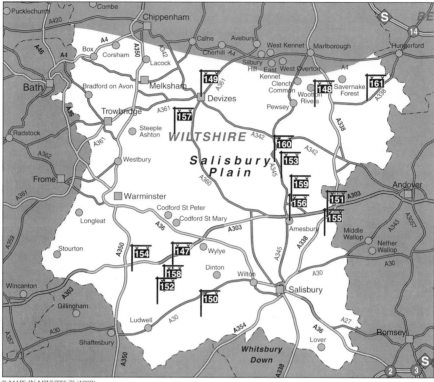

© MAPS IN MINUTES ™ (1999)

Please note all cross references refer to page numbers

South Wiltshire

Salisbury and south Wiltshire are a part of traditional England with 6,000 years of history, and a delight for visitors from all over the world. Salisbury, with its glorious Cathedral, is one of the most beautiful cities in the kingdom, and elsewhere in the region are the chalk downs and river valleys, the stately homes and picturesque villages, the churches, the ancient hill forts and, above all, Stonehenge, one of the great mysteries of the prehistoric world.

The region's more recent, industrial heritage is also evident in many forms, from brewing at Devizes to Wilton's carpet factory.

PLACES OF INTEREST

AMESBURY

Queen Elfrida founded an abbey here in 979 in atonement for her part in the murder of her son-in-law, Edward the Martyr, at Corfe Castle. Henry II rebuilt the abbey's great Church of St Mary and St Melor, whose tall central tower is the only structure to survive from the pre-Norman monastery. A mile to the north of Amesbury, the A345 passes along the eastern side of **Woodhenge**, a ceremonial monument even older than Stonehenge. It was the first major prehistoric site to be discovered by aerial photography, its six concentric rings of post holes having been spotted as cropmarks by Squadron Leader Insall in 1925. Like Stonehenge, the A345 passes along the eastern side of the A345 passes along the eastern side of the A345 passes along the eastern nomical calendar. When major excavation was carried out in the 1920s, a number of neolithic tools and other artefacts were found, along with

Stonehenge

the skeleton of a three-year-old child whose fractured skull suggested some kind of ritual sacrifice.

Two miles west of Amesbury at the junction of the A303 and A344/A360 stands **Stonehenge** itself, perhaps the greatest mystery of the prehistoric world, one of the wonders of the world, and a monument of unique importance. The World Heritage Site is surrounded by the remains of ceremonial and domestic structures, many of them accessible by road or public footpath. The great stone blocks of the main ring are truly massive, and it seems certain that the stones in the outer rings - rare bluestones from the Preseli Hills of west Wales - had to be transported over 200 miles. Stonehenge's orientation on the rising and setting sun has always been one of its most remarkable features, leading to theories that the builders were from a sun-worshipping culture or that the whole structure is part of a huge astronomical calendar ... or both. The mystery remains, and will probably remain for ever.

BRADFORD-ON-AVON

An historic market town at a bridging point on the Avon, which it spans with a superb nine-arched bridge with a lock-up at one end. The town's oldest building is the **Church of St Lawrence**, believed to have been founded by St Aldhelm around 700. It 'disappeared' for over

140

1,000 years, when it was used variously as a school, a charnel house for storing the bones of the dead, and a residential dwelling. It was re-discovered by a keen-eyed clergyman who looked down from a hill

Kennet & Avon Canal, Bradford-on-Avon

Iford Manor Gardens

and noticed the cruciform shape of a church. The surrounding buildings were gradually removed to reveal the little masterpiece we see today. Bradford's Norman church, restored in the 19th century, has an interesting memorial to Lieutenant-General Henry Shrapnel, the army officer who, in 1785, invented the shrapnel shell. Another of the town's outstanding buildings is the mighty **Tithe Barn**, once used to store the grain from local farms for Shaftesbury Abbey, now housing a collection of antique farm implements and agricultural machinery. The centrepiece of the museum in Bridge Street is a pharmacy which has stood in the town for 120 years before being removed lock, stock and medicine bottles to its new site.

Off the A363 on the northern edge of town, **Barton Farm Country Park** offers delightful walks in lovely countryside by the River Avon and the Kennet & Avon Canal. It was once a medieval farm serving Shaftesbury Abbey. Barton Bridge is the original packhorse bridge built to assist the transportation of grain from the farm to the tithe barn.

Half a mile south of town by the River Frome is the Italian-style **Peto Garden** at **Iford Manor**. Famous for its romantic, tranquil beauty, its steps and terraces, statues, colonnades and ponds, the garden was laid out by the architect and landscape gardener Harold Ainsworth Peto between 1899 and 1933. He was inspired by the works of Lutyens and Jekyll to turn a difficult hillside site into "a haunt of ancient peace".

East of Bradford, off the A366, the charming 15th century Westwood Manor has many in-teresting features, including Jacobean and Gothic windows and ornate plasterwork.

CLENCH COMMON

A lovely part of the world for walking or cycling. The Forestry Commission's West Woods, particularly notable for its bluebells in May has a picnic site. The Wansdyke Path, a long earthwork of a single bank and ditch, forms part of the wood's boundary. Also nearby is Martinsell Hill, topped by an ancient fort. Downland to the east of the fort is particularly beautiful in early spring and summer.

CODFORD ST PETER & CODFORD ST MARY

Sister villages beneath the prehistoric remains of **Codford Circle**, an ancient hilltop meeting place which stands 617' up on Salisbury Plain. The church in Codford St Peter has one of Wiltshire's finest treasures in an exceptional 9th century Saxon stone carving of a man holding a branch and dancing. East of Malmpit Hill and visible from the A36 is a rising sun emblem carved by Australian soldiers during World War l. In the military cemetery at Codford St Mary are the graves of Anzac troops who were in camp here. Anzac graves may also be seen at nearby Baverstock.

CORSHAM

"Corsham has no match in Wiltshire for the wealth of good houses", asserted Pevsner. Many of the town's fine buildings are linked to the prosperity that came from the two main industries of cloth-weaving and stone-quarrying. Corsham Court, based on an Elizabethan house dating from 1582, was bought by Paul Methuen in 1745 to house a fabulous collection of paintings and statuary. The present house and grounds are principally the work of Capability Brown, John Nash, Thomas Bellamy and Humphrey Repton a top-pedigree setting for the treasures inside, which include paintings by Caravaggio, Fra Filippo Lippi, Reynolds, Rubens and Van Dyke and furniture by Chippendale. Among other important buildings in Corsham are the row of 17th century Flemish weavers' cottages, the old market house and the superb almshouses built in 1668 by Dame Margaret Hungerford. A unique attraction is the Underground Quarry Centre, the only shaft stone mine open to the public in the world, opened in 1810 and reached by 159 steps. Helmets, lamps and an experienced guide are provided for this fascinating underground tour.

In 1998 Gill Habgood, Mark and Beau moved from Oxford, fell in love with Corsham and bought **Cheviot House**, a handsome Georgian building in a quiet part of the main street. Gill had offered B&B accommodation in Oxford and continues to do so here, in two en suite bedrooms - a double/family room and a twin decorated and furnished in keeping with the character of the house but also provided with modern amenities such as remote-control TVs. The original rubble wall of the house, once a schoolhouse, is still visible, but the rest of the old core was made 'grand' with ashlar frontage, moulded cornices and parapets when the local stone industry expanded. Cheviot House was named after a type of tweed by a master tailor who owned the property before the First World War. Behind the house, which is Grade ll listed, are lovely gardens, where Pierre the peacock struts his stuff, and an old malthouse, now residential, which was opened by that same tailor, Alf Butt, and later saw service as a place of recreation for war casualties, a glove factory, a cardboard box factory and a laundry.

DEVIZES

At the western edge of the Vale of Pewsey, Devizes is the central market town of Wiltshire. The town was founded in 1080 by Bishop Osmund, nephew of William the Conqueror. The bishop was responsible for building a timber castle between the lands of two powerful manors, and this act brought about the town's name, which is derived from the Latin ad divisas, or 'at the boundaries'. After the wooden structure burnt down, Roger, Bishop of Sarum, built a stone castle in 1138 that survived until the end of the Civil War, when it was demolished. Bishop Roger also built two fine churches in Devizes. Long Street is lined with elegant Georgian houses and also contains the Wiltshire Archaeological and Natural History Society's **Devizes Museum**, which has a splendid collection of artefacts from the area, and a gallery with a John Piper window and regularly changing exhibitions.

The newly opened **Devizes Visitor Centre** offers a unique insight into the town. The Centre is based on a 12th century castle and takes visitors back to medieval times, when Devizes was home to the finest castle in Europe and the scene of anarchy and unrest during the struggles between Empress Matilda and King Stephen. An interactive exhibition shows how the town came to be at the centre of the 12th century Civil War and thrived as a medieval town, many traces of which remain today, and on into the present.

Many more of the town's finest buildings are situated in and around the old market place, including the Town Hall and the Corn Ex-

Market Cross, Devizes

142

change. Also here is an unusual **market cross** inscribed with the story of Ruth Pierce, a market stall-holder who stood accused, in 1753, of swindling her customers. When an ugly crowd gathered round her, she stood and pleaded her innocence, adding "May I be struck dead if I am lying". A rash move, as she fell to the ground and died forthwith.

Devizes stands at a key point on the Kennet & Avon Canal, and the **Kennet & Avon Canal Museum** tells the complete story of the canal in fascinating detail. Many visitors combine a trip to the museum with a walk along the towpath, which is a public footpath. Each July the Canalfest, a weekend of family fun designed to raise funds for the upkeep of the canal, is held at the Wharf, which is also the start point, on Good Friday, of the annual Devizes-Westminster canoe race.

DINTON

Two National Trust properties to visit near this lovely hillside village. **Little Clarendon** is a small but perfectly formed Tudor manor house; **Philipps House** is a handsome white-fronted neo-Grecian house with a great Ionic portico. The work of the early 19th century architect Jeffrey Wyattville, it stands in the beautiful grounds of Dinton Park.

LACOCK

The National Trust village of Lacock is one of the country's real treasures. The quadrangle of streets - East, High, West and Church - holds a delightful assortment of mellow stone buildings, and the period look (no intrusive power

Lacock Abbey

cables or other modern-day eyesores) keeps it in great demand as a film location. Every building is a well-restored, well-preserved gem, and overlooking everything is **Lacock Abbey**, founded in 1232 by Ela, Countess of Salisbury in memory of her husband William Longsword, stepbrother to Richard the Lionheart. In common with all monastic houses Lacock was dissolved by Henry Vlll, but the original cloisters, chapter houses, sacristy and kitchens survive.

Much of the remainder of what we see today dates from the mid 16th century, when the abbey was acquired by Sir William Sharington. He added an impressive country house and the elegant octagonal tower that overlooks the

Lacock Village Street

Avon. The estate next passed into the hands of the Talbot family, who held it for 370 years before ceding it to the National Trust in 1944.

The most distinguished member of the Talbot family was the pioneering photographer William Henry Fox Talbot, who carried out his experiments in the 1830s. The **Fox Talbot Museum** commemorates the life and achievements of a man who was not just a photographer but a mathematician, physicist, classicist, philologist and transcriber of Syrian and Chaldean cuneiform. He also remodelled the south elevation of the abbey and added three new oriel windows. One of the world's earliest photographs shows a detail of a latticed oriel window of the abbey; made in 1835 and the size of a postage stamp, it is the earliest known example of a photographic negative.

LONGLEAT

1999 saw the 50th anniversary of the opening of **Longleat House** to the public. The magnificent home of the Marquess of Bath was built by an ancestor, Sir John Thynne, in a largely symmetrical style, in the 1570s. The inside is a treasure house of old masters, Flemish tapestries, beautiful furniture, rare books.....and Lord Bath's murals. The superb grounds of Longleat House were landscaped by Capability Brown and now contain one of the country's best known venues for a marvellous day out. In the famous **safari park** the Lions of Longleat, first introduced in 1966, have been followed by a veritable Noah's Ark of exotic creatures, including elephants, rhinos, zebras and white tigers. The park also features safari boat rides, a narrow-gauge railway, children's amusement area, garden centre and the largest hedge maze in the world.

LOVER

In the vicinity of this charmingly-named village is the National Trust's **Pepperbox Hill** topped by an early 17th century octagonal tower known as **Eyre's Folly**. Great walking, great views.

LUDWELL

Near the village is the National Trust-owned **Win Green Hill**, the highest point in Wiltshire, crowned by a copse of beech trees set around an ancient bowl barrow. From the summit there are wonderful views as far as the Quantock Hills to the northwest and the Isle of Wight to the southeast.

PEWSEY

In the heart of the beautiful valley that bears its name, this is a charming village of half-timbered houses and thatched cottages. It was once the personal property of Alfred the Great, and a statue of the king stands at the crossroads in the centre. The parish church, built on a foundation of sarsen stones, has an unusual altar rail made from timbers taken from the San Josef, a ship captured by Nelson in 1797.

Attractions for the visitor include the old wharf area and the **Heritage Centre**. In an 1870 foundry building it contains an interesting collection of old and unusual machine tools and farm machinery. The original **Pewsey White Horse**, south of the village on Pewsey Down, was cut in 1785, apparently including a rider, but was redesigned by a Mr George Marples and cut by the Pewsey Fire Brigade to celebrate the coronation of King George VI. **Pewsey Carni-**

val takes place each September, and the annual Devizes to Westminster canoe race passes through **Pewsey Wharf**.

A minor road runs past the White Horse across Pewsey Down to the isolated village of **Everleigh**, where the Church of St Peter is of unusual iron-framed construction. Rebuilt on a new site in 1813, it has a short chancel and narrow nave, an elegant west gallery and a neo-medieval hammerbeam roof.

SALISBURY

The glorious medieval city of Salisbury stands at the confluence of four rivers, the Avon, Wylye, Bourne and Nadder. Originally called New Sarum, it grew around the present Cathedral, which was built between 1220 and 1258 in a sheltered position two miles south of the site of its windswept Norman predecessor at Old Sarum. Over the years the townspeople followed the clergy into the new settlement, creating a flourishing religious and market centre whose two main aspects flourish to this day.

One of the most beautiful buildings in the world, **Salisbury Cathedral** is the only medieval cathedral in England to be built in the same Early English style - apart from the spire, the tallest in England which was added some years later and rises to an awesome 404 feet. The Chapter House opens out of the cloisters and contains, among other treasures, one of the four surviving originals of Magna Carta. Six hundred thousand visitors a year come to marvel at this and other priceless treasures, including a number of magnificent tombs. The oldest working clock in Britain and possibly in the world is situated in the fan-vaulted north transept; it was built in 1386 to strike the hour and has no clock face. The Cathedral is said to contain a door for each month, a window for each day and a column

Salisbury Cathedral Spire

144

for each hour of the year. A small statue inside the west door is of Salisbury's 17th century **Boy Bishop**. It was a custom for choristers to elect one of their number to be bishop for a period lasting from St Nicholas Day to Holy Innocents Day (6-28 December). One year the boy bishop was apparently literally tickled to death by the other choristers; since he died in office, his statue shows him in full bishop's regalia.

The Close, the precinct of the ecclesiastical community serving the cathedral, is the largest in England and contains a number of museums and houses open to the public. **Salisbury Museum**, in the 17th century King's House, is home of the Stonehenge Gallery and the winner of many awards for excellence. Displays include Early Man, Romans and Saxons, the Pitt Rivers collection (see under Tollard Royal), Old Sarum, ceramics, costume, lace, embroidery and Turner watercolours. A few doors away is **The Royal Gloucestershire, Berkshire and Wiltshire Museum** housed in a 13th century building called the Wardrobe, which was originally used to store the bishop's clothes and documents. The museum tells the story of the county regiments since 1743 and the exhibits include Bobbie the Dog, the hero of Maiwand, and many artefacts from foreign campaigns. The house has a riverside garden with views of the famous water meadows. The historic **Medieval Hall** is the atmospheric setting for a 30-minute history of Salisbury in sound and pictures. **Mompesson House**, a National Trust property, is a perfect example of Queen Anne architecture notable for its plasterwork, an elegant carved oak staircase, fine period furniture and the important Turnbull collection of 18th century drinking glasses. In the Market Place is the **John Creasey Museum** and the **Creasey Col-**

lection of **Contemporary Art**, a permanent collection of books, manuscripts, objects and art. Also in the Market Place, in the library, is the Edwin Young Collection of 19th and early 20th century oil paintings of Salisbury and its surrounding landscape. There are many other areas of Salisbury to explore on foot and a short drive takes visitors to the ruins of **Old Sarum**, abandoned when the bishopric moved into the city. Traces of the original cathedral and palace are visible on the huge uninhabited mound, which dates back to the Iron Age. Old Sarum became the most notorious of the 'rotten boroughs', returning two Members of Parliament, despite having no voters, until the 1832 Reform Act stopped the cheating. A plaque on the site commemorates Old Sarum's most illustrious MP William Pitt the Elder.

SAVERNAKE FOREST

The ancient woodland of **Savernake Forest** is a magnificent expanse of unbroken woodland, open glades and bridle paths. King Henry Vlll hunted wild deer here and married Jane Seymour, whose family home was nearby. Designated an SSSI (Site of Special Scientific Interest), the forest is home to abundant wildlife, including a small herd of deer and 25 species of butterfly.

STEEPLE ASHTON

The long main street of this village is lined with delightful old buildings, many featuring half-

Steeple Ashton

timbering and herringbone brickwork. The Church of St Mary the Virgin, without a steeple since it was struck by lightning in 1670, houses the Samuel Hey Library whose highlight is the early 15th century Book of Hours.

STOURTON

The beautiful National Trust village of Stourton lies at the bottom of a steep wooded valley and is a particularly glorious sight in the daffodil

Mompesson House

season. The main attraction is, of course, **Stourhead**, one of the most famous examples of the early 18th century English landscape movement. The lakes, the trees, the temples, a grotto and a classical bridge make the grounds a paradise in the finest 18th century tradition, and the gardens are renowned for their striking vistas and woodland walks as well as a stunning selection of rare trees and specimen shrubs, including tulip trees, azaleas and rhododendrons. The house itself, a classical masterpiece built in the 1720s in Palladian style for a Bristol banker, contains a wealth of Grand Tour

Stourhead Gardens

paintings and works of art, including furniture by Chippendale the Younger and wood carvings by Grinling Gibbons. On the very edge of the estate, some three miles by road from the house, the imposing King Alfred's Tower stands at the top of the 790' Kingsettle Hill. This 160' triangular redbrick folly was built in 1772 to commemorate the king, who reputedly raised his standard here against the Danes in 878.

TROWBRIDGE

The county of town of Wiltshire, and another major weaving centre in its day. A large number of industrial buildings still stand, and the Town Council and Civic Society have devised an interesting walk that takes in many of them. The parish church of St James, crowned by one of the finest spires in the county, contains the tomb of the poet and former rector George Crabbe, who wrote the work on which Benjamin Britten based his opera *Peter Grimes*. Trowbridge's most famous son was Isaac Pitman, the shorthand man, who was born in Nash Yard in 1813.

WARMINSTER

The largest centre of population is a historic wool, corn-trading and coaching town with many distinguished buildings, including a famous school with a door designed by Wren. In addition to the 18th and 19th century buildings, Warminster has a number of interesting monuments: the Obelisk with its feeding troughs and pineapple top erected in 1783 to mark the enclosure of the parish; the Morgan Memorial Fountain in the Lake Pleasure Grounds; and *Beyond Harvest*, a statue in bronze by Colin Lambert of a girl sitting on sacks of corn. Warminster's finest building is the Church of St Denys, mainly 14th century but almost completely rebuilt in the 1880s to the design of Arthur Blomfield. The **Dewey Museum**, in the public library, displays a wide range of local history and geology. To the west of town is the 800' **Cley Hill**, an Iron Age hill fort with two Bronze Age barrows. Formerly owned by the Marquess of Bath, the Hill was given to the National Trust in the 1950s and is a renowned sighting place for UFOs. (The region is also noted for the appearance of crop circles and some have linked the two phenomena.)

On the northern edge of Warminster **Arn Hill Nature Reserve** along public footpaths forms a circular walk of two miles through woodland and open downland.

WESTBURY

Westbury, at the western edge of the chalk downlands of **Salisbury Plain**, was a major player in the medieval cloth and wool trades, and still retains many fine buildings from the days of great prosperity, including some cloth works and mills, Westbury was formerly a 'rotten borough' and returned two MPs until 1832. Scandal and corruption were rife, and the **Old Town Hall** in the market place is evidence of such goings-on, a gift from a grateful victorious candidate in 1815. This was Sir Manasseh Massey Lopes, a Portuguese financier and slave-trader who 'bought' the borough to advance his political career.

All Saints Church, a 14th century building on much earlier foundations, has many unusual and interesting features, including a stone reredos, a copy of the Erasmus Bible and a clock with no face made by a local blacksmith in 1604. It also boasts the third heaviest peal of bells in the world.

On the southern edge of town is another church well worth a visit. Behind the simple, rustic exterior of St Mary's, Old Dilton, are a three-decker pulpit and panelled pew boxes with original fittings and individual fireplaces. Just west of Westbury, at Brokerswood, is Woodland Park and Heritage Centre, 80 acres of ancient broadleaf woodland with a wide range of trees, plants and animals, nature trails, a lake with fishing, a picnic and barbecue area, a tea room and gift shop, a museum, a play area and a narrow-gauge railway.

By far the best-known Westbury feature is the famous Westbury White Horse, a chalk carving measuring 182' in length and 108' in height. The present steed dates from 1778, replacing an earlier one carved to celebrate King Alfred's victory over the Danes at nearby Ethandun (Edington) in 878. The white horse is well looked after, the last major grooming being in 1996. Above the horse's head are the ruins of Bratton Castle, an Iron Age hill fort covering 25 acres.

WILTON

The third oldest borough in England, once the capital of Saxon Wessex. It is best known for its carpets, and the Wilton Carpet Factory on the River Wylye continues to produce top-quality Wilton and Axminster carpets. Visitors can tour the carpet-making exhibition in the historic courtyard then go into the modern factory to see the carpets made on up-to-date machinery using traditional skills and techniques. Alongside the factory is the Wilton Shopping Village offering high-quality factory shopping in a traditional rural setting.

Wilton House is the stately home of the Earls of Pembroke. When the original house was destroyed by fire in 1647, Inigo Jones was commissioned to build its replacement. He designed both the exterior and the interior, including the amazing Double Cube Room, and the house was further remodelled by James Wyatt. The art collection is one of the very finest, with

Wilton House

works by Rembrandt, Van Dyke, Rubens and Tintoretto; the furniture includes pieces by Chippendale and Kent. There's plenty to keep children busy and happy, notably the Wareham Bears (a collection of 200 miniature costumed teddy bears), a treasure hunt quiz and a huge adventure playground. There's a Tudor kitchen, a Victorian laundry and 21 acres of landscaped grounds with parkland, cedar trees, water and rose gardens and an elegant Palladian bridge. During World War ll the house was used as an operations centre for Southern Command and it is believed that the Normandy landings were planned here. Open daily late March-end October.

The Church of St Mary and St Nicholas is a unique Italianate church built in the style of Lombardy by the Russian Countess of Pembroke in 1845. The interior is resplendent with marble, mosaics, richly carved woodwork and early French stained glass.

WOOTTON RIVERS

An attractive village with a real curiosity in its highly unusual church clock. The Jack Sprat Clock was built by a local man from an assortment of scrap metal, including old bicycles, prams and farm tools, to mark the coronation of King George V in 1911. It has 24 different chimes and its face has letters instead of numbers.

WYLYE

Peace arrived in Wylye in 1977, when a bypass diverted traffic from the busy main roads. It had long been an important junction and staging post on the London-Exeter coaching route. A statue near the bridge over the River Wylye (from which the village, Wilton and indeed Wiltshire get their names) commemorates a brave postboy who drowned here after rescuing several passengers from a stagecoach which had overturned during a flood.

Above the village is the little-known Yarnbury Castle, an Iron Age hill fort surrounded by two banks and an outer bank. To the west is a triangular enclosure from Roman times which could have held cattle or sheep. From the 18th century to World War l Yarnbury was the venue of an annual sheep fair.

The Black Dog

147

Salisbury Road,
Chilmark,
Wiltshire SP3 5AH
Tel: 01722 716344
Fax: 01722 716124

Directions:

From the A303, about 18 miles southwest of Andover, turn left on a minor road to Chilmark (1.5 miles). You will see The Black Dog on your left as you enter the village

It was the Romans who were the first to quarry the fine creamy limestone at Chilmark and in medieval times this lovely stone was used in the building of Salisbury Cathedral. The quarries have recently been re-opened to hew stone for use in the restoration of this magnificent structure. The quarries used to belong to Wilton Abbey but when Henry VIII dissolved all religious houses the estate was granted to William Herbert, later created 1st Earl of Pembroke. A century later the 4th Earl chose Chilmark stone for the building of Wilton House, his sumptuous mansion a few miles to the east of the village. The house has remained in the same family ever since and today is the home of the 17th Earl.

Chilmark stone was also used when **The Black Dog** was built back in the 15th century. The original inglenook fireplaces with their bread and salt ovens are still intact and the inn's beamed ceilings and planked floors all add to the charm. This outstanding hostelry run by Alaric Campbell Hill, a welcoming host who is a great believer in customer care. The cuisine is exceptional, prepared by "the best chef in the south" according to one customer and the choice of beverages ranges from real ales to superb wines. The candlelit restaurant with its crisp linen tablecloths and gleaming crystal is housed in what was originally the Brewhouse. Look out for the ammonite fossils, believed to be 160 million years old, contained in the Chilmark stone of the Brewhouse walls.

Opening Hours: Mon-Sat: 11.00-15.00; 18.00-23.00. Sun: 12.00-15.00; 19.00-22.30

Food: A la carte menu featuring top quality cuisine

Credit Cards: All major cards accepted

Facilities: Off road parking

Local Places of Interest/Activities:
Farmer Giles Farmstead, 2 miles; Dinton Park (NT), 3 miles; Regimental Badges Hill Carving, 5 miles; Wilton House, 9 miles

148 The Bruce Arms

Easton Royal,
nr Pewsey,
Wiltshire
SN9 5LR
Tel: 01672 810216

Directions:

From Marlborough take the A346 south towards Ludgershall. After 6 miles, at the roundabout, turn right on the B3087, towards Pewsey. Easton Royal is about 1 mile along this road

Easton Royal stands at the eastern end of the lovely Vale of Pewsey, with the charming little town of Pewsey just a couple of miles away. Also within easy reach is the Kennet & Avon Canal with its extensive towpath walks. At Pewsey Wharf boat trips are available during the summer. Northwards stretches the expanse of Savernake Forest with its impressive Grand Avenue and many woodland walks.

Entering into **The Bruce Arms** is like stepping back some 60 years or so. The bar was fitted in 1934 and very little has changed since then. The tables and benches are believed to be more than 150 years old and the building itself dates back to around 1800. Jaqui and John Butler run this atmospheric old hostelry and a very friendly and welcoming couple they are. Their menu offers excellent cheese and onion rolls. The pub keeps no fewer than 2 real ales on tap and occasionally 1 guest ale and for lovers of pub games there's a separate room for skittles, pool, darts and shove ha'penny. Outside is a pleasant garden and a licensed caravan site. If you enjoy pubs with a character of their own, The Bruce Arms should definitely not be missed.

Opening Hours: Mon-Sun: 11.00-14.00; 18.00-23.00

Food: Rolls

Credit Cards: Not accepted

Facilities: Garden; caravan site; parking

Entertainment: Skittles; pool; darts; shove ha'penny

Local Places of Interest/Activities:
Vale of Pewsey to the west; Kennet & Avon Canal, 1 mile; Savernake Forest, 2 miles; Crofton Beam Engines, 4 miles

Internet/Website:
www.brucearms.co.uk

The Cavalier | 149

Eastleigh Road,
Devizes,
Wiltshire SN10 3EG
Tel: 01380 723285

Directions:

From Devizes town centre, follow the signs for Andover (A342) along Nursteed Road and turn left into Eastleigh Road just before the football club.

Standing at the western end of the picturesque Vale of Pewsey, Devizes is an attractive and historic market town which was founded in 1080 by William the Conqueror's nephew, Bishop Osmund. A fine Norman church tower of around 1130 still stands, surrounded by some lovely old buildings. There are yet more handsome buildings all around the spacious Market Place and in Long Street which is lined with elegant Georgian dwellings. Just a few minutes from the town centre, **The Cavalier** is well-known for offering "good value for money food" and a choice of up to 5 real ales on tap at any one time. Landlord and landlady Steve and Nicky Wragg are a lively couple and there always seems to be something going on. Pool, darts and skittles, and even petanque. There's a piste to the side of the pub and matches are played with other local teams. And if you visit on a Thursday evening, you can take part in the regular Quiz Night.

Nicky is in charge of the kitchen and her menus offer a very wide range of main meals, starters and light meals, sandwiches, "name your own filling" baguettes, jacket potatoes and sandwiches. In addition, there are at least half a dozen Daily Specials. Steve is a Fellow of the Institute of Innkeepers and his innkeeping skills have been recognised by a Cask Marque awarded for his real ales and an Investors in People award.

Opening Hours: Mon-Sat: 11.00-23.00; Sun: 12.00-22.30

Food: Wide choice of main courses, bar meals, snacks and sandwiches

Credit Cards: All major cards except Amex and Diners

Facilities: Beer Garden with Petanque piste; function room; ample parking

Entertainment: Pool, darts, skittles, petanque. Quiz night every Thursday with bonus rollover

Local Places of Interest/Activities: Kennet & Avon Canal & Museum in Devizes; towpath walks; scenic walks and drives in the Vale of Pewsey to the east, and across Salisbury Plain to the south

Internet/Website: cavalier.devizes@lineone.net

150 The Crown Inn

Alvediston,
Salisbury,
Wiltshire SP5 5JY
Tel: 01722 780335

Directions:

From Shaftesbury take the A30 towards Wilton & Salisbury. After 7 miles turn right on minor road to Alvediston (3 miles).

Alvediston village is set in the beautiful Chalke Valley which runs from Coombe Bissett near Salisbury to Ludwell

near Shaftesbury. This peaceful spot was chosen as his final resting place by the former Prime Minister, Anthony Eden, 1st Earl of Avon. After a long and distinguished career, - he was three times Foreign Secretary, Eden followed Winston Churchill as Premier in 1955. His period of office was dominated by the Suez crisis and following that débâcle he resigned in 1957, pleading ill health. He retired to Jamaica where he died in 1977. His grave lies on the edge of Alvediston churchyard, near the car parking area.

Just up the road from the church, **The Crown Inn** looks absolutely ravishing with its pink-washed walls, thatched roof and creepers trying to smother the windows. Mike Jenkins, the landlord, is an extrovert personality and he and his wife Pauline have built up a young, friendly team of waiting and kitchen staff. The food is largely homemade and based on fresh local produce. Everything from a sandwich to a substantial restaurant meal is available, - fresh fish dishes, homemade pies and curries, and traditional favourites such as liver & bacon and sausages with bubble & squeak. Tuesday night is Steak Night, and there's a monthly charity quiz on the first Sunday of every month. The inn has three beautiful letting rooms, all en suite, and they help make The Crown an inviting and convenient base, especially in wintertime when there are cheap breaks available.

Opening Hours: Mon-Sat: 11.00-15.00; 18.00-23.00. Sun: 12.00-16.00; 19.00-22.30

Food: Bar & restaurant food available until 14.30 and 21.30

Credit Cards: Mastercard and Visa

Accommodation: 2 doubles, 1 twin, all en suite

Facilities: Large garden; children's play area; covered patio; non-smoking area; children & pets welcome if well-behaved

Entertainment: Darts & the locals! Monthly charity quiz

Local Places of Interest/Activities: Riding, golf and fishing nearby; Dinton Park Gardens (NT), 8 miles; Wilton House, 8 miles; City of Salisbury, 12 miles

Crown Inn

Cholderton,
nr Salisbury,
Wiltshire SP4 6NW
Tel/Fax: 01980 629247

Directions:

From the A303, take the A338 towards Salisbury. Cholderton is about 1 mile along this road. The Crown Inn is at the southern end of the village.

Located close to the Hampshire border, the small village of Cholderton sits beside the River Avon with Salisbury Plain rolling off to the north and east. A major family attraction just a mile or so outside the village is the Cholderton Rare Breeds Farm. This interesting establishment specialises in centuries-old breeds of domestic animals, including pigs, sheep, cattle and over 50 breeds of rabbit. Baby animals are on show during the spring and summer months, and amusing pig races are held at peak times. The farm also offers trailer rides, a nature trail, water garden and adventure playground.

In Cholderton itself, the **Crown Inn** is as pretty as a picture with its thatched roof, hanging baskets and quaint thatched wishing well. Inside, low-beamed ceilings, lots of brasses, miniatures and prints, and open log fire testify to the inn's antiquity. There are two bars and a separate dining area, candlelit in the evening, offering very superior fare. The blackboard menus show separate listings for vegetarian, meat and fish dishes. Amongst the latter you might find lumpfish roe 'caviar style', served on ice with water biscuits but whichever menu you choose from, all of chef Lynne Hunt's creations are both imaginative and appetising. Her husband Jeremy, in addition to his landlord role, is also responsible for the witticisms published on a chalk board outside! The Crown has a lovely garden, patio area, children's play area and, on a 2-acre site to the rear, facilities for campers and caravanners.

Opening Hours: All day, every day

Food: Quality meals and bar snacks every lunchtime and evening

Credit Cards: All major cards accepted

Facilities: Beer garden; patio; children's play area; caravan and camping site; ample parking

Local Places of Interest/Activities: Rare Breeds Farm, 1.5 miles; Stonehenge, 7 miles; Salisbury Cathedral, 13 miles

152 The Crown Inn

Church Street,
Tisbury,
Wiltshire SP3 6NH
Tel: 01747 870221
Fax: 01747 871858

Directions:

From the A30, about 5 miles northeast of Shaftesbury, take the minor road on the left to Ansty and Tisbury (3 miles)

An undulating lane to the north of Ansty descends into the beautiful valley of the upper Nadder. Tisbury is an attractive community which boasts the largest surviving tithe barn in England. More than 5400 square feet of thatch cover the whole of its 200ft long roof, protecting an internal space of around one third of an acre. With its complex arrangement of beams and timber uprights, the barn has an almost cathedral-like quality. Tisbury's lovely riverside church is also well worth visiting. It has a splendid carved roof, a striking pulpit, pews and font cover all dating from the 1600s and, in the churchyard, the graves of Rudyard Kipling's parents.

Along the road from the church is another impressive building, **The Crown Inn**, a former coaching inn which still has its arched opening through which the coach would pass. Inside, the solid wood floors, timber ceiling and exposed stonework all contribute to the period charm. Mine hosts at The Crown are Anne and Stewart Skinner who offer their customers an excellent choice of food, (everything from a filled baguette to a hearty meal), real ales, comfortable en suite accommodation in recently converted cottage style bedrooms, and a lively atmosphere with lots of pub games available. Outside, there's a pleasant beer garden, patio and a secluded courtyard with a children's play area.

Opening Hours: Thu-Sun: All day, every day

Food: Full meals and bar snacks

Credit Cards: All major cards accepted

Accommodation: 4 doubles, all en suite

Facilities: Pool; bar billiards; bagatelle; cribbage; beer garden; patio; secure courtyard play area; function room; ample parking

Entertainment: Music nights; theme nights in summer; barbecue evenings

Local Places of Interest/Activities: Old Wardour Castle, 3 miles; Farmer Giles Homestead, 5 miles; Dinton Park Gardens (NT), 6 miles

The Dog & Gun Inn | 153

Salisbury Road,
Netheravon,
Wiltshire
SP4 9RQ
Tel/Fax:
 01980 671287

Directions:

From the A303, 14 miles west of Andover, turn right on the A345 towards Devizes and Marlborough. Netheravon is about 5 miles along this road.

Netheravon developed alongside the River Avon and to the west of the village stretches the virtually treeless expanse of Salisbury Plain. Some historians attribute the lack of woodland on the Plain to the intensive agriculture carried out here by the same pre-historic tribes who created the awe-inspiring pagan monument of Stonehenge, just a few miles down the road from Netheravon.

The Dog and Gun Inn can't really compete with the antiquity of Stonehenge, - its history extends to a mere 300 years. The olde-worlde atmosphere is almost palpable. Ancient beams support the ceilings, open log fires crackle a warm welcome, half-panelled walls add to the charm. There's even a separate little snug for 'meetings of a confidential nature!'. Hanging on the walls are wickedly satirical caricatures of the inn's regulars, along with an interesting collection of regimental plaques. Mine host at the Dog and Gun is Steve Gurling. In 1997 he took over a moribund hostelry and speedily brought it back to life. Music nights and themed evenings are undoubtedly part of the appeal but it's the consistent quality and value for money of the food and drink served here that provides the major attraction. Everything on the menu is freshly cooked to order. If the weather is kind, you can enjoy your meal in the attractive beer garden where there's also a secure children's play area and pets' corner.

Opening Hours: All day, every day

Food: Value for money, home-cooked pub food

Credit Cards: All major cards accepted

Facilities: Beer garden; secure children's area; pets' corner; ample parking

Entertainment: Pool room; darts; music

nights; themed evenings

Local Places of Interest/Activities: Woodhenge, 4 miles; Stonehenge, 6 miles; Salisbury Plain to east and west

154 The Grosvenor Arms

Hindon,
Salisbury,
Wiltshire
SP3 6DJ
Tel: 01747 820696
Fax: 01747 820869

Directions:

From the A350, 8 miles north of Shaftesbury, turn right on the B3089 to Hindon (2 miles). The Grosvenor Arms is in the centre of the village

An ancient sign on the wall of **The Grosvenor Arms** promises 'GOOD STALL STABLEING & LOCK UP COACH HOUSES', a relic of the days when the inn served stage coach and other travellers en route between London and Exeter. This delightful old hostelry has been recently refurbished in keeping with its original Georgian character, - still serving a pint of real ale and keeping an open log fire blazing away in the bar with its stone-flagged floors.

A particular attraction at The Grosvenor Arms is the excellent cuisine on offer and you can watch your meal being prepared in the glass fronted theatre-style kitchen. Only the finest and freshest local produce is used to create dishes such as Dorset loin of lamb in a rosemary and tomato jus, or caramelised sautéed Brixham scallops on a Thai-flavoured risotto finished with lobster oil. The recent refurbishment now allows the hotel to offer 7 individually named and appointed guest rooms, one of which has the extra luxury of a 4-poster bed. All the rooms are en suite and provided with crisp white sheets, heavy plump towels and all the modern facilities to ensure the comfort of the hotel's guests.

Opening Hours: Hotel, - 24 hours

Food: Quality food available every lunchtime & evening

Credit Cards: All major cards accepted

Accommodation: 7 en suite bedrooms

Facilities: Gardens to side and rear; spacious patio; residents' lounge

Local Places of Interest/Activities: Farmer Giles' Homestead, 6 miles; Stourhead, 11 miles; Stonehenge, 16 miles

The Malet Arms
155

Newton Toney,
Salisbury,
Wiltshire
SP4 0HJ
Tel: 01980 629279
Fax: 01980 629459

Directions:

From the A303, 9 miles west of Andover, turn left on the A338 towards Salisbury. After about 2.5 miles, turn left on a minor road to Newton Toney

The small village of Newton Toney lies close to the Hampshire border, with the cathedral cities of Salisbury and Winchester both within easy reach. The major prehistoric sites of Stonehenge and Woodhenge lie even closer. The village developed along the banks of the River Bourne which still flows along one side of the main street.

On the other side you'll find **The Malet Arms**, an early 19th century hostelry run by Ann and Noel Cardew and their business partner, David. They are an imaginative and enthusiastic threesome with, between them, many years experience in the wine and restaurant trade in London. So there's a constantly changing menu which offers some inspired creations and also remarkably good value for money. A typical example: Four Queen Scallops grilled in their shells with honey, ginger and fresh rosemary, with a rocket and pine nut salad. The wine list has clearly been compiled by someone with a very well-educated palate, but if your beverage of choice is real ale then check out the church hymn board for the 'Hymm and Hers' real ales. An additional attraction at this inviting inn is the decor, - an eclectic mix of church pews and horse brasses, settles and vintage prints, all of them adding to the charm.

Opening Hours: Daily: 11.00-15.00; 18.00-23.00

Food: Value for money food available every lunchtime & evening

Credit Cards: All major cards except Amex

Facilities: Ample off road parking

Places of Interest/Activities: River Bourne, just across the road; Stonehenge, 8 miles; City of Salisbury, 10 miles

156   The New Inn

High Street,
Amesbury,
Wiltshire SP4 7DL
Tel/Fax: 01980 622110

Directions:

Amesbury is 8 miles north of Salisbury at the junction of the A345/A303. The New Inn is in the centre of the town, on the High Street

When King Arthur died, according to Sir Thomas Malory his widow Guinevere retreated to a nunnery at Amesbury. There's considerably more evidence that a later queen, Elfrida, founded an abbey here around 979 in reparation for her complicity in the murder of her son-in-law, Edward the Martyr, at Corfe Castle. Almost two centuries later, Henry II rebuilt the abbey church, adding a noble central tower which is all that survives of the ancient monastery.

Located at the heart of this appealing little town set around a loop of the River Avon is **The New Inn**. Originally a coaching inn, it was recorded in the 18th century as the Three Tuns and was at that time run by the Widow Vincent. Your hosts today are Alan and Natasha Dunford who recently took over from Natasha's father. Over the years, he had built up the New Inn's reputation for providing good food and drink, and a welcoming atmosphere. The inn has a separate dining room, small but quiet and intimate, and offering the very best in home cooked food. A recent addition to the New Inn's amenities is a charming function room created from the former stables and approached from the old world charm of the enclosed courtyard. Children are welcome here, - there's even a garden for them, and jazz devotees are attracted by the Jazz Nights held once a month.

Opening Hours: Mon-Fri: 10.30-15.00; 18.00-23.00. Sat-Sun: Open all day

Food: Comprehensive choice available every lunchtime & evening

Credit Cards: All major cards except Amex

Facilities: Children's garden; function rooms; off road parking

Entertainment: Jazz night once a month

Places of Interest/Activities: Salisbury Plain to the north; Stonehenge, 3 miles; City of Salisbury, 8 miles

The Rose & Crown | 157

108 High Street,
Worton, Devizes,
Wiltshire SN10 5SE
Tel: 01380 724202

Directions:

From Devizes take the A360 towards Salisbury. After 2 miles turn right near the Wiltshire Fire Service headquarters. After 1 mile turn right into the village of Worton. The Rose & Crown is in the village centre.

Located in the heart of this attractive village, the **Rose & Crown** has a long history stretching back to 1726 when it was first recorded as a cider house. But it was known to have existed as a blacksmith's and ale house before then. The original buildings remain, as do the old fireplaces and low ship's beams, - they really are low so do watch out! Since coming here in 1996, Tracey and Brian Greene have really turned around the fortunes of the only pub in the village. It's well known for having the best skittles alley in the area and some 20 men's, ladies and mixed teams are based here. When there is not a match in progress, anyone can try their skill in the alley but for those who like something a little less energetic, there are plenty of other traditional pub games to play, such as cribbage and dominoes.

Before 'retiring' Brian was a master chef in the Army and, with Tracey's help, he provides an excellent range of freshly prepared, cooked to order meals, served in either the cosy dining room or the bar. Ranging from delicious sandwiches to a full à la carte menu as well as a daily specials board. However, it is the interesting and unusual list of curries that has really put the pub on the culinary map.The curry menu not only features the more familiar dishes such as mild Korma and hot Vindaloo, but also curries from Morocco, Thailand and elsewhere. The inn is also developing a small but select list of European wines and there's always a good selection of real ale on tap.

Opening Hours: Daily: 12.00-15.00; 18.00-23.00

Food: All home made: grills, omelettes, fish bar, authentic Indian and other curries

Credit Cards: Not accepted

Facilities: Skittle Alley, Beer Garden, children's play area, ample parking

Entertainment: Fun Quiz Night on Sunday; occasional live music at weekends;

Music Festival organised for village

Local Places of Interest/Activities: The White Horse hill carving at Westbury, 7 miles; Caen Hill lock staircase on the Kennet and Avon Canal; scenic drives and walks through the Vale of Pewsey to the east and Salisbury Plain to the south

Internet/Website:
brian@greene52.freeserve.co.uk

158 | The South Western Hotel

Station Road,
Tisbury,
Wiltshire SP3 6JT
Tel: 01747 870160

Directions:

From the A30, about 5 miles northeast of Shaftesbury, take the minor road on the left to Ansty and Tisbury (3 miles). The South Western Hotel is at the southern end of the village, opposite the railway station

The charming riverside village of Tisbury is notable for having one of England's largest surviving medieval tithe barns, some charming old houses and a lovely church with a striking carved roof and some fine 17th century pieces. In its graveyard are buried the parents of Rudyard Kipling and a royalist heroine of the Civil War. Lady Blanche lived at nearby Wardour Castle, a unique hexagonal tower house built in 1393. The castle was besieged by Cromwell's troops and although she had only a handful of men to support her, the 60-year-old Lady Blanche held out against a force of over a thousand. When she eventually surrendered she was imprisoned for a while but later released. Her ghost is said to haunt the splendid castle which is well worth visiting.

The South Western Hotel was built to service travellers on the London South Western Railway and indeed it still does since rather surprisingly the village has somehow managed to keep its main line service. The hotel is run by Patricia Ost, a lady with a splendid sense of humour who says she reckons that her job is really her hobby, she enjoys it so much. With a choice of real ales on offer, most of the hotel's business is 'wet' but there's also a small selection of appetising home made dishes available which are served in the cosy dining room. In good weather customers can enjoy the pleasant beer garden and if you are planning to stay in this scenic corner of the county, the hotel has 4 rooms, some of them en suite.

Opening Hours: Mon-Thu: 12.00-15.00, 18.00-23.00; Fri and Sat: 12.00-23.00; Sun: 12.00-15.00, 18.00-22.30

Food: Small selection of home made dishes

Credit Cards: All major cards accepted

Accommodation: 4 rooms, some en suite

Facilities: Beer garden; ample parking

Entertainment: Occasional live music

Local Places of Interest/Activities: Old Wardour Castle, 3 miles; Farmer Giles Homestead, 5 miles; Dinton Park Gardens (NT), 6 miles

The Stonehenge Inn | 159

2 Stonehenge Road,
Durrington,
Wiltshire SP4 8BN
Tel: 01980 655205

Directions:
From the A303, about 14 miles west of Andover turn right on the A345 towards Marlborough. At the first roundabout (1 mile) turn right into Durrington.

The whole world knows about Stonehenge; not so many know about the even older Woodhenge, a mile or so to the southwest of Durrington. It was constructed around 2200BC, - predating Stonehenge by several hundred years. As with its more famous neighbour, the timber uprights at Woodhenge were aligned to mark the sun's position on Midsummer's Day. The posts have long since disappeared but their position is now indicated by concrete markers. Interestingly, the site was one of the first to have been discovered by aerial reconnaissance, the six concentric rings of post holes showing clearly from the air in a photograph taken in 1925.

The Stonehenge Inn is a much more recent arrival, - the original coaching inn opened here in 1804 and was rebuilt in the 1920s. This spacious hostelry is owned and run by Paul and Doreen Banks and it enjoys a particularly good reputation for the quality of the food on offer. The main menu includes steaks, seafood and poultry dishes but there's another menu of traditional dishes, and yet another featuring a whole range of Italian favourites. Vegetarians have their own selection of meals and for lighter appetites there's a choice of jacket potatoes and filled baguettes. If you are planning to stay in this historic area, the inn has 6 guest rooms, all en suite.

Opening Hours: Mon-Tue; 11.00-15.00, 18.00-23.00; Wed - Sun 11.00-23.00

Food: Traditional English, and Italian cuisine

Credit Cards: All major cards accepted

Accommodation: 6 en suite rooms

(doubles, twins and family)

Facilities: Families welcome; large car park

Entertainment: Quiz Nights; Music Nights

Local Places of Interest/Activities:
Woodhenge, 1 mile; Stonehenge, 3 miles; Cholderton Rare Breeds Farm, 4 miles

160   The Swan at Enford

Long Street,
Enford,
nr Pewsey,
Wiltshire SN9 6DD
Tel: 01980 670338
Fax: 01980 671318

Directions:

From the A303, 14 miles west of Andover, turn right on the A345 towards Devizes and Marlborough. Enford is about 7 miles along this road.

Set in the heart of Salisbury Plain, the tiny village of Enford sits on the west bank of the River Avon, its houses clustered around an ancient church. The parish boundaries in this fertile valley run up the hillsides, an arrangement that assured each parish its fair share of both upland grazing and the richer soil in the valley bottom.

The Swan at Enford is a delightfully picturesque building with a sweeping thatched roof. Dating back to the 1600s, part of the building is whitewashed, part has its mellow old bricks exposed. A former coaching inn, The Swan is the epitome of a traditional country pub with a hospitable and welcoming atmosphere. An interesting feature is the exquisite collection of porcelain and pottery decorating the walls. This inviting hostelry is owned and run by Bob and Phyllis Bone, a friendly couple who manage to combine a relaxed manner with complete professionalism. Bob spent his younger days at the London Dorchester and his extensive menu shows that this is a man who takes good food very seriously. Everything is home cooked from fresh ingredients and if there's a game dish on the menu, the game will have been shot by Bob himself. Real ales and quality wines are available, and in good weather you can take advantage of the peaceful garden at the rear or the lawned area to the front.

Opening Hours: Mon-Sat: 12.00-15.00, 19.00-23.00; Sun 12.00-15.00, 19.00-23.30

Food: Every lunchtime and evening except Sunday evening

Credit Cards: All major cards accepted

Facilities: Garden; patio; parking in adjacent lay-by

Local Places of Interest/Activities: Woodhenge, 4 miles; Stonehenge, 6 miles; Salisbury Plain to east and west

Internet/Website: e-mail: theswanatenford@easynet.co.uk

The Tipsy Miller | 161

Marten,
nr Marlborough,
Wiltshire
SN8 3SH
Tel: 01264 731372

Directions:

From Marlborough take the A346 south to Burbage (6 miles). At the roundabout go left on the A338 towards Hungerford. About 3.5 miles along this road you will see The Tipsy Miller on the left

It's not known whether **The Tipsy Miller** derived its name from a real character but there's certainly a real mill nearby. Wilton Windmill is the only working windmill to have survived in Wiltshire. It stands 170ft above sea level, a mile or so south of the Kennet & Avon Canal, a local attraction which provides some pleasant towpath walks. Right beside the canal is another important example of England's industrial heritage, the Crofton Pumping Station. The Georgian Engine House here contains 2 restored Cornish Beam pumping engines dating back to 1812 and still working. A few miles further north is Savernake Forest, a magnificent expanse of woodland criss-crossed by paths and bridle ways.

Back in Marten, the Tipsy Miller is an inviting, white-washed building around a hundred years old. A free house, it is run by Alan and Diana Woodham, their son Daniel and daughter Joanne. Daniel has worked in Italy, a fact which explains why pasta dishes are a speciality of the house. But there's also a wide choice of other fare, ranging from à la carte meals in the separate restaurant to bar meals and snacks in the main bar with its polished brasses and copper items. The inn also boasts a whole acre of formal, lawned garden in which there's a superbly furnished and fitted chalet, available for self-catering guests.

Opening Hours: Mon-Sat: 11.30-15.00; 18.30-23.00. Sun: 12.00-15.00; 19.00-22.30

Food: Everything from à la carte meals to sandwiches

Credit Cards: All major cards except Amex and Diners

Accommodation: Self-catering chalet in the grounds sleeping 3

Facilities: One acre garden; patio; ample parking

Local Places of Interest/Activities: Wilton Windmill, 1.5 miles; Crofton Beam Engines, 2 miles; Savernake Forest, 6 miles

The Hidden Inns of the South of England

This page is intentionally left blank

6 North Hampshire

PLACES OF INTEREST:

PUBS AND INNS:

The Hidden Inns of the South of England

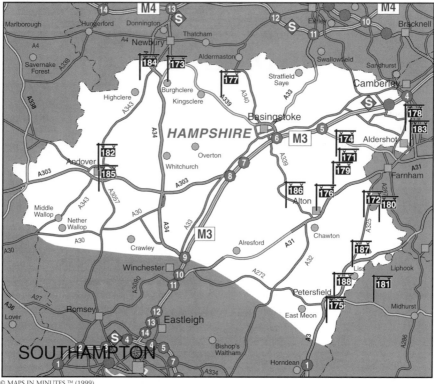

© MAPS IN MINUTES ™ (1999)

171 **The Anchor Inn**, Lower Froyle, nr Alton

172 **Blues Tavern II**, Sleaford, nr Bordon

173 **Carpenters Arms** , Burghclere, nr Newbury

174 **The Chequers Inn**, Well, nr Long Sutton

175 **The Five Bells**, Buriton, nr Petersfield

176 **The French Horn**, Alton

177 **George & Dragon** , Townsend, nr Wolverton

178 **The George Inn**, Ash Vale, nr Aldershot

179 **The Hen & Chicken Inn**, Upper Froyle, nr Alton

180 **The Holly Bush**, Headley, nr Bordon

181 **The Keepers Arms**, Trotton, nr Petersfield

182 **The Lamb Inn**, Andover

183 **The Lion Brewery**, Ash, nr Aldershot

184 **The Rampant Cat**, Woolton Hill, nr Newbury

185 **The Royal Oak**, Goodworth Clatford, nr Andover

186 **The Star Inn**, Bentworth, nr Alton

187 **The Temple Inn**, Liss Forest, nr Liss

188 **The White Hart**, Petersfield

Please note all cross references refer to page numbers

North Hampshire is quite heavily populated, dotted with prosperous, sprawling towns such as Aldershot and Basingstoke. What is surprising is that, once you turn off the busy main roads, you can find yourself driving along narrow country lanes where, if you meet an approaching vehicle, a diploma in Advanced Driving Skills could be very helpful.

This area forms part of the North Downs. Honouring the perverse tradition of English place-names, the Downs are actually uplands, softly-rolling, wooded hills in whose folds lie scores of picturesque villages. As the crow flies, central London is little more than 30 miles away; for many of the northeastern Hampshire villages, even today, the metropolis might just as well be 300 miles distant.

There are few grand houses in the area, although The Vyne near Basingstoke and the Duke of Wellington's home, Stratfield Saye House, are both very imposing. Two smaller dwellings, however, attract hundreds of thousands of visitors to this corner of the county: Jane Austen's House at Chawton, near Alton, and a few miles to the south in the village of Selborne, The Wakes, home of the celebrated naturalist, Gilbert White. Lovers of steam railways can combine a visit to these two houses with a ride on the Watercress Line which runs between Alton and Alresford.

Some of Hampshire's grandest scenery lies in the northwestern part of the county as the North Downs roll westwards towards Salisbury Plain. There's just one sizeable town, Andover, and one major city, Winchester: the rest of the region is quite sparsely populated (for southern England) with scattered villages bearing evocative names such as Nether Wallop. Winchester is of course in a class of its own with its dazzling Cathedral, but there are many other attractions in this area, ranging in time from the Iron Age Danebury Ring, through the Victorian extravaganza of Highclere Castle, to Stanley Spencer's extraordinary murals in the Sandham Memorial Chapel at Burghclere.

PLACES OF INTEREST

ALDERSHOT

Back in 1854, Aldershot was a village of some 800 inhabitants. Then the Army decided to build a major camp here and the population has grown steadily ever since to its present tally of around 55,000. The story of how Aldershot became the home of the British Army is vividly recounted at the **Aldershot Military Museum** which stands in the middle of the camp and is a must for anyone with an interest in military history. Housed in the last two surviving Victorian barrack blocks, its tiny appearance from the outside belies the wealth of fascinating information contained inside. For example, there's a detailed cutaway model of a cavalry barracks showing how the soldiers'

rooms were placed above the stables, an economic form of central heating described as "warm, but aromatic".

It was the army at Aldershot who became the first aviators in Britain, using Farnborough Common for their flying, and building their aircraft sheds where the Royal Aircraft Establishment stands today. The **Airborne Forces Museum** has many interesting exhibits illustrating the part these pioneers played during the early days of the 20th century and during two World Wars. In memory of those who lost their lives in these conflicts, **The Heroes Shrine** in Manor Park, commemorates the dead of World War I, while the nearby walled and sunken garden, shaded by a huge deodar tree, honours the fallen of World War II.

166

Another celebrated military figure, the Duke of Wellington, is celebrated by an imposing bronze statue on Round Hill. It originally stood in London on top of the Triumphal Arch at Hyde Park Corner and was removed to Aldershot in 1885.

ALRESFORD

Pronounced Allsford, Alresford was created around 1200 by a Bishop of Winchester, Geoffrey de Lucy, as part of his grand plan to build a waterway from Winchester to Southampton. Where the river Arle flows into the Itchen, he constructed a huge reservoir covering 200 acres, its waters controlled to keep the Itchen navigable at all seasons. The **Bishop's Reservoir** is now reduced to some 60 acres but it's still home to countless wildfowl and many otters. Known today as Old Alresford Pond, it's one of the most charming features of this dignified Georgian town. Alresford can also boast one of the county's most beautiful streets, historic **Broad Street**, lined with elegant, colourwashed Georgian houses interspersed with specialist shops and inviting hostelries.

Alresford's most famous son was Admiral Lord Rodney, a contemporary of Lord Nelson, who built the grand Manor House near the parish church, but the town can also boast two famous daughters. One was Mary Sumner, wife of the Rector of Alresford, who founded the Mother's Union here in 1876. The other was Mary Russell Mitford, author of the fascinating collection of sketches of 18th century life, Our Village, published in 5 volumes between 1824-1832. Mary's prolific literary output was partly spurred on by the need to repay the debts of her spendthrift father. Dr Mitford managed to dissipate his own inherited fortune of many thousands of pounds; his wife's lavish dowry which almost doubled that income disappeared equally quickly, and when Mary at the age of ten won the huge sum of £20,000 in a lottery, the good doctor squandered that as well. Mary's classic book tells the story

One of Alresford's attractions that should not be missed is the **Watercress Line**, Hampshire's only preserved steam railway, so named because it was once used to transport watercress from the beds around Alresford to London and beyond. The line runs through 10 miles of beautiful countryside to Alton where it links up with main line services to London. Vintage steam

Watercress Line, Alresford

locomotives make the 35-minute journey up to 8 times a day, and there are regular dining trains as well as frequent special events throughout the year.

ALTON

Surrounded by hop-fields and some of Hampshire's loveliest countryside, Alton is an appealing market town with a history stretching back far beyond Roman times. (The name actually means "Old Town"). Alton boasts a large number of old coaching inns, and the impressive, partly-Norman **St. Lawrence's Church** which was the setting for a dramatic episode during the Civil War. A large force of Roundheads drove some eighty Royalists into the church where 60 of them were killed. The Royalist commander, Colonel Boles, made a last stand from the splendid Jacobean pulpit, firing repeatedly at his attackers before succumbing to their bullets. The church door and several of the Norman pillars are still pock-marked with bullet holes fired off during this close-combat conflict. More cheerful are the comical carvings on these pillars of animals and birds, amongst them a wolf gnawing a bone and two donkeys kicking their heels in the air.

Nearby is the old cemetery and the well-tended Grave of Fanny Adams. The expression "Sweet Fanny Adams" arose from the revolting murder in 1867 of a young girl in the town who was hacked into pieces by her assassin. With macabre humour, sailors used the phrase "Sweet Fanny Adams" to describe the recently-issued tinned mutton for which they had a certain mistrust. Over the years, the saying became accepted as a contemptuous description for anything considered valueless. A poor memorial for an innocent girl.

There's a different sort of monument in Amery Street, a narrow lane leading off the market place. On a small brick house is a plaque commemorating the Elizabethan poet Edmund Spenser who came to Alton around 1590 to enjoy its "sweet delicate air".

Well worth a visit while you are in Alton is the **Allen Gallery** in Church Street (free), home to an outstanding collection of English, Continental and Far Eastern pottery, porcelain and tiles. Housed in a group of attractive 16th and 18th century buildings the Gallery's other attractions include the unique Elizabethan Tichborne Spoons, delightful watercolours and oil paintings by local artist William Herbert Allen and a comfortable Coffee Lounge. Across the road, the Curtis Museum (free) concentrates on exploring 100 million years of local history with displays devoted to the "shocking tale of Sweet Fanny Adams", other local celebrities such as Jane Austen and Lord Baden Powell, and a colourful Gallery of Childhood with exhibits thoughtfully displayed in miniature cases at an ideal height for children.

A good time to visit the town is mid-July when the **Alton Show** takes place. Established in 1840, this is one of southern England's most important agricultural gatherings with a wide range of events featuring such attractions as Heavy Horses, llamas, beagles, gun dogs and birds of prey.

ANDOVER

Andover has expanded greatly since the 1960s when it was selected as a "spillover" town to relieve the pressure on London's crowded population. But the core of this ancient town, which was already important in Saxon times, retains much of interest. One outstanding landmark is **St Mary's Church**, completely rebuilt in the 1840s at the expense of a former headmaster of Winchester College. The interior is said to have been modelled on Salisbury Cathedral and if it doesn't quite match up to that sublime building, St Mary's is still well worth a visit.

Equally striking is the **Guildhall** of 1825, built in classical style, which stands alone in the Market Place where markets are still held every Tuesday and Saturday. Andover has also managed to retain half a dozen of the 16 coaching inns that serviced 18th century travellers at a time when the fastest stage coaches took a mere 9 hours to travel here from London. As many as 50 coaches a day stopped at these inns to change horses and allow the passengers to take refreshments.

For a fascinating insight into the town's long history, do pay a visit to the **Andover Museum** (free) in Church Close. There are actually two museums here, both of them housed in buildings which began life as an elegant Georgian town house in 1750 and were later extended to serve as Andover's Grammar School from the 1840s to 1925. The Andover Museum traces the story of the town from Saxon times to the present day with a range of colourful exhibits.

Another good way of getting to know the town is to join one of the guided tours along the **Andover Heritage Trail**. Scheduled tours, lasting about 90 minutes, take place on Tuesday and Saturday afternoons but can also be arranged for groups at other times.

Two miles east of Andover, **Finkley Down Farm Park** provides a satisfying day out for families with young children. Youngsters can feed and handle the animals, groom a pony, ride on a mini-tractor, and expend any excess energy in the well-equipped playground. Romany caravans and farming bygones are on display and other attractions include a tea room, gift shop and picnic area.

Another good family day out can be enjoyed at **The Hawk Conservancy**, 4 miles west of the town. With more than 200 birds to see in 22 acres of grounds, the Hawk Conservancy is one of the largest collections of raptors in the world. Flying demonstrations take place three times daily and include species such as owls, eagles, vultures and condors, falcons, kites, hawks and secretary birds.

BASINGSTOKE

It comes as something of a surprise to discover that this busy, prosperous town with its soaring multi-storey buildings can boast no fewer than 25 parks and open spaces. A useful leaflet available from the Tourist Information Centre gives details of them all, ranging from the 16-hectare **War Memorial Park**, an 18th century park complete with bandstand, aviary and sports facilities, to **Southview Cemetery**, a site with a fascinating history. Some 800 years ago, during the reign of King John, England languished under an Interdict pronounced by the Pope. Throughout the six years from 1208 to 1214, any baby christened, or dead person buried, lacked the official blessing of Mother Church. At Basingstoke during those years, the

168

deceased were interred in the graveyard known as **The Liten** and when the Interdict was finall lifted, the ground was consecrated and a chapel built, the **Chapel of the Holy Ghost**. Today, it's a striking ruin surrounded by a well-managed site which provides a peaceful refuge from the bustling town.

As befits such a thriving place, Basingstoke offers visitors a wide choice of attractions: theatre, cinema, a vast Leisure Park, and an "Old Town" area which is a lively cosmopolitan mix of bars, theme pubs and restaurants. Here too is the excellent **Willis Museum** (free) which charts the town's history with lively displays featuring characters such as "Fred", a Roman skeleton, and "Pickaxe", a 19th century farm worker "forced to scrape a living from the streets of Basingstoke as a scavenger".

Just to the east of Basingstoke, **Basing House** was once one of the grandest residences in the realm. Built during the reign of Henry VIII, it rivalled even the king's extravagant mansions. Less than a hundred years later, during the Civil War, Cromwell's troops besieged the house for an incredible three years, one of them reporting that the mansion was 'as large as the Tower

The Vyne, Nr Basingstoke

of London'. When Basing House was finally captured the victorious New Army burnt it to the ground, but a magnificent 16th century barn survived, its timber roof a marvel of the carpenter's craft.

The Vyne (National Trust), 4 miles north of Basingstoke, has enjoyed a much happier history. Built in the early 1500s for Lord Sandys, Lord Chamberlain to Henry VIII, the house enjoys an idyllic setting with lawns sweeping down to a shimmering lake. A classical portico was added in 1654, the first of its kind in England. The Vyne's treasures include a fascinating Tudor chapel with Renaissance glass, a

Palladian staircase, and a wealth of old panelling and fine furniture.

BURGHCLERE

The village is home to the **Sandham Memorial Chapel**, which was built in the 1920s to remember the dead of World War I. What, however, makes this chapel so interesting are the internal murals which entirely cover the walls that are considered by many to be Stanley Spencer's greatest achievement. An extraordinary project, the murals illustrate the artist's experiences as a medical orderly during the war and he celebrates the everyday routine of a soldier's life. The pictures reach a climax with the huge Resurrection of the Soldiers which completely fills the east wall. This modern chapel is found amidst beautiful and tranquil scenery with views across Watership Down.

CHAWTON

From the outside, the home in which Jane Austen spent the last eight years of her life, **Chawton House**, and where she wrote three of her most popular novels (*Mansfield Park*, *Emma* and *Persuasion*), is a disappointingly dull, blank-faced building. Sadly, once you step inside, the interior is equally dispiriting. You can

Chawton House

see the sitting-room in which she penned those cleverly-crafted novels, the bedroom to which she retired, but the house is curiously empty, as elusive as the author herself. Unless you are a really dedicated Jane-ite, this is a literary shrine which radiates only a minimum charge of magic.

The Wakes, the home of Gilbert White in **Selborne**, about 3 miles south of Chawton, is quite different. A humble curate of the parish from 1784 until his death in 1793, Gilbert spent his spare hours meticulously recording observations on the weather, wild-life and geology

The Wakes, Selborne

ing the fall of Adam and Eve. Only four of these wonderful fonts are known to exist in England and East Meon's is generally regarded as the most magnificent of them.

Just across the road is the 15th century **Courthouse** which also has walls 4ft thick. It's a lovely medieval manor house where for generations the Bishops of Winchester, as Lords of the Manor, held their courts. It would have been a familiar

of the area. Astonishingly, a percipient publisher to whom Gilbert submitted his notes recognised the appeal of his humdrum, day-to-day accounts of life in what was then a remote corner of England. *The Natural History and Antiquities of Selborne* was first published in 1788, has never been out of print, and still provides what is perhaps the most entertaining and direct access to late-18th century life, seen through the eyes of an intelligent, sceptical mind.

CRAWLEY

Crawley is a possibly unique example of an early-20th century model village. The estate was bought by the Philippi family in 1900 who enthusiastically set about adding to the village's store of genuine traditional cottages with faithful fakes built in the same style. (They also provided their tenants with a state-of-the-art bath house and a roller skating rink). Sensitive to tradition and history, they did nothing to blemish the partly Norman church, leaving its unusual interior intact. Instead of stone pillars, St Mary's has mighty wooden columns supporting its roof, still effective more than 500 years after they were first hoisted into place.

EAST MEON

Tucked away in the lovely valley of the River Meon and surrounded by high downs East Meon has been described as "the most unspoilt of Hampshire villages and the nicest". As if that weren't enough, the village also boasts one of the finest and most venerable churches in the county. The central tower, with walls 4ft thick, dates back to the 12th century, and is a stunning example of Norman architecture at its best. Inside, the church's greatest treasure is its remarkable 12th century Tournai font of black marble, exquisitely carved with scenes depict-

HIGHCLERE

About 5 miles east of Faccombe, **Highclere Castle** is an example of Victorian neo-Gothic architecture at its most exuberant. If the central tower reminds you of another well-known building, that may be because the Castle was designed by Sir Charles Barry, architect of the Houses of Parliament. It stands on the site of a former Palace of the Bishops of Winchester, overlooking an incomparably lovely park, one of Capability' Brown's greatest creations. The ornate architecture and furnishings of the Castle interior delights many, others feel somewhat queasy at its unrelenting richness. Highclere is the family home of the 7th Earl and Countess of Carnavon and it was the present Earl's grandfather who in 1922 was with Howard Carter at the opening of Tutankhamun's tomb. A small museum in the basement of the Castle recalls that breath-taking moment. Another display reflects the family's interest in horse racing. For more than a century, Earls of Carnavon have owned, bred and raced horses, and the present Earl is racing manager to the Queen. In addition to the superb parkland, there's also a Walled Garden, planted entirely with white blooms, a gift shop, restaurant and tea rooms.

MIDDLE WALLOP

The village of Middle Wallop became famous during the Battle of Britain when the nearby airfield was the base for squadrons of Spitfires and Hurricanes. Many of the old buildings have been incorporated into the **Museum of Army Flying** which traces the development of Army Flying from the balloons and kites of pre-World War I years, through various imaginative dioramas, to a helicopter flight simulator in which visitors can test their own skills of 'hand and eye' co-ordination. Other attractions include a Museum Shop, licensed café & restaurant, and a grassed picnic area. More details on 01980 674421.

About 3 miles east of Middle Wallop, **Danebury Ring** is Hampshire's largest Iron Age hill fort. Intensively occupied from about 550 BC until the arrival of the Romans, the site has been meticulously excavated over the last 30 years and the finds are now displayed at the Museum of the Iron Age in Andover. Visitors can wander the 13 acre site and with the help of explanatory boards, reconstruct the once-bustling community with its clearly defined roads, shops, houses and what were probably temples.

NETHER WALLOP

The names of the three Wallops (Over, Middle and Nether) have provided a good deal of amusement to visitors over the centuries, so it's slightly disappointing to discover that Wallop is just a corruption of the Old English word *waell-hop*, meaning a valley with a stream. At Nether Wallop the stream is picturesquely lined with willow trees, while the village itself is equally attractive with many thatched or timbered houses. The most notable building in Nether Wallop, though, is **St Andrew's Church**, partly because of its Norman features and handsome West Tower of 1704, but also because of its striking medieval wall paintings which provide an interesting contrast with Stanley Spencer's at Burghclere. Some 500 years old, they lay hidden for generations under layers of plaster and were only rediscovered in the 1950s. The most impressive of them shows St George slaying the dragon. Outside St Andrew's stands an item of great interest for collectors of churchyard oddities. It's a dark grey stone pyramid, 15ft high, with red stone flames rising from its tip. This daunting monument was erected at his own expense and in memory of himself by Francis Douce, 'Doctor of Physick', who died in 1760. Dr Douce also left an endowment to build a village school on condition that the parishioners would properly maintain the pyramid.

PETERSFIELD

An appealing market town, Petersfield is dominated by the bulk of **Butser Hill**, 900ft high and the highest point of the South Downs offering grand panoramic views over the town and even, on a clear day, to the spire of Salisbury Cathedral, some 40 miles distant. In the 1660s, Samuel Pepys noted his stay in Petersfield, at a hotel in which Charles II had slept before him. Another king is commemorated in the Square where William III sits on horseback, incongruously dressed in Roman costume. Unusually, the statue is made of lead.

Most of the elegant buildings around the Square are Georgian, but the **Church of St Peter** is much older, dating back to Norman times and with a fine north aisle to prove it. Just off the Square, the **Flora Twort Gallery** was once the home and studio of the accomplished artist of that name who moved to Petersfield at the end of World War I. Her delightful paintings and drawings capture life in the town over some 40 years - "reminders of some of the things we have lost" as she put it shortly before her death at the age of 91 in 1985.

From the Gallery, a short walk along Sheep Street, (which has some striking timber-framed 16th century houses and Georgian cottages), brings you to **The Spain**, a pleasant green surrounded by some of the town's oldest houses. It apparently acquired its rather unusual name because dealers in Spanish wool used to hold markets there.

STRATFIELD SAYE

Stratfield Saye House was just one of many rewards a grateful nation showered on the Duke of Wellington after his decisive defeat of Napoleon at Waterloo. The Duke himself doesn't seem to have been reciprocally grateful: only lack of funds frustrated his plans to demolish the gracious 17th century house and replace it with an even more impressive mansion which he intended to call Waterloo Palace. Quite modest in scale, Stratfield Saye fascinates visitors with its collection of the Duke's own furniture and personal items such as his spectacles, handkerchiefs and carpet slippers. More questionable are the priceless books in the library, many of them looted from Napoleon's own bibliotheque. A good number of the fine Spanish and Portuguese paintings on display share an equally dubious provenance, "relieved" during the Duke's campaign in those countries as "spoils of war". That was accepted military practice at the time and, these quibbles apart, Stratfield Saye House is certainly one of the county's "must-see" attractions.

The Anchor Inn | 171

Lower Froyle,
nr Alton,
Hampshire
GU34 4NA
Tel: 01420 23261

Directions:

Lower Froyle is just off the A31 Guildford to Winchester road, about 16 miles west of Guildford.

Located in the picturesque village of Lower Froyle **The Anchor Inn** was already offering hospitality to locals and travellers way back in the 1300s. The present building has a really old world atmosphere with very low beams, some exposed stone walls, real fires and lots of memorabilia on display. A Free House, the inn is owned and run by John and Frances Jenkins partnered by Linda and Michael Howard. It's very much a family business since Frances and Linda are sisters and their mum, Irene, is also involved. The family has been here for more than 20 years and has built up a formidable reputation for the quality of the fare on offer.

Food is available every lunchtime, from noon until 14.00, and Monday - Saturday evenings from 18.30 until 22.00. The extensive menu of main meals and bar snacks is supplemented by three or four daily specials. Children and vegetarians are well-catered for, there's a non-smoking area, and to complement your meal there's a well-chosen wine list and a choice of at least 3 real ales. Desserts include a good old-fashioned Treacle Sponge & Custard as well as delicious apple and blackberry crispy pancakes. The inn boasts not just one but two beautifully maintained beer gardens and there's also a large paddock for children to play in. Disabled visitors will find access to the inn is easy and disabled toilets are provided.

Opening Hours: Open every session

Food: Available every lunchtime & evening except Sunday evening

Credit Cards: All major cards accepted

Facilities: Two large beer gardens; spacious paddock as children's play area; good disabled access & toilets; ample parking

Local Places of Interest/Activities:
Birdworld, 4 miles; 'Watercress Railway', 6 miles; Jane Austen's House, Chawton, 8 miles

172 Blues Tavern II

Farnham Road,
Sleaford, Bordon,
Hampshire GU35 9LJ
Tel/Fax: 01420 472227
Mobile: 07787 762208

Directions:

From the A3, six miles north of Petersfield, take the A325 towards Farnham. Sleaford is about 5 miles along this road, at the junction with the B3004. The Blues Tavern II is located at this junction.

Formerly known as The New Inn, the **Blues Tavern II** is a picturesque half-timbered building which dates back to the 16th century. It's a Grade I Listed Building and in the days of stage coaches it was an important stopping place on the road to Portsmouth.

As the name suggests, the inn is the second of its line. The first Blues Tavern was created by Peter Zedd at Heath End near Aldershot. In 1998 Pete and Tina Zedd took over the New Inn at Sleaford and again offered their customers a satisfying mix of good food, fine ales and excellent music. Tragically, Peter died in 1999 but Tina has continued to run this popular inn. It is closed on Mondays (except Bank Holidays) but every night of the week there is live music from 8.30 pm. Tuesday is 'Jamming Night' when you can bring along your own instrument and join in; Wednesday is acoustic night, Thursday and Sunday evenings are demo nights with performances by up and coming bands. On Friday and Saturday evenings professional bands perform and on these two evenings there's a small door charge. During the summer, Tina also arranges all day music festivals. To accompany the entertainment there's a wide choice of meals and bar snacks and a choice of 3 real ales along with all the popular brews. In good weather, you can enjoy your refreshments outside. Although regular musical performances are a familiar feature of Irish pubs, they are very rare in England so it's a pleasure to discover it happening here - and in such an attractive hostelry.

Opening Hours: Closed Mondays except Bank Holidays

Food: Main meals & bar snacks available until 22.30 every day

Credit Cards: Not accepted: cash or cheque only

Facilities: Ample parking

Entertainment: Live music 6 days a week from 20.30; all day music festivals in summer

Local Places of Interest/Activities: Bohunt Manor, 8 miles; Gilbert White's house, Selborne, 6 miles; Jane Austen's house, Chawton, 10 miles

Internet/Website: www.bluestavern.co.uk

Carpenters Arms | 173

Harts Lane,
Burghclere,
nr Newbury,
Hampshire
RG20 9JY
Tel: 01635278251

Directions:

From the A34, about 4 miles south ofNewbury, follow signs to Burghclere. On entering the village, the Carpenters Arms is on your right.

Burghclere is well known to admirers of the maverick English painter, Stanley Spencer. Some of his most inspired work can be seen at the Sandham Memorial Chapel, erected in 1926 by the Behrend family in memory ofa relative who died in World War I. The exterior of the building is unprepossessing but the interior contain a remarkable series of 19 murals, one of which, *The Resurrection of the Soldiers,* completely covers the east wall. The chapel overlooks the well-known beauty spot, Watership Down. In the village itself, the **Carpenters Arms** is a spacious building with a history stretching back to 1826. The inn has retained many of its original features and the open log fire in the lounge bar certainly adds to the warm and cosy atmosphere of this typical country inn.

Your hosts are Christopher and Audrey Ayling who between them have more than 40 years experience as innkeepers. They offer a full a la carte menu which is served in the elegant conservatory restaurant and includes a good range of fish, meat and vegetarian dishes. Bar meals, snacks and sandwiches are also available. Real ale fans will find a choice of 3 brews, one of them a guest beer, and wine lovers are presented with an extensive selection of wines available by the bottle or by the glass.

Opening times: Mon-Sat: 11.00-15.00; 18.00-23.00. Sun: 11.00-23.00

Food: Restaurant a la carte meals; bar meals, snacks & sandwiches

Credit Cards: All major cards except Amex and Diners; also Barter Cards

Facilities: Large Beer Garden with barbecue area; extensive car park

Local Places of Interest/Activities: Sandham Memorial Chapel (NT), 100yds; Watership Down, 1 mile; Highclere Castle, 4 miles; Beacon Hill, 5 miles

174 The Chequers Inn

Well,
nr Long Sutton,
Hampshire
RG29 1TL
Tel: 01256 862605
Fax: 01256 862133

Directions:

From West Street in Farnham, take the minor road signposted to Crondall and Well. Follow the signs for Well

The Chequers Inn looks absolutely delightful in summer when the covered terrace at the front is smothered in flowers, well set off by the whitewashed walls. Dating back to the 1600s, the Chequers has always been an inn but its name suggests that it also doubled as "a place where taxes are paid". It has a wonderfully traditional atmosphere with low beamed ceilings, wooden plank floors and walls, and an inglenook fireplace where log fires blaze in winter. The separate comfortable restaurant has high, ornate ceilings.

Your hosts at the Chequers are Shawn and Desiree Blackey who originate from South Africa and took over the inn in 1998. They are both members of the Institute of Innkeepers and take great pride in providing their customers with quality food and drink. The chalkboard menu offers a wide variety of dishes although fish is a speciality of the house, - not just the familiar cod and plaice but also swordfish, marlin, snapper and bream. All the beers on offer have received the independent Cask Marque seal of approval and wine lovers will find a wide selection of wines from around the world. If you enjoy taking your refreshments outside, there's a pleasant, shady garden at the rear which looks out over unspoiled countryside, and the charming covered terrace at the front.

Opening Hours: Mon-Fri: 11.00-15.00; 18.00-23.00; Sat & Bank Holidays: 11.00-23.00; Sun: 12.00-22.30

Food: Restaurant & bar meals; fish dishes a speciality

Credit Cards: All cards except Amex & Diners

Facilities: Beer garden at rear; covered terrace at front; large car park

Entertainment: Live jazz in garden during summer

Local Places of Interest/Activities: Good walking nearby; Bird World , 5 miles; Watercress Railway, Alton, 6 miles; Jane Austen's House, Chawton, 9 miles

The Five Bells

High Street, Buriton,
nr Petersfield,
Hampshire GU31 5RX
Tel: 01730 263584
Fax: 01730 263845

Directions:

From the A3, at the roundabout 4 miles south of Petersfield, take the B2070 and almost immediately turn right on a minor road to Buriton (1 mile).

Buriton's ancient church, surrounded by trees and overlooking a large pond, is flanked by an appealing early 18th century Manor House built by the father of Edward Gibbon, the celebrated historian. Gibbon wrote much of his magnum opus, *The Decline and Fall of the Roman Empire*, in his study here. He was critical of the position his father had chosen for the house, "at the end of the village and the bottom of the hill", but was highly appreciative of the view over the Downs: "the long hanging woods in sight of the house could not perhaps have been improved by art or expense".

Named after the five bells of Buriton church, **The Five Bells** inn is on record as far back as 1639. Much of the building dates back to that era, as witnessed by the low-beamed ceilings and the large inglenook fireplace with its roaring log fire. The present kitchen and restaurant were added in the 18th century with what is now the restaurant serving as a farrier's. Mine host at this charming old inn is Bridget Slocombe, a lady with a very welcoming smile and a friendly, infectiously happy personality. Bridget also has an obvious flair for producing tasty food. Her extensive menu covers fish, game, meat and vegetarian dishes as well as a large selection of curries and an excellent choice of home made sweets. Also on offer at lunchtime is a range of appetising snacks. In good weather, these can be enjoyed in the pleasant garden to the rear, or on the sheltered patio. The Five Bells lays on live music, ranging from pop to jazz, every Wednesday evening, and if you are planning to stay in the area offers 2 comfortable self-catering units, both with en suite double bedrooms.

Opening Hours: Mon-Fri: 11.00-14.30, 17.30-23.00; Sat: 11.00-15.00, 17.30-23.00; Sun: 12.00-15.00, 19.00-22.30

Food: Available every lunchtime and evening. Specialities are game in season and fish

Credit Cards: All major cards accepted

Facilities: Floodlit beer garden; occasional barbecues; off road parking

Entertainment: Darts; cribbage; dominoes; board games; live music on Wednesday evenings

Local Places of Interest/Activities: Queen Elizabeth Country Park, 2 miles; Butser Ancient Farm, 4 miles; Uppark (NT), 6 miles

176   The French Horn

The Butts, Alton,
Hampshire GU34 1RT
Tel/Fax: 01420 83269

Directions:

Alton is just off the A31 Guildford to Winchester road, about 20 miles southwest of Guildford. The French Horn is located on the edge of the town, overlooking The Butts.

Surrounded by hop fields and some of Hampshire's loveliest countryside, Alton is an appealing market town with a history stretching back far beyond Roman times. It has an impressive, partly-Norman church which was the setting for a dramatic episode during the Civil War. Some 80 Royalists sought refuge in the church from a large force of Roundheads. A pitched battle took place inside, with the Royalist commander making a last stand from the splendid Jacobean pulpit. Sixty Royalists were killed. The church door and several of the Norman pillars are still pock-marked with bullet holes.

Almost exactly 100 years after that incident, in 1746, the two cottages that now form **The French Horn** were built. It was apparently named after the owners of the old cottages, Frenchie, with the 'Horn' derived from Hern, or Heron. The interior is delightfully olde worlde with lots of beams and inglenook fireplaces. An interesting feature is the upright Aquarium in the bar. The inn is well known for its excellent food, served either in the separate restaurant, in the bar, or outside in one of the two gardens. (Children are welcome in one of them; the other is known as the 'Quiet Garden'). It's always a good idea to book ahead if you want to eat in the restaurant. The inn has its own, separate, skittle alley and once a year mine hosts Helen and Nigel Collins hold an Old Fashioned Cricket Day with barbecues and a jazz band in attendance. If you are planning to stay in this attractive part of the county, there are two well-equipped chalets to let, both doubles, which are available either on a self-catering or a bed & breakfast basis.

Opening Hours: Lunchtime and evening sessions

Food: A la carte meals & bar snacks

Credit Cards: All major cards accepted except Amex

Accommodation: 2 chalets, both doubles, available for self-catering or B&B

Facilities: Two beer gardens (one for children); ample parking

Entertainment: Separate skittle alley; Annual Old Fashioned Cricket Day with barbecue & jazz band

Local Places of Interest/Activities: 'Watercress Railway' nearby; Jane Austen's House, Chawton, 3 miles; Gilbert White's house, Selborne, 6 miles

George & Dragon   **177**

Townsend,
Wolverton,
Hampshire RG26 5ST
Tel: 01635 298292
Fax: 01635 297700

Directions:

From the A339 Basingstoke to Newbury road, turn right at the sign to Townsend, Baughurst, Wolverton and Stoney Heath. Townsend is about 1 mile along this road and the George & Dragon is on the right as you enter the village.

Originally built as a farmhouse some 300 years ago, the **George & Dragon** is a charming, whitewashed building with Dutch gables at each end. It was originally part of the Duke of Wellington but had to be sold to pay off death duties. The interior is as inviting as the outside. Lionel and Paula Shore, who have been here since 1985, have enlarged the bar and revealed the pub's natural features, with big log fires and oak beams. There's a games room, with darts and bar billiards, for winter evenings, and a large garden for the summer. In a new building at the rear, Lionel and Paula have built a new skittle alley and function room which is completely self-contained with its own kitchen, toilets and bar with real ales. The room can seat 70 people and accommodate up to 130 for a buffet or dancing. Way back in the 1800s, the George & Dragon was a coaching inn and the old coach house has been skilfully converted into 4 luxury en suite double rooms quite separate from the pub.

Paula is an accomplished cook and her wholesome home cooking includes giant Steak & Kidney Pies, steaks, curries, chilli con carne, and a range of appetising snacks. Specials on the blackboard include venison, fish and vegetarian dishes. Complement your meal with one of the 5 real ales on tap, or a selection from the extensive wine list.

Opening hours: Mon-Sat: 12.00-15.00; 17.30-23.00. Sun: 12.00-15.00; 19.00-22.30

Food: Main meals & bar snacks, lunchtime and evening

Credit Cards: All major cards accepted except Diners

Facilities: Function room accommodating up to 100; large car park

Entertainment: Skittle alley; darts; bar billiards

Accommodation: 4 luxury en suite double rooms

Local places of Interest/Activities: Newbury Race Course, 10 miles; Highclere Castle, 8 miles, Watership Down, 4 miles

Internet/Website: www.georgeanddragon.wolverton.co.uk

178   The George Inn

Frimley Road,
Ash Vale,
Aldershot,
Hampshire
GU12 5PD
Tel/Fax: 01252 543539

Directions:

From the A331 just south of Farnborough, take the B3166 to Ash Vale. After about 1 mile, turn right on the B3411. The George Inn is on this road

One of Ash Vale's most attractive amenities is undoubtedly the Basingstoke Canal which forms its eastern boundary. It was built in 1794 to transport timber and agricultural produce from Basingstoke by way of the Wey navigation and the River Thames to London. When it was supplanted by the railways, the canal fell into disuse for more than a century. Then in 1973 canal enthusiasts began restoration work and today walkers have access to 30 miles of peaceful towpath. The canal is also noted for its wealth of plants and colourful dragonflies.

Just a short walk from the canal, **The George Inn** is a spacious mid-Victorian hostelry that looks very inviting with its white-washed walls and abundance of hanging baskets and window boxes. Mine host here is Ian Roberts and he is also the chef, offering a menu of good, wholesome food that ranges from hearty steaks to freshly prepared sandwiches. Lunch is served from 11.30 to 14.30; evening meals from 17.30 to 19.30, except on Sunday evening. There are always 4 real ales on tap: Courage is permanently available, the others change regularly. Outside, there's a peaceful beer garden where you can enjoy your refreshments in good weather. The inn has 7 letting rooms and guests can stay on either a bed and breakfast or bed, breakfast and evening meal basis.

Opening Hours: All day, every day

Food: Main meals and bar snacks every lunchtime and evening except Sunday evening

Credit Cards: Not accepted

Accommodation: 7 standard rooms (2 twin, 5 single)

Facilities: Beer garden; ample parking

Entertainment: Pool; darts; dominoes; Aunt Sally in summer; quiz on Wednesday evenings; live music or karaoke, each once a month on a Friday

Local Places of Interest/Activities: Fishing, 0.5 miles; Basingstoke Canal, 1 mile; North Downs Way, 3 miles; Guildford Cathedral, 6 miles

The Hen & Chicken Inn ■ 179

Upper Froyle,
nr Alton,
Hampshire
GU34 4JH
Tel: 01420 22115
Fax: 01420 23021

Directions:
From Farnham, take the A31 towards Alton. After about 7 miles, turn right on minor road to Froyle. The Hen & Chicken Inn is well signposted on the right hand side after the turn off

Historically, the area around Froyle was important for hop growing and today hop fields still surround **The Hen & Chicken Inn**. Old documents record that every year on 11th July 1798 until about 1860 the farmers and growers of the district would assemble at the inn for a dinner. The meal evidently provided a basis for business of greater importance, - the laying of wagers on the forthcoming hop crops. The connection with hop growing is recalled by the dried hops swathing the old beams and posts of the inn, with copper kettles, mugs and colanders dotted amongst them.

Your hosts at the Hen & Chicken are Hughen and Joyce Riley who have been in the licensed trade for more than 20 years. Football fans will remember Hughen as a professional footballer playing for Rochdale, Crewe, Bury and Bournemouth. Some of his football memorabilia is on display. Today, his skills are exercised in the kitchen with the aid of 2 chefs. All food is freshly prepared to order and based on produce from local farms, supplemented by fresh fish which is a speciality of the house. Bar food is available throughout the day, and there's also a children's menu. To complement your food, there's a choice of 4 real ales and a wide range of wines from around the world, 9 of which are available by the glass. A lovely garden at the rear and picnic benches on the front patio provide a pleasant alternative for fair weather days.

Opening Hours: Mon-Sat: 11.00-23.00; Sun: 12.00-22.30

Food: A la carte meals available every lunchtime & evening; bar food always available

Credit Cards: All major cards accepted

Facilities: Beer garden at rear; seating at front; large car park

Local Places of Interest/Activities: Bird World, 3 miles; Watercress Railway, Alton, 4 miles; Jane Austen's House, Chawton, 6 miles

180   The Holly Bush

High Street,
Headley,
nr Bordon,
Hampshire
GU35 8PP
Tel: 01428 712211
Fax: 01428 714889

Directions:

From the A3, 11 miles northeast of Petersfield, turn left on the B3002 to Headley (5 miles). The Holly Bush is located in the centre of the village.

Headley is one of those peaceful little English villages which have never hit the headlines, never become involved in any strife or warfare, or suffered any notable disaster. It has a settled, tranquil atmosphere that is very soothing for the visitor.

At the heart of the village is **The Holly Bush**, an impressive late-Victorian building of mellow red brick. Norma and Tony Bishop took over here in late 1999 and very quickly established the inn's reputation for good food, well-tended ales and a welcoming atmosphere. The cuisine on offer is definitely not the usual 'Pub Grub'. Amongst the starters there's an appetising Seafood Basket, Torpedo Prawns (prawns wrapped in filo pastry with sweet & sour sauce), and 'Wings of Fire', - chicken wings marinated in a hot chilli sauce and served with salad. Main courses include a wide range of meat, poultry and fish dishes and if you are a real ale fan, there's a choice of no fewer than 5 brews on tap. Meals can be enjoyed in the 30-seater restaurant, in the lounge or outside in the pleasant beer garden. At the time of writing two guest rooms (1 double, 1 twin) are being refurbished and these should be available in late 2000.

Opening Hours: Every session and all day on Saturday

Food: Main meals and bar snacks available every lunchtime and evening except Sunday evening

Credit Cards: All major cards accepted

Accommodation: 2 rooms (1 double; 1 twin) available late 2000

Facilities: Beer garden; outside bar; small functions catered for; barbecues in summer

Entertainment: Pool; darts; fruit machine; pub quiz alternate Thursdays; food theme nights; occasional discos.

Local Places of Interest/Activities: Bohunt Manor, 6 miles; Gilbert White's house, Selborne, 7 miles; Jane Austen's house, Chawton, 12 miles

The Keepers Arms **181**

Trotton,
Rogate,
Petersfield,
Hampshire GU31 5ER
Tel/Fax: 01730 813724

Directions:

On the A272 about 6 miles east of Petersfield

Trotton is set beside the River Rother, crossed at this point by an impressive five arch bridge. Trottons' 13th Century Church is on the west side of the bridge and **The Keepers Arms** is on a sharp bend to the east of the bridge. (People travelling east often opt to go up the hill and turn around rather than chance the right hand turn !).

Walking in to The Keepers Arms feels rather like walking into someone's living room. The Bar has an oak floor with Turkish rugs and the open fire is surrounded by a number of settees and comfortable leather armchairs. All around you is a selection of ethnic artifacts and momentoes of Steve and Jenny's many years of travelling. At night the whole pub is lit by candles and a huge Moroccan lamp by the fireside.

The extensive menu, which includes imaginative vegetarian dishes, is all written on blackboards and changes daily. As the first West Sussex member of the Campaign for Real Food, everything is cooked fresh on the premises with a number of organic ingredients. From May to September they specialise in a Fresh Seafood Platter on Friday evenings and in the winter The famous Keepers Game Pie is a permanent fixture with many of the ingredients being provided locally and then topped with Jenny's homemade suet crust pastry. As a true freehouse The Keepers Arms serves real ales from local breweries such as Ballards and the Cheriton Brewhouse. Wine lovers will find an excellent selection of wines to interest you including a regularly changing wine of the month. It is advisable to book ahead at all times, especially for the Friday Seafood.

Opening Hours: Tue-Fri, 11.00-15.00, 18.30-23.00; Sat, 12.00-15.00, 18.30-23.00; Sun 12.00-15.00; closed Sun eves and all day Mon; Open Bank Holiday Mon lunch only

Food Served: Full menu served lunch and evenings : Tue-Sat,12.00-14.00, 19.00-21.00; Sun 12.00-14.00

Facilities: Disabled entrance, South facing Terrace & ample parking

Places of interest: Cowdray Ruins; 3 miles, Uppark; 5 miles, Southdowns Way; 3 miles and many other local walks

Internet/Website:
e-mail: stephenoxley@keepersarms.co.uk

182 | The Lamb Inn

Winchester Street,
Andover,
Hampshire
SP10 2EA
Tel/Fax: 01264 323961

Directions:

Andover is just off the A303, 19 miles west of Basingstoke. The Lamb Inn is in the centre of the town

An outstanding landmark in Andover is St Mary's Church which was completely re-built in the 1840s at the personal expense of a former headmaster of Winchester College. The interior is said to have been modelled on Salisbury Cathedral. Equally striking is the classical style Guildhall of 1825 which stands in solitary splendour in the Market Place where markets are still held every Tuesday and Saturday. Two miles east of the town, Finkley Down Farm Park provides a satisfying day out for families with young children, and another good family day out can be enjoyed at the Hawk Conservancy, four miles to the west. With more than 200 birds to see in 22 acres of grounds, the hawk Conservancy offers one of the largest collections of raptors in the world.

Back in Andover, **The Lamb Inn** is known as "the country pub in town", a good description of the traditional atmosphere of this inviting hostelry whose history goes back some 450 years. There are lots of horse brasses and bygones on display, and a real fire for chilly evenings. Turn left from the small entrance hall and you enter the bar, a popular student hang-out; turn right and you step into a cosy little lounge, "just like someone's front room". The landlady at the Lamb is very special, - Léonie Rickard is now in her 80s, has been licensee here for almost 40 years and is also very active in arranging functions for charities. Her right-hand man, John Lancaster, has more than 12 years to his credit. The inn offers a choice of snacks, 'sandwedges' and meals at lunchtimes, Monday to Saturday, with occasional 'Curry Evenings' and other special events.

Opening Hours: Open every session

Food: Available lunchtimes, Mon-Sat

Credit Cards: Not accepted

Facilities: Parking nearby

Entertainment: Darts; board games;

piano; occasional live entertainment

Local Places of Interest/Activities:
Finkley Down Farm Park, 2 miles; Hawk Conservancy, 4 miles; Stonehenge, 16 miles

The Lion Brewery

183

104 Guildford Road, Ash,
Aldershot,
Hampshire GU12 6BT
Tel/Fax: 01252 650486

Directions:

From the A331, east of Aldershot, take the A323 towards Guildford. Ash is about 1 mile along this road

The little town of Ash lies just to the east of Aldershot with the Basingstoke Canal forming its northern edge. Back in 1854, Aldershot was a village of some 800 inhabitants. Then the Army decided to build a major camp here and the population has grown steadily ever since to its present tally of around 55,000. Anyone with an interest in military matters will find the Aldershot Military Museum fascinating. It was the army at Aldershot who became the first aviators in Britain. They used Farnborough Common as their flying field, building their aircraft sheds where the Royal Aircraft Establishment stands today. The exploits of these pioneer airmen are recalled at the Airborne Forces Museum at Farnborough.

The Lion Brewery in Ash has been run by Mike and Susan Armitage since 1980, celebrating their 20 years as mine hosts in September 2000. Their spacious old inn was built in the early 1800s and was a beer and meat only house until after the war. Today it's a popular venue for local people. The Lion Brewery is highly regarded for the quality of the food and ales on offer. Included on the menu are house specials such as Steak & Kidney Pie and Cottage Pie, 'Nice'n'Spicy' chilli con carne, fish and pasta dishes, ploughman's, burgers, jacket potatoes, sandwiches and baguettes. At least 5 real ales are available and meals can be enjoyed either inside or on the secluded patio. The inn has 7 guest rooms situated in the public house or the adjoining cottage.

Opening Hours: All day, every day

Food: Quality bar meals and snacks served all day

Credit Cards: All the major cards

Accommodation: 7 rooms (1 double, 2 twin, 2 three bedded rooms and 2 family rooms) ;

Facilities: Beer garden; patio; separate function room; barbecue facilities

Entertainment: Live music Thursday & weekend evenings; occasional quiz nights; annual Music Festival in aid of charity

Local Places of Interest/Activities: Basingstoke Canal, 0.5 miles; Fishing, 1 mile; North Downs Way, 3 miles; Guildford Cathedral, 6 miles; local golf courses Merrist Wood and Roker Park

Internet/Website:
e-mail michael@armitagej.freeserve.co.uk
website: www.thelionbrewery.co.uk

184 The Rampant Cat

Broad Layings
Woolton Hill, nr Newbury
Hampshire RG20 9TP
Tel: 01635 253474

Directions:

From the A34 just south of Newbury take the A343 to Andover. After short distance turn right to Woolton Hill. After 200yds turn right to Broad Layings. After another 200 yards turn right and The Rampant Cat is on the left.

It's intriguing to speculate about the origins of an inn named **The Rampant Cat**. There he is on the pub sign, a fine beast nattily attired for a night out on the tiles. The inn itself is an attractive building with a shingled upper storey, a patio with picnic tables at the front and a large garden to the rear with lawns and a fish pond. Inside, there's a spacious bar with old beams and an adjoining, non-smoking, fully licensed restaurant. Located just off the A34, the Rampant Cat is conveniently placed for visiting one of Berkshire's top attractions, Highclere Castle. An example of Victorian neo-Gothic architecture at its most exuberant, the castle is the family home of the Earl and Countess of Caernavon. It was present Earl's grandfather who in 1922 was with Howard Carter at the opening of Tutankhamun's tomb. In addition to the flamboyant castle, there's a park landscaped by 'Capability' Brown and a walled garden planted entirely with white blooms. Also close to the Rampant Cat is the Sandham Memorial Chapel with its sublime murals created by Stanley Spencer.

Your hosts here are the Molyneux family, - John and Antoinette, and their son Nigel. They offer an extensive à la carte menu and a specials board which changes regularly. As a sample, you might well find Crock of Pheasant with caramelised oranges and a port wine sauce. Bar meals are also available. Complement your meal with a selection from the lengthy wine list or with a pint of one of the 4 real ales which also change regularly. The Molyneuxs are happy to cater for weddings and other functions.

Opening hours: Mon-Sat 12.00-15.00 (closed Monday lunchtime); 18.00-23.00. Sun 12.00-15.00, 19.00-22.30

Food: Extensive menu which changes regularly. Bar meals. Real ales.

Credit Cards: All major cards accepted

Facilities: Large garden with fish pond, patio and lawns

Entertainment: Quality live music every Thursday

Local places of interest/Activities: Sandham Memorial Chapel (NT), 3 miles; Highclere Castle, 4 miles, Kennet & Avon Canal 4 miles.

The Royal Oak 185

Goodworth Clatford
Andover
Hampshire SP11 7QY
Tel: 01264 324105
Fax: 01264 323280

Directions:

From the A303 at Andover, turn south on the A3057 towards Stockbridge. Take the 3rd turning to the right, signposted to Goodworth Clatford (0.5 mile)

During World War II, the airfield at Middle Wallop, about 4 miles away, was a major base for Spitfires and Hurricanes. The area became a prime target during the Blitz and it was during one of the air raids that the old **Royal Oak** was completely destroyed. It was rebuilt in 1950 and has recently been thoroughly refurbished and given an attractive decor of Royal blue and cream. The inn boasts an outstanding garden, - about half an acre in all with lawns, shrubs and rose borders. There's a safe play area for children and a BBQ site for warm summer evenings.

The Royal Oak is well known locally for the excellence of its cuisine, created by chef/patron Jon Hawes. Jon regularly changes his menus, "to avoid menu fatigue" he says, but you'll always find a very wide choice of wholesome, freshly prepared food. Starters include a home made soup, Hot Mozza Melts, and Mushrooms d'Amour, while the main course options comprise a range of traditional pub fayre, chargrilled dishes, and house specialities such as Tarragon & Honey Chicken or Loin of Tuna. There are separate menus for vegetarians and for children. Children can also order half portions of some of the main dishes. Guests can enjoy their meals either in the restaurant or more informally in the bar areas. Jon always has 4 real ales on tap, (they change regularly), and also offers really well-chosen wine list, - Jon and his family spent three days tasting different wines before arriving at their final selection!

Opening hours: Summer: Mon-Sun 11.00-23.00. Winter: Mon-Sun 11.00-14.30, 18.30-23.00

Food: Traditional Pub Fayre, light meals & snacks. Vegetarian choices; children's menu

Credit Cards: Visa, Mastercard, Switch

Parking: Ample, to the front and side

Facilities: Games Room, patio & Beer

Garden, play area, BBQ area

Entertainment: Occasional theme nights, Thursday

Local Places of Interest/Activities:
Andover, 2 miles; Museum of Army Flying, Middle Wallop (4 miles); Danebury Ring Iron Age hill fort, 5 miles; Hawk Conservancy, Monxton, 5 miles. Walking in the Test Valley

186 The Star Inn

Church Street,
Bentworth, Alton,
Hampshire
GU34 5RD
Tel: 01420 561224

Directions:

From Alton take the A339 towards Basingstoke. About 4 miles along this road, turn left on a minor road signposted to Bentworth (1 mile). Follow this road to a T-junction and turn left. At the next mini-roundabout you will find The Star Inn.

One of the most popular visitor attractions in this corner of Hampshire is the home of a humble curate in the little village of Selborne. Gilbert White was the parish priest here from 1784 until his death in 1793. He spent his spare hours meticulously recording observations on the weather, wild-life and geology of the area. Rather surprisingly, a publisher to whom Gilbert submitted his notes recognised the appeal of his humdrum, day-to-day accounts of life in what was then a remote corner of England. *The Natural History and Antiquities of Selborne* was first published in 1788 and has never been out of print.

Also well worth visiting is **The Star Inn** at the heart of Bentworth village. This appealing old hostelry was built as an inn in 1841 and has been dispensing hospitality ever since. The interior has lots of character with ancient beams, quarry tiled floor and real fires. An interesting feature is the array of cabinets displaying an extensive collection of cricket club ties. Yours hosts at The Star, Karen and Matt, offer an appetising menu with fish dishes as the speciality of the house. The regular menu is supplemented by daily specials but if you still can't find exactly what you want just ask, - Karen and Matt will do their best to accommodate you. Tuesday is Curry Night at The Star with a different curry each week, and there are special prices for steaks Monday to Friday. The inn offers a choice of at least 3 real ales and if you are lucky with the weather you can enjoy your refreshments in the peaceful beer garden.

Opening Hours: Open every session

Food: Quality food available every lunchtime & evening; fish dishes a speciality

Credit Cards: All major cards accepted

Facilities: Beer garden; children welcome; off road parking

Entertainment: Darts; dominoes; live music on Friday nights; occasional barbecues

Local Places of Interest/Activities: 'Watercress Line' steam railway, 5 miles; Jane Austen's house, Chawton, 6 miles; Gilbert White's house, Selborne, 9 miles

The Temple Inn 187

82 Forest Road,
Liss Forest, Liss,
Hampshire
GU33 7BP
Tel: 01730 892134

Directions:

From Petersfield, take the A3 north. Five miles along this road, at the roundabout, take the B3006 to Liss (1.5 miles). In the centre of Liss, follow the signs for Liss Forest. The Temple Inn is on this road.

There was a settlement at Liss long before the Romans arrived. Flint arrowheads, spearheads and axes have all been uncovered nearby but the strangest artefact to be unearthed was the hollowed-out trunk of a tree in which lay a hard black lump resembling a piece of coal. After it had been indoors for some time, however, the 'coal' gradually unfurled itself and proved to be the hair of a woman. It was estimated that the lady who owned these ebony tresses had been buried in her tree-coffin some 2500 years ago.

The Temple Inn's history doesn't stretch back quite that far. It was built in 1871 as The Temple Inn and its pub sign shows a knight who is believed to represent Richard the Lionheart. Inside, gleaming horse brasses are displayed along the walls and around the frames, and an interesting feature is a collection of lovely old vases on display. Landlady Anne Manning is also the chef here, offering a quality menu of home cooked food every lunchtime and evening except on Mondays (unless it's a Bank Holiday). Lunch is served from noon until 2pm; dinner from 6.30 to 9.45 (later at weekends). Guests can take their meal in the separate restaurant, in the lounge or outside in the peaceful garden which is also a safe place for children. The inn boasts its own petanque court and hosts a Pub Quiz on the first Sunday of each month. Occasionally, there also live music evenings.

Opening Hours: Every session; all day Wed, Sat & Sun

Food: Available every lunchtime and evening, except Mondays (unless it's a Bank Holiday)

Credit Cards: Not accepted, cash or cheque only

Facilities: Spacious beer garden; petanque court; children welcome; off road parking

Entertainment: Pub Quiz, first Sunday of the month; occasional live music

Local Places of Interest/Activities: Golf, 5 miles; Gilbert White's house, Selborne, 5 miles; Bohunt Manor, 6 miles; Hollycombe Steam, 8 miles

188   The White Hart

20 College Street,
Petersfield,
Hampshire
GU31 4AD
Tel: 01730 262270

Directions:

Petersfield is just off the A3, about 24 miles southwest of Guildford. The White Hart is in the centre of the town

An appealing market town, Petersfield is dominated by the bulk of Butser Hill, 900ft high and the loftiest point of the South Downs. On a clear day the view extends some 40 miles to the spire of Salisbury Cathedral. In the Square there's an equestrian statue of William III, incongruously garbed in Roman costume. Unusually, the statue is made of lead. A visit to the Flora Twort Gallery is highly recommended. Flora moved to Petersfield at the end of World War I and her delightful paintings and drawings capture life in the town over some 40 years, - "reminders of some of the things we have lost" she said shortly before her death at the age of 91 in 1985.

When Lynne-Marie and Philip Beckett arrived at **The White Hart** in the late spring of 2000, the inn was in a parlous state. In an incredibly short time they effected a transformation and their pub now offers an excellent choice of food and drink in stylish and comfortable surroundings. There's a delightful conservatory restaurant overlooking the garden which has a secure children's play area. For anyone who appreciates superbly prepared fresh fish dishes, a visit to the White Hart is a treat but the menu also includes a good range of meat, poultry and vegetarian options, and there are always at least 4 real ales on tap. (The Becketts are in the course of converting the adjoining building to provide quality accommodation, probably by late 2000).

Opening Hours: Mon-Fri: lunchtime & evening; Sat-Sun: all day

Food: Available every lunchtime, and evenings Mon-Sat. Seafood a speciality

Credit Cards: All major cards accepted

Accommodation: rooms available towards end of 2000

Facilities: Conservatory restaurant; secluded beer garden; safe children's play area; barbecues in summer; parking

Entertainment: Quiz Night on Thursdays

Local Places of Interest/Activities: South Downs Way, 3 miles; Queen Elizabeth Country Park, 4 miles; Uppark (NT), 5 miles; Gilbert White's House, Selborne, 7 miles

7 South Hampshire

PLACES OF INTEREST:

PUBS AND INNS:

The Hidden Inns of the South of England

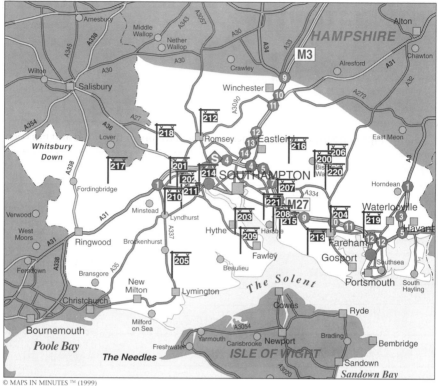

© MAPS IN MINUTES ™ (1999)

200 The Chase Inn, Waltham Chase	**210** The Mailmans Arms, Lyndhurst
201 The Compass Inn, Winsor, nr Cadnam	**211** The New Forest Hotel, Ashurst
202 The Gamekeeper, Woodlands, nr Southampton	**212** The Old House at Home, Romsey
203 Gleneagles, Butts Ash, nr Hythe	**213** The Osborne View, Fareham
204 The Gordon Arms, Fareham	**214** The Peg & Carrot, Totton
205 The Hobler Inn, Battramsley, nr Lymington	**215** The Rising Sun, Warsash
206 The Hunters Inn, Swanmore, nr Bishops Waltham	**216** The Robin Hood Inn, Durley
207 The Jolly Sailor, Old Bursledon	**217** The Royal Oak, Fritham, nr Lyndhurst
208 The Ketch Rigger, Hamble	**218** The Shoe Inn, Plaitford, nr Romsey
209 The Langley Tavern, Blackfield, nr Southampton	**219** Uncle Toms Cabin, Cosham
	220 The Vintage Inn, Shedfield, nr Wickham
	221 Ye Olde Whyte Harte, Hamble

Please note all cross references refer to page numbers

South Hampshire

A goodly proportion of Hampshire's 1.2 million inhabitants live along the coastal crescent that stretches from Southampton through Portsmouth to Havant. Inland, though, there are parts of the South Downs as peaceful and scenic as anywhere in the county.

Southampton boasts one of the finest natural harbours in the world and has been the leading British deep-sea port since the days of the Norman Conquest. Portsmouth did not develop as a port until the 16th century but makes up for its shorter history by its romantic associations with such legendary ships as HMS Victory, the Mary Rose, and HMS Warrior. Portsmouth is also a popular seaside resort providing, together with its neighbour, Hayling Island, some seven miles of sandy beaches. Southsea Castle and the massive Portchester Castle have interesting historical associations, and the ruins of Netley Abbey and the Bishop's Palace at Bishop's Waltham are both outstandingly picturesque.

Like most major ports, Southampton and Portsmouth have something of a cosmopolitan air about them, making an intriguing contrast with the rural charms of the inland villages.

The New Forest, as is the way with English place-names, is neither New nor a Forest, although much of it is attractively wooded. Some historians believe that 'Forest' is a corruption of an ancient British word, gores or gorest, meaning waste or open ground. 'Gorse' comes from the same root word. The term New Forest came into use after William the Conqueror proclaimed the area a royal hunting ground, seized some 15,000 acres that Saxon farmers had laboriously reclaimed from the heathland, and began a programme of planting thousands of trees. To preserve wildlife for his sport, (the deer especially), William adopted all the rigorous venery laws of his Saxon royal predecessors and added some harsh measures of his own. Anyone who killed a deer would himself be killed. If he shot at the beast and missed, his hands were cut off. And, perhaps most ruthless of all, anyone who disturbed a deer during the breeding season had his eyes put out.

There are still plenty of wild deer roaming the 145 square miles of the Forest Park, confined within its boundaries by cattle grids, (known to Americans as Texas Gates). You are much more likely though to see the famous New Forest ponies, free-wandering creatures which nevertheless are all privately owned. They are also something of a hazard for drivers, so do take care, especially at night.

The largest wild area in lowland Britain, the Forest is ideal walking country with vast tracts virtually unpopulated but criss-crossed by a cat's cradle of footpaths and bridle-ways. The Forestry Commission has also established a network of waymarked cycle routes which make the most of the scenic attractions and are also designed to help protect the special nature of the Forest. A map detailing the cycle network is available, along with a vast amount of other information about the area, from the New Forest Museum and Visitor Centre in Lyndhurst. Visitors can watch an audio visual show, see life-sized models of Forest characters, make use of its Resource Centre and Library, and explore a gift shop specialising in locally made Forest crafts.

BEAULIEU

The ruins of a 13th century Cistercian Abbey, a stately home which grew up around the Abbey's imposing gatehouse, and the **National Motor Museum** sited in its grounds are three good reasons why the village of Beaulieu has become one of the county's major visitor attractions. When Lord Montagu of Beaulieu first opened his family home to the public in the 1950s, he organised a display of a few vintage motor vehicles in homage to his father who had been a pioneer of motoring in Britain. That modest clutch of cars has now expanded to include some 250 of the oldest, newest, slowest and fastest motor-cars and bikes in British motoring history, plus some rare oddities. The motoring theme is continued in fun features such

National Motor Museum, Beaulieu

as Go Karts, Miniature Motors, and 'Fast Trax', described as the 'best in virtual racing simulators'.

It was an ancestor of Lord Montagu, the 2nd Duke of Montagu, who created the picturesque riverside village of **Buckler's Hard** in the early 1700s. It was designed as an inland port to receive and refine sugar from the Duke's West Indian estates and His Grace planned his model village on a grand scale: the streets, for example, were to be 80ft wide. Unfortunately, the enterprise failed and only a single street was built. That 18th century street remains intact and unspoiled, and one of its buildings has been converted into a **Maritime Museum** reflecting the subsequent history of the village when it became a ship-building centre. More than 50 naval ships were built at Buckler's Hard, amongst them one of Nelson's favourite ships, the *Agamemnon*.

Just across the Beaulieu River from Buckler's Hard, as the crow flies, is **Exbury Gardens**. By road, that's about a 10-mile detour but one which is definitely worth making. One visitor described the Exbury Gardens as "Heaven with the gates open". Created by Lionel de Rothschild in the 1920s, Exbury is still run by his descendants, Mr & Mrs Edmund de Rothschild. They welcome visitors to share their own appreciation of these spectacular gardens where you can wander through some 200 acres of breathtakingly landscaped displays of noble trees, shrubs and botanical rarities.

BISHOP'S WALTHAM

Bishop's Waltham is a charming and historic small town. It was the country residence of the Bishops of Winchester for centuries and through the portals of their sumptuous **Palace** have passed at least 12 reigning monarchs. Amongst them were Richard the Lionheart returning from the Crusades, Henry V mustering his army before setting off for Agincourt, and Henry VIII entertaining Charles V of Spain (then the most powerful monarch in Europe) to a lavish banquet. The Palace's days of glory came to a violent end during the Civil War when Cromwell's troops battered most of it to the ground. The last resident Bishop was forced to flee, concealing himself beneath a load of manure. The ruins remain impressive, especially the Great Hall with its 3-storey tower and soaring windows. The Palace is now in the care of English Heritage and entrance is free.

The town itself offers visitors a good choice of traditional and specialist shops, amongst them a renowned fishmonger, butcher, baker - even a candle-maker. And just north of the town you can visit one of the country's leading vineyards.

South of Bishop's Waltham, at **Waltham Chase, Jhansi Farm Rare Breed Centre** is dedicated to the conservation of rare breed farm animals, some of them critically endangered. The Farm has a pets' corner housing a large variety of pure bred rabbits, guinea pigs, chipmunks and birds, a souvenir and pet shop, tea room, picnic and play area, nursery and water gardens, with events such as sheep shearing and hand spinning taking place throughout the season.

HAMBLE

Famous throughout the world as a yachting centre, Hamble takes its name from the river, a mere 10 miles long, that flows past the village into **Southampton Water**. Some 3,000 vessels have berths in the **Hamble Estuary**, so there's an incredible variety of boats thronging the river during the season, anything from vintage barges to the sleekest of modern craft.

Anyone interested in England's industrial heritage should travel a couple of miles north from Hamble to **Bursledon**. Ships have been built here since medieval times, the most famous being the *Elephant*, Nelson's flagship at the Battle of Copenhagen. The yard where it was built, now renamed the Elephant Boatyard is still in business. On a rise to the north of the village stands **Bursledon Windmill**, the only working windmill in Hampshire. Built in 1814 at a cost of £800, its vanes ground to a halt during the great agricultural depression of the 1880s. Happily, all the machinery remained intact and after a lengthy restoration between 1976 and 1991, the sails are revolving once again whenever a good northerly or southerly wind is blowing, producing stoneground flour for sale. The windmill is open to visitors at weekends, or whenever the sails are turning! Tel: 01703 404999.

The village can boast yet another unique industrial site. When **Bursledon Brickworks** was established in 1897 the machinery installed was at the very forefront of brickmaking technology. The works closed in 1974 but a Charitable Trust has now restored its gargantuan machines, thus preserving the last surviving example of a steam-driven brickworks in the country. More details on 01489 576248.

Heritage of a different kind can be found a couple of miles northwest of Hamble, at ruined **Netley Abbey** (English Heritage), a wonderfully serene spot surrounded by noble trees. "These are not the ruins of Netley" declared Horace Walpole in the mid-1700s, "but of Paradise". Jane Austen was equally entranced by the Abbey's romantic charm and she made many visits. Dating back to 1300, the extensive ruins provide a spectacular backdrop for open air theatre performances during the summer.

HAYLING ISLAND

A traditional family resort for more than a century, Hayling Island manages to provide all the usual seaside facilities without losing its rural character. Much of the foreshore is still open ground with wandering sand dunes stretching well back from the 4-mile long shingle beach. Bathing is safe here and West Beachlands even boasts a European Blue Flag which is only awarded to beaches meeting 26 environmental criteria. One of Hayling's more unusual beach facilities is the line of old-fashioned beach huts all of which are available to rent.

Hayling is something of a Mecca for board sailors. Not only does it provide the best sailing in the UK for beginners and experts alike, it is also the place where board-sailing was invented. Many places claim that honour but Peter Chilvers has a High Court ruling to prove it. In 1982 a Judge decided that Mr Chilvers had indeed invented the sailboard at Hayling in 1958. As a boy of ten, he used a sheet of plywood, a tent fly-sheet, a pole and some curtain rings to sail up an island creek.

LYNDHURST

The most striking building in this compact little town is the **Church of St Michael**, rebuilt in mid-Victorian times in what John Betjeman described as 'the most fanciful, fantastic Gothic style that I ever have seen'. The rebuilding coincided with the heyday of the Pre-Raphaelite movement so the church contains some fine stained glass by Burne-Jones, produced by the firm of William Morris, as well as a splendidly lush painting by Lord Leighton of *The Wise and Foolish Virgins*.

In St Michael's churchyard is the Grave of Alice Liddell who, as a young girl, was the inspiration for Lewis Carroll's Alice in Wonderland. As Mrs Reginald Hargreaves, Alice lived all her married life in Lyndhurst and was very active in local affairs.

Next to the church is the **Queen's House** which rather confusingly is re-named the King's House whenever the reigning sovereign is male. Originally built as a royal hunting lodge, its medieval and Tudor elements are still visible. Many Kings and Queens have lodged here and the last monarch to stay, George III, graciously allowed loyal villagers to watch through the

194

window as he ate dinner. The House is now the headquarters of the Forestry Commission and is also home to the Verderer's Court, an institution dating back to Norman times which still deals with matters concerning the forest's ancient commoning rights.

This little town is noted for its variety of small shops where you can find "anything from fresh food to Ferraris!" Many are located in the High Street, an attractive thoroughfare of mostly Edwardian buildings, which gently slopes down the hill to Bolton's Bench, a tree-crowned knoll where grazing ponies can usually be found and there are excellent views over Lyndhurst and the surrounding forest. At the other end of the town, **Swan Green**, surrounded by picturesque thatched cottages, provides a much-photographed setting where cricket matches are held in summer.

MILFORD-ON-SEA

This sizeable coastal village is most notable for its fine, remarkably well-preserved 13th century Church of All Saints, its grand views across The Solent to the Isle of Wight, and the odd-looking construction called **Hurst Castle**. At the centre of Hurst Castle is a squat fort built by Henry VIII to guard the Solent entrance against incursions by the French. Its tower is flanked by two long low wings added in the 1860s for gun emplacements, the square openings making them look rather like shopping arcades. The Castle was used as a garrison right up until World War II but is now in the care of English Heritage which has an on-site exhibition explaining its history.

Hurst Castle stands at the tip of a long gravel spit which stretches out across the Solent to within three quarters of a mile of the Isle of Wight coast. It can only be reached by a mile and a half walk along the shingle beach, or by ferries operated by Hurst Castle Ferry & Cruises at Keyhaven Quay, one mile east of Milford on Sea.

MINSTEAD

The village of Minstead offers two interesting attractions, one of which is the **Church of All Saints**. During the 18th century, the gentry and squirearchy of Minstead seem to have regarded church attendance as a necessary duty which, nevertheless, should be made as agreeable as

possible. Three of the village's most affluent residents paid to have the church fabric altered so that they could each have their own entrance door leading to a private "parlour", complete with open fireplace and comfortable chairs. The squire of Minstead even installed a sofa on which he could doze during the sermon. It's easy to understand his concern since these sermons were normally expected to last for at least an hour; star preachers seem to have thought they were short-changing their flock if they didn't prate for at least twice as long. It was around this time that churches began introducing benches for the congregation.

Admirers of the creator of Sherlock Holmes, Sir Arthur Conan Doyle, will want to pay their respects at his grave in the churchyard here. A puzzle worthy of Sir Arthur's great detective is the idiosyncratic sign outside the Trusty Servant pub in the village. Instead of showing, as one might expect, a portrait of a dutiful domestic, the sign actually depicts a liveried figure with the feet of a stag and the face of a pig, its snout clamped by a padlock. A 10-line poem underneath this peculiar sign explains that the snout means the servant will eat any old scraps, the padlock that he will tell no tales about his master, and the stag's feet that he will be swift in carrying his master's messages.

Minstead's other main attraction is **Furzey Gardens**, eight acres of delightful, informal landscape with extensive views over the New Forest towards the Isle of Wight. Beautiful banks of azaleas and rhododendrons, heathers and ferns surround an attractive water garden, and amongst the notable species growing here are incandescent Chilean Fire Trees and the strange 'Bottle Brush Tree'.

NEW MILTON

If you were allowed to see only one visitor attraction in New Milton, you would have a difficult choice. One option is the town's splendid **Water Tower** of 1900. Late-Victorian providers of water services seem to have enjoyed pretending that their storage towers and sewage treatment plants were really castles of the Middle Ages. They built these mock-medieval structures all around the country, but the one at New Milton is particularly striking. Three storeys high, with a castellated parapet, the octagonal building has tall, narrow windows - ideal for Water Authority archers seeing off customers who have dared to dispute their water bill.

Devotees of vintage motor-cycles will make for a very different attraction: the **Sammy Miller Museum** to the west of the town, widely regarded as one of the best motorcycle museums in the world. Sammy Miller is a legend in his own lifetime, still winning competitions almost half a century after his first racing victory. More than 200 rare and classic motorcycles are on display here.

If you are more interested in the arts, you'll be pleased to hear about **Forest Arts** in New Milton. Hampshire is particularly fortunate in having a network of arts centres that specialises in bringing their audiences something 'just that little bit different'. Forest Arts is a typical example, a very busy multi-artform venue and a unique venue for the arts activities on offer in the New Forest District.

PORTSMOUTH

Currently, any brochure promoting Portsmouth always adds the words "Flagship City". With good reason, since the port is home to the most famous flagship in naval history, *HMS Victory*. From the outside it's a majestic, three-masted ship: inside it's creepily claustrophobic, except for the Admiral's and Captain's spacious, mahogany-panelled quarters. Visitors can pace the very same deck from which Nelson masterminded the decisive encounter with the French navy off Cape Trafalgar in 1805. Standing on this deck, ostentatiously arrayed in the gorgeous uniform of a British Admiral of the Fleet, Nelson presented a clear target to a sharp-sighted French sniper. The precise spot where Nelson fell and the place on the sheltered orlop (lowest) deck where he died are both marked by plaques.

The death of Nelson was a tragedy softened by a halo of victory: the loss of the *Mary Rose*, some 260 years earlier was an unmitigated disaster. Henry VIII had ordered the ship, the second largest in his fleet, to be built. He was standing on Southsea Common above Portsmouth in 1545, watching the *Mary Rose* manoeuvre, when it suddenly heeled over and sank. All seven hundred men on board drowned. "And the King he screeched right out like any maid, 'Oh, my gentlemen! Oh, my gallant men!'" More than four centuries later, in 1982, the hulk of the *Mary Rose* was carefully raised from the seabed where it had lain for so long. Some seventeen years after that recovery, its oak frame is still drying out, the impressive remains now housed in the timber-clad **Mary Rose Museum** and open to visitors.

Another ship you can see at Portsmouth doesn't possess the same historical glamour as the *Victory* or the *Mary Rose*, but *HMS Warrior* merits a visit because when this mighty craft was commissioned in 1860, she was the Navy's first ironclad warship. A great advance in technology, but the distinctions between the officers' and crew accommodation show little difference from those obtaining in Nelson's day.

Like Southampton, Portsmouth suffered badly during World War II, losing most of its 17th and 18th century buildings. **St George's Church**, a handsome Georgian building of 1754 with large galleries, was damaged by a bomb but has been fully restored, and just to the north of the church, the barn-like **Beneficial Boy's School**, built in 1784, is another survivor. One of the most interesting buildings is to be found in Southsea, the city's resort area. **Southsea Castle** was built in 1544 as one of Henry VIII's series of forts protecting the south coast from French attacks. It has been modified several times since then but the original Keep is still intact and there are good views across the Solent from the gun platforms.

Portsmouth also offers visitors a wealth of varied museums, three of which deserve special mention. The **Royal Armouries**, housed in the huge Victorian Fort Nelson, claims to be 'Britain's Loudest Museum', with live firings every day; the **Charles Dickens Birthplace Museum** at 393, Old Commercial Road, has been restored and furnished to show how the house looked when the great novelist was born here in 1812; and the **D-Day Museum** in Southsea commemorating the Allied invasion of Europe in 1944 and most notable for the 83 metre long Overlord Tapestry, a 20th century equivalent of the Bayeux Tapestry which is well worth seeing.

Standing at the head of Portsmouth Harbour, **Portchester Castle** is not only the grandest medieval castle in the county but also stands within the best-preserved site of a Roman fort in northern Europe. Sometime around 280 AD, the Romans enclosed 8 acres of this strategic headland and used it as a base for their ships clearing the Channel of pirates. The original walls of the fort were 20ft high and 10ft thick, their depth much reduced by local people pillaging the stone for their own buildings.

The medieval castle dates back to 1120 although the most substantial ruins are those of the royal palace built for Richard II between 1396 and 1399. Richard was murdered in 1399 and never saw his magnificent castle. Also within the walls of the Roman enclosure is **Portchester Church**, a superb Norman construction built between 1133 and 1150 as part of an Augustinian Priory. For some reason, the Priors moved inland to Southwick, and the church remained disused for more than five and a half centuries until Queen Anne personally donated £400 for its restoration. Apart from the east end, the church is entirely Norman and, remarkably, its 12th century font of wondrously carved Caen stone has also survived the centuries.

RINGWOOD

Wednesday morning is a good time to visit Ringwood, since that is when its market square is filled with a notable variety of colourful stalls. The town has expanded greatly in recent years but its centre still boasts a large number of elegant Georgian houses, both large and small. **Ringwood Meeting House**, built in 1727 and now a Museum, is an outstanding example of an early Nonconformist chapel, complete with the original, rather austere, fittings. **Monmouth House** is of about the same period and stands on the site of an earlier house in which the luckless Duke of Monmouth was confined after his unsuccessful uprising against James II. The Duke had been discovered hiding in a ditch just outside the town and despite his abject pleas to the King to spare his life he was beheaded at Tower Hill a few days later.

Five miles west of the town stretch the great expanses of **Ringwood Forest**, which includes the **Moors Valley Country Park**. Since this area lies across the River Avon and is therefore in East Dorset, it really belongs in the next chapter but its landscape makes it clearly part of the New Forest. One of the most popular attractions in the Moors Valley Country Park is the **Moors Valley Railway**, a delightful narrow gauge steam railway with rails just 7¼ inches apart. The railway has eleven locomotives, all in different liveries, and 33 passenger vehicles. At busy periods, there may be up to six trains on the track so signalling is taken seriously and strictly controlled in accordance with British Rail procedures. The signal box at Kingsmere, the main station, was purpose-built but all the equipment inside comes from old redundant signal boxes - the main signal lever frame for example came from the Becton Gas Works in East London. At Kingsmere Station, in addition to the Ticket Office and the Engine and Carriage Sheds, there's also a Railway Shop, Buffet and Model Railway Shop. The route southwards runs alongside the Moors Lake, a manmade feature which also serves as a flood diversion area when the River Moors, notorious for causing flooding in the area, is running high. The southern terminus of the railway is at Lakeside Station where there's a Visitor Centre, Information Point, Tearoom and Country Shop.

A mile or so south-east of Ringwood, in the hamlet of **Crow**, the **New Forest Owl Sanctuary** is home to the largest collection of owls in Europe, housed in more than 100 aviaries. There are flying displays, both inside and out, daily lectures to entertain visitors of all ages, a café and shop. In the hospital units Bruce Berry, founder of the sanctuary, and his dedicated staff have prepared hundreds of birds for release back into the world. The Sanctuary is open daily from March to November; weekends only during the winter.

ROMSEY

"Music in stone", and "the second finest Norman building in England" are just two responses to **Romsey Abbey**, a majestic building containing some of the best 12th and 13th century architecture to have survived. Built between 1120 and 1230, the Abbey is remarkably complete. Unlike so many monastic buildings which were destroyed or fell into ruin after the Dissolution, the Abbey was fortunate in being bought by the town in 1544 for £100. Subsequent generations of townspeople have carefully maintained their bargain purchase. The

Romsey Abbey

Abbey's most spectacular feature is the soaring Nave which rises more than 70ft and extends for more than 76ft. Amongst the Abbey's many treasures is the Romsey Rood which shows Christ on the cross with the hand of God descending from the clouds.

Just across from the Abbey, in Church Court, stands the town's oldest dwelling, King John's House, built around 1240 for a merchant. It has served as a royal residence but not, curiously, for King John who died some 14 years before it was built. He may though have had a hunting lodge on the site. The house is now a museum and centre for cultural activities.

Romsey's most famous son was undoubtedly the flamboyant politician Lord Palmerston, three times Prime Minister during the 1850s and 1860s. Palmerston lived at Broadlands, just south of the town, and is commemorated by a bronze statue in the town's small triangular Market Place.

In addition to its Abbey, Romsey also boasts one of the finest stately homes in the county, **Broadlands**, a gracious Palladian mansion built by Lord Palmerston's father in the mid-1700s. The architect was Henry Holland, the landscape was modelled by the ubiquitous 'Capability'

Broadlands, Nr Romsey

Brown. The important collections of furniture, porcelain and sculpture were acquired by the 2nd Viscount Palmerston. The house passed to the Mountbatten family and it was Lord Louis Mountbatten who first opened Broadlands to the public shortly before he was killed in 1979. The present owner, Lord Romsey, has established the Mountbatten Exhibition in tribute to his grandfather's remarkable career as naval commander, diplomat, and last Viceroy of India. An audio-visual film provides an overall picture of the Earl's life and exhibits include his dazzling uniforms, the numerous decorations he was awarded, and an astonishing collection of the trophies, mementoes and gifts he received in his many rôles.

| SOUTHAMPTON | **197** |

From this historic port, Henry V set sail for Agincourt in 1415, the Pilgrim Fathers embarked on their perilous journey to the New World in 1620, and, on April 10th, 1912, the Titanic set off on its maiden voyage, steaming majestically into the Solent. The city's sea-faring heritage is vividly recalled at the excellent **Maritime Museum** (free), housed in the 14th century **Wool House**. The museum tells the story of the port from the age of sail to the heyday of the great ocean liners.

As a major sea-port, Southampton was a prime target for air raids during World War II and suffered grievously. But the city can still boast a surprising number of ancient buildings. Substantial stretches of the medieval Town Walls have miraculously survived, its ramparts interspersed with fortifications such as the oddly-named 15th century **Catchcold Tower** and **God's House Gate and Tower**, which now houses the city's archaeological museum. Perhaps the most impressive feature of the walls is **Bargate**, one of the finest medieval city gates in the country. From its construction around 1200 until the 1930s, Bargate remained the principal entrance to the city. Its narrow archway is so low that Southampton Corporation's trams

Bargate, Southampton

had to be specially modified for them to pass through. Inside the arch stands a statue of George III, cross-dressing as a Roman Emperor. Bargate now stands in its own pedestrianised area, its upper floor, the former Guildhall, now a Museum of local history and folklore.

Another remarkable survivor is the **Medieval Merchant's House** in French Street which has been expertly restored and authentically furnished, now appearing just as it was when it was built around 1290. One of the most popular visitor attractions in Southampton is the **Tudor House Museum & Garden**, a lovely 15th

Tudor House Museum, Southampton

century house with an award-winning Tudor Garden complete with fountain, bee skeps and 16th century herbs and flowers.

There's so much history to savour in the city, but Southampton has also proclaimed itself "A City for the New Millennium". West Quay, one of the largest City Centre developments in Europe, is scheduled to open in 2000; a £3.4m injection from the Heritage Lottery Fund will enhance Southampton's already highly acclaimed central parks; the £27m Leisure World offers a wide range of leisure activities; and the new, state-of-the-art Swimming & Diving Complex incorporates separate championship, diving and fun pools.

Another major development is **Ocean Village**, an imaginatively conceived waterfront complex with its own 450-berth marina, un-

dercover shopping, excellent restaurants and a multi-screen cinema.

As you'd expect in a city with such a glorious maritime heritage, there's a huge choice of boat excursions, whether along the River Hamble, around the Solent, or over to the Isle of Wight. Blue Funnel Cruises operate from Ocean Village; Solent Cruises from Town Quay.

The city also occupies an important place in aviation history. A short step from Ocean Village, the **Hall of Aviation** presents the story of aviation in the Solent and incorporates the **R.J. Mitchell Memorial Museum**. Mitchell lived and worked in Southampton in the 1930s and not only designed the Spitfire but also the S6 Seaplane which won the coveted Scheider Trophy. The centrepiece of the Hall of Aviation is the spectacular Sandringham Flying Boat which you can board and sample the luxury of air travel in the past - very different from the Cattle Class standards of today's mass travel.

WINCHESTER

One of the country's most historic cities, Winchester was adopted by King Alfred as the capital of his kingdom of Wessex, a realm which then included most of southern England. There had been a settlement here since the Iron Age and in Roman times, as Venta Belgarum, it became an important military base. **The Brooks Experience**, located within the modern Brooks Shopping Centre, has displays based on excavated Roman remains with its star exhibit a reconstructed room from an early-4th century town-house.

When the Imperial Legions returned to Rome, the town declined until it was refounded by Alfred in the late 800s. His street plan still provides the basic outline of the city centre. A Saxon cathedral had been built in the 7th century but the present magnificent **Cathedral**, easily the most imposing and interesting building in Hampshire, dates back to 1079. It's impossible in a few words to do justice to this glorious building and its countless treasures such as the famous Winchester Bible. Winchester Cathedral boasts the longest nave in Europe, a dazzling 14th century masterpiece in the Perpendicular style, a wealth of fine wooden carvings, and gems within a gem such as the richly decorated Bishop Waynflete's Chantry of 1486. Sumptuous medieval monuments, like the effigy of William of Wykeham, founder of Winchester College, provide a striking contrast to

Winchester Cathedral

and 1236. Nikolaus Pevsner considered it "the finest medieval hall in England after Westminster Hall". Other buildings of interest include the early-14th century Pilgrim Hall (free), part of the **Pilgrim School**, and originally used as lodgings for pilgrims to the shrine of St Swithun, and **Wolvesey Castle** (English Heritage), the residence of the Bishops of Winchester since 963. The present palace is a gracious, classical building erected in the 1680s, flanked by the imposing ruins of its 14th century predecessor which was one of the grandest buildings in medieval England. Also well worth a visit is the 15th century **Hospital of St Cross**, England's oldest almshouse. Founded in 1132 by Henri du Blois, grandson of William the Conqueror, it was extended in 1446 by Cardinal Beaufort, son of John of Gaunt. It is still home to 25 Brothers and maintains its long tradition of hospitality by dispensing the traditional Wayfarer's Dole to any traveller who requests it.

the simple black stone floorslabs which separately mark the graves of Izaak Walton and Jane Austen.

Just south of the Cathedral, on College Street, are two other buildings of outstanding interest. No. 8, College Street, a rather austere Georgian house with a first-floor bay window, is **Jane Austen's House** in which she spent the last six weeks of her life in 1817. The house is private but a slate plaque above the front door records her residence here. Right next door stands **Winchester College**, the oldest school in England, founded in 1382 by Bishop William of Wykeham to provide education for seventy 'poor and needy scholars'. Substantial parts of the 14th century buildings still stand, including the beautiful Chapel. The Chapel is always open to visitors and there are guided tours around the other parts of the College from April to September. If you can time your visit during the school holidays, more of the College is available to view.

Two years after Jane Austen was buried in the Cathedral, the poet John Keats stayed in Winchester and it was here that he wrote his timeless *Ode to Autumn* - "Season of mists and mellow fruitfulness". His inspiration was a daily walk past the Cathedral and College and through the Water Meadows beside the River Itchen. A detailed step-by-step guide to Keats' Walk is available from the Tourist Information Centre.

The city's other attractions are so numerous one can only mention a few of the most important. **The Great Hall**, (free), off the High Street, is the only surviving part of the medieval Castle rebuilt by Henry III between 1222

200 The Chase Inn

Winchester Road,
Waltham Chase,
Southampton,
Hampshire SO32 2LL
Tel: 01489 892229
Fax: 01489 890336

Directions:

Situated on the B2177 Winchester Road at Waltham Chase, between Bishops Waltham and Wickham

A Chase (or Chace) was a piece of land reserved by the Crown or local lord for his own hunting. Waltham Chase was a preserve of the Bishops of Winchester who had their summer palace at nearby Bishop's Waltham. The deer with which the Chase was stocked were a continual nuisance to the labouring tenants whose crops they ate, but it wasn't until the 18th century that the 'Waltham Blacks' appeared. Disguised and with their faces blackened, these young men stole the Bishop's deer and went on to rob stage coaches. Their misdemeanours led to the passing of the 'Black Act' which made scores of crimes punishable by death.

Waltham today is a peaceful enough place, a lively village with a thriving community spirit. At its heart is **The Chase Inn**, a free house owned and run by Chris and Jane Staples. The inn has a separate, non-smoking restaurant offering a menu that changes every fortnight but always includes the specialities of the house, - steaks and fresh fish dishes. In the main bar, there's a good choice of main meals and bar snacks, and a children's menu. Three real ales are on tap and if you are lucky with the weather you can enjoy your drink in the pleasant beer garden, or on the patio. And if you're visiting the bar on a Saturday evening or Sunday lunchtime, swing along with the live music, - mellow jazz and pop numbers from the 40s and 50s. Chris and Jane also arrange themed evenings about once a month when the cuisine is devoted to one particular country.

Opening Hours: All sessions, all day Sat, Sun

Food: Available every lunchtime & evening

Credit Cards: All major cards accepted

Accommodation: 3 rooms available for bed and breakfast

Facilities: Beer garden; patio; barbecues on Bank Holidays; adjacent parking

Entertainment: Live music Sat evening, Sun lunchtime; themed food evenings once a month

Local Places of Interest/Activities: Bishop's Palace, Bishop's Waltham, ½ mile; Marwell Zoo 4 miles; Manor Farm Country Park, 5 miles; Winchester, Portsmouth, Southampton 12 miles

The Compass Inn   201

Winsor Road,
Winsor,
nr Cadnam,
Hampshire
SO40 2HE
Tel: 023 8081 2237

Directions:

From Exit 1 of the M27, take the A336 towards Totton. About 2 miles along this road, turn left on minor road to Winsor (1 mile)

"A riot of colour" may be a cliché but it's really the only way to describe the front of **The Compass Inn** during the summer when the cream-coloured walls are almost smothered with a profusion of hanging baskets, window boxes and tubs. The beer garden at the rear is equally colourful. Beautifully arranged baskets of flowers hang from the covered arbour, some 35ft long, and there's more colour inside in the form of a striking mural painted by a local artist. The interior of this 400-year-old inn continues the floral theme with many dried flower arrangements adding to the period charm of the old beams, wooden floors and cosy atmosphere.

Mop Draper has been running the Compass Inn since 1996 together with her daughter Sophie. During that time, their inn has won many awards and not surprisingly has featured in the ***New Forest Country*** magazine as one of the area's Great Pub Gardens. The inn is also renowned for its food, - good home cooking served in generous portions and at value for money prices. Meals are served every lunchtime and evening, and during the afternoon you can tuck into a Cream Tea, a special Curry Night on Monday evenings, and a British Beef Night on Tuesdays. There are always half a dozen real ales on tap including the local brew, H.S.B. and Ringwood. Booking is strongly advised at the weekends.

Opening Hours: Mon-Sat: 11.00-23.00; Sun: 12.00-22.30

Food: Available every lunchtime & evening; Cream Teas in afternoon

Credit Cards: All major cards accepted

Facilities: Outstanding beer garden; own car park

Entertainment: Irish music, Thursday evenings; Beer festivals on May & August Bank Holidays

Local Places of Interest/Activities: New Forest, 2 miles; City of Southampton, 8 miles; Furzey Gardens, 8 miles

202 | The Gamekeeper

268 Woodlands Road,
Woodlands,
Southampton
SO40 7GH
Tel: 02380 293093

Directions:

From Exit 2 of the M27 take the A326. After about 3 miles, turn right on the A336 towards Cadnam. After about half a mile, turn left on minor road to Woodlands (1.5 miles). As you enter the village you will see The Gamekeeper on the right

This sizeable village stands on the edge of the New Forest, a huge 'lung' extending over 145 square miles that has been protected from development ever since the days of William the Conqueror. The area is covered by a cats-cradle of footpaths, bridleways and, a more recent amenity, a network of waymarked cycle routes. There are plenty of wild deer still roaming the Forest, confined within its boundaries by cattle grids (known to Americans as Texas Gates). But you are much more likely to see the famous New Forest ponies, free-wandering creatures which nevertheless are all privately owned.

The Gamekeeper is a good place to start a tour of the Forest. It's an inviting-looking inn with a history that goes back to the early 1800s when it was called The Royal Oak. There are many olde-worlde features, - low beams, exposed brick pillars, quarry tiled and wooden floors, lots of bygones and a wood-burning stove. But there's also an attractive modern conservatory restaurant, overlooking the well-tended garden. Your hosts here are Heather and Derek Heather is an exceptional cook and her blackboard menu offers a choice of at least 5 daily main course specials, "99.9% of them home made". If you plan to eat here at the weekend, booking is strongly recommended. Real ale fans will find anything from 3 to 5 brews on tap and the inn also stocks a wide range of popular beers, and other brews.

Opening Hours: Mon-Fri: Lunchtime & evening; Sat-Sun: open all day

Food: Available every lunchtime & evening, except Sunday evening

Credit Cards: All major cards accepted

Facilities: Beer garden; patio; children's play area; camping in field to the rear

Entertainment: Jazz once a month; occasional Murder Mystery nights

Local Places of Interest/Activities: Walking/Riding in New Forest; Furzey Gardens, Minstead, 4 miles; National Motor Museum, Beaulieu, 8 miles

Gleneagles

Butts Ash Lane, Butts Ash,
Dibden Purlieu, Hythe,
Southampton,
Hampshire SO45 3RF
Tel: 02380 842162

Directions:

From Exit 2 on the M27, take
the A326 towards Hythe. About
9 miles along this road, you will
come to Dibden Purlieu. Ask for
Butts Ash Lane.

Only the A326 separates Dibden Purlieu from the verdant expanses of the New Forest. The protected parkland stretches for some 15 miles to the east, a sparsely-populated area that provides a peaceful environment for walkers, riders and cyclists. Also within easy reach of the town is the National Motor Museum at Beaulieu. When Lord Montagu of Beaulieu first opened his family home to the public in the 1950s, he organised a display of a few vintage motor vehicles in homage to his father who had been a pioneer of motoring in Britain. That modest clutch of cars has now expanded to include some 250 of the oldest, newest, slowest and fastest motorcars and bikes in British motoring history.

Geoff Mercer's passion is not motoring but golf, which is why he renamed the inn he runs with his wife Sandie, **Gleneagles**. Naturally, there's lots of golfing memorabilia on display, including many cups and trophies that Geoff has won over the years. This is a very family-friendly inn. Not only is there a secure play area outside, complete with trampolines and swings, but also a play zone inside the pub. Adults are also well-provided for, with a choice of lovingly prepared, home made food on offer. The regular Curry Nights are especially popular. In good weather, you can enjoy your meal in the delightful beer garden and if you are a devotee of real ales you'll find up to 4 different brews to choose from. The inn has just won the Whitbread Pub Partnerships Beer Pub of the South for 2000. This lively hostelry also lays on live music every Thursday evening, a quiz on Sunday evenings and many charity events throughout the year.

Opening Hours: Open all day, every day

Food: Available Mon-Fri lunchtimes & evenings, (except Thu evening); Sat-Sun, all day

Credit Cards: All major cards accepted

Facilities: Large beer garden; safe children's play area with trampolines, swings; also children's play zone inside; ample parking

Entertainment: Darts; cribbage; fruit machines; quiz machine; live music, Thursday evenings; Quiz, Sunday evenings; many charity events

Local Places of Interest/Activities: New Forest to the west; National Motor Museum, Beaulieu, 4 miles; Exbury Gardens, 5 miles;

Internet/Website:
e-mail: gleneagles@btinternet.com

204   The Gordon Arms

Gordon Road,
Fareham,
Hampshire
PO16 7TG
Tel: 01329 280545

Directions:

From the M27 at Exit 11 take the A27 to Fareham. The Gordon Arms is in Gordon Road which runs adjacent to Fareham High Street

Jolting horseback along the atrocious roads of Tudor England, this country's first travel writer, John Leland, paused for a moment to record Fareham in the 1540s as a 'fiscar town' (fishing village). Almost half a millennium later, that little fishing village on the northwestern tip of Portsmouth Harbour has burgeoned into an affluent waterside community. Fareham prospered greatly during the 18th century and an extraordinary number of the elegant Georgian buildings constructed during that period have survived, - Fareham's High Street has been authoratively described as the 'finest street in Hampshire'.

A few steps away from the High Street, **The Gordon Arms** is an attractive building with colourful parasol-protected picnic tables on its front patio. One visitor described the interior as "just like my Granny's old front room". He loved his Granny's old front room and so will most visitors to its clone here. Your hosts at this free house are Arthur and Penny Bath. Arthur was born and bred in Fareham; Penny has lived in the area for more than 20 years. They possess a genuine gift for hospitality, a trait which is clearly apparent in the lovingly-prepared meals and friendly service. The Gordon Arms, as the old guide books used to say, is *'well worth a detour'*. (And it's only a few miles from the M27).

Opening Hours: All day, every day

Food: Available from 11am "until Penny gets fed up with cooking"

Credit Cards: Not accepted

Facilities: South facing beer garden; patio

Entertainment: Pool; darts; cribbage; dominoes; chess; live music Saturday evenings; Quiz on Sunday evenings

Local Places of Interest/Activities: Fort Nelson, 4 miles; Manor Farm Country Park, 8 miles; City of Portsmouth, 9 miles;

The Hobler Inn

Southampton Road,
Battramsley,
Lymington,
Hants SO41 8PT
Tel: 01590 623291
Fax: 01590 622857

Directions:

From Exit 1 of the M27, take the A337 through Lyndhurst and Brockenhurst. About 2 miles beyond Brockenhurst you will come to Battramsley, - The Hobler Inn is on the left.

Battramsley sits right on the edge of the New Forest, a village so small it doesn't even have its own church. It does have its own pub though, **The Hobler Inn**, a charming old building in warm red brick. From here you can strike off along one of the countless footpaths, bridleways and cycle paths that criss-cross the New Forest. Keen gardeners will want to pay a visit to the nearby Spinners garden, a superb woodland garden stocked with a fascinating range of choice plants, trees and shrubs.

Inside the Hobler Inn there are three distinct areas. At the front there's a lounge which would remind you of your granny's parlour if it weren't for the fact that walls are papered with music sheets; then a central bar area, and beyond that an area called the Gun Room with settles as seats. The whole inn has a wonderfully relaxing atmosphere and is well known for the quality of food on offer so booking ahead is always advisable. The menu offers something for every palate, with steaks and the pork goulash proving particularly popular. The inn has a good range of real ales on tap and in good weather refreshments can be enjoyed in the spacious beer garden. The owner of the Hobler Inn, Pip Steven, has personally run the pub for more than 15 years and he also owns The Sausage, Pie & Mash House in Lyndhurst which, like the Hobler Inn, is well worth a visit.

Opening Hours: Open every session

Food: Available every lunchtime & evening

Credit Cards: All major cards except Diners

Facilities: Large beer garden; secure children's play area; large car park

Entertainment: Occasional live entertainment

Local Places of Interest/Activities: New Forest to the west & north; Spinners Gardens, 1 mile; Isle of Wight ferry, 3 miles; National Motor Museum, Beaulieu, 7 miles

206 | The Hunters Inn

Cott Street,
Swanmore,
nr Bishops Waltham,
Hampshire
SO32 2PZ
Tel: 01489 877214
Fax: 01489 877418

Directions:

From the A32, about 7 miles north of Fareham, take a minor road to the left, signposted to Swanmore.

A sizeable village flanked by orchards, Swanmore was once surrounded by Bere Forest, a popular place for hunters. It's believed that **The Hunters Inn** was originally built as a shooting lodge. It's a delightful old building, dating back in parts to the 16th century. There has been an alehouse on this site for more than 300 years and the original house is still standing but has been extended many times in its long history. Originally, The Hunters Inn served only the local farmworkers and beer was often hand-delivered to the men working in the fields. During the early 1900s, a lounge bar was built to attract the farmworkers' wives and the local gentry. A dance hall was later added, (now part of the Tavern Bar), and dances held every Saturday night.

The inn acquired a rather dubious reputation during the war years, with coach loads of sailors arriving regularly from Portsmouth, - this led to the loss of the licence for a short period! The Hunters remained a drinking only inn right up to 1969 when Mr Westmacott and his wife took over and added food to the menu. The inn now has an enviable reputation for outstanding home cooked food. It has its own bakery and butchery, ensuring wonderfully fresh bread and pies; fresh fish is also available depending on the day's catch. The menu includes a selection of Smaller Meals and also a 'Kiddies Corner', and you'll always find 3 real ales on tap, as well as a choice of wines from around the world. Mention must also be made of the beautifully laid out beer garden with its pergolas and tiled patio.

Opening Hours: Every session and all day Sat, Sun

Food: Quality home cooked food available every lunchtime & evening

Credit Cards: All major cards accepted

Facilities: Delightful beer garden; children's play area; occasional barbecues; ample parking

Entertainment: Rock & Blues music every Thursday from 21.00

Local Places of Interest/Activities: Kings Way footpath, close by; Bishop's Palace, Bishop's Waltham, 3 miles; Vineyard & Winepress, Hambledon, 7 miles; Manor Farm Country Park, 8 miles

The Jolly Sailor

Lands End Road,
Old Bursledon,
Southampton,
Hampshire
SO31 8DN
Tel: 02380 405557
Fax: 02380 402050

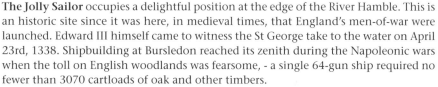

Directions:

Take the A27 from Southampton towards Fareham. In Bursledon, just before the railway bridge, turn right, then left into the railway station car park. From the car park, follow the path signposted to The Jolly Sailor

The Jolly Sailor occupies a delightful position at the edge of the River Hamble. This is an historic site since it was here, in medieval times, that England's men-of-war were launched. Edward III himself came to witness the St George take to the water on April 23rd, 1338. Shipbuilding at Bursledon reached its zenith during the Napoleonic wars when the toll on English woodlands was fearsome, - a single 64-gun ship required no fewer than 3070 cartloads of oak and other timbers.

The Jolly Sailor has been standing on this site since at least Tudor times although the present frontage was built in the days of Queen Anne. Inside, there's a wealth of maritime memorabilia, - a bar with portholes, a lifebelt from the cruise liner *Carmonia*, and many prints and watercolours of sailing craft and of the Hamble. Low-beamed ceilings, stone-flagged floors and old bow windows all add to the charm. The inn is well-known for its fresh fish dishes but you'll also find a good choice of other options available either from the à la carte menu, the chalkboard specials or the bar snacks list. There are 5 real ales on tap and the Jolly Sailor has been awarded a Cask Marque for the quality of its traditional brews. Wine lovers have an excellent choice of wines, (including Olde English wines and liqueurs), and there's a good range of wines available by the glass. You can enjoy your meal either in the cosy bar, in one of the two shady gardens, or on the riverside patio and pier.

Opening Hours: Mon-Sat: 11.00-23.00; Sun: 12.00-22.30

Food: Available from noon until 21.30 every day

Credit Cards: All major cards accepted

Facilities: Waterfront patio & pier; gardens

Entertainment: Only the constantly changing scene on the River Hamble!

Local Places of Interest/Activities: Bursledon Brickworks, 1 mile; Manor Farm Country Park, 1.5 miles; Royal Victoria Country Park, 3 miles

208 The Ketch Rigger

*Hamble Point
Marina,
School Lane,
Hamble,
Hampshire
SO31 4NB
Tel: 02380 455601
Fax: 02380 454642*

Directions:

From Exit 8 of the M27, take the A3025 and then the B3397 to Hamble (4 miles). In Hamble follow the signs for Hamble Point Marina. When you reach the Marina you will see The Ketch Rigger on the quayside.

Famous throughout the world as a yachting centre, Hamble takes its name from the river, a mere 10 miles long, that flows past the village into Southampton Water. Some 3,000 vessels have berths in the Hamble Estuary so there's an incredible variety of boats thronging the river during the season, everything from vintage barges to the sleekest of modern craft. For a contrasting scene, pay a visit to the ruins of Netley Abbey, one of Jane Austen's favourite locations. "These are not the ruins of Netley" declared Horace Walpole in the mid-1700s, "but of Paradise".

The Ketch Rigger is a smart modern building enjoying a harbourside location overlooking the busy Marina. For fairweather days, there's seating outside; inside, the inn is furnished and decorated with a maritime theme. The Ketch Rigger is well known for the quality of its food. Chef Derek Webber has been here 10 years and in catering for more than 30 years. There are separate menus for lunchtimes and evenings but both offer a good selection of meat, fish and vegetarian dishes. On Saturday and Sunday mornings the restaurant is also open from 8.00 until 9.45 for breakfast. The Ketch Rigger is owned and run by John and Susan Nutter who used to own a Flying Club near Southampton. A qualified flying instructor, John still has his own aeroplane and still gives lessons.

Opening Hours: Open all day, most days

Food: Home made food available every lunchtime and evening; also breakfast, Sat & Sun

Credit Cards: All major cards accepted

Facilities: Outside seating; ample parking

Local Places of Interest/Activities:
Bursledon Windmill, 2 miles; Bursledon Brickworks, 2 miles; Netley Abbey (English Heritage), 3 miles

The Langley Tavern | 209

Lepe Road, Blackfield,
Southampton,
Hampshire SO45 1XR
Tel: 02380 891402

Directions:

From Exit 2 of the M27, take the A326 towards Hythe and Fawley. About 11 miles along this road, at the roundabout just before Fawley, turn right onto a minor road to Blackfield. The Langley Tavern is located just half a mile from beach

Blackfield village sits right on the edge of the New Forest with the National Motor Museum at Beaulieu and Exbury Gardens both within easy reach. One visitor described the latter as "Heaven with the gates open". Created by Lionel de Rothschild in the 1920s, Exbury is still run by his descendants, Mr & Mrs Edmund de Rothschild. They welcome visitors to share their own appreciation of these spectacular gardens where you can wander through some 200 acres of breathtakingly landscaped displays of noble trees, shrubs and botanical rarities.

Located only half a mile from The Solent beach, **The Langley Tavern** is an impressive 1930s building set in spacious grounds. Your hosts, René and Hannie Brand, come from Holland where they worked in the hospitality business for more than 30 years before arriving at The Langley early in 2000. So there's a continental flavour to the cuisine but English traditional dishes are also on offer. The Langley has 5 guest rooms, all en suite, and you can stay on either a B&B or B&B and dinner basis. As an alternative to breakfast in the hotel, the Brands will give you a £4 voucher redeemable at a café on the beach where you can watch the busy traffic passing through The Solent. The Langley boasts what must be one of the largest and most pleasant beer gardens in the country, complete with a Koi Carp pond stocked with some 800 fish, a secure children's play area with bouncy castle and trampolines, and a barbecue area.

Opening Hours: Open all day, every day

Food: Available every lunchtime & evening except Sunday evening

Credit Cards: Not accepted

Accommodation: 5 guest rooms (4 double, 1 single), all en suite

Facilities: Very extensive beer garden; secure and well-stocked children's play area; barbecue area

Entertainment: Pool table; darts; fruit machine; large screen digital television; karaoke, quiz or disco, Saturday evenings; Race Nights

Local Places of Interest/Activities: Lepe Foreshore Country Park, 1 mile; Exbury House Gardens, 3 miles; National Motor Museum, Beaulieu, 5 miles

210 The Mailmans Arms

71 High Street,
Lyndhurst,
Hampshire SO43 7BE
Tel: 02380 284196

Directions:

From Exit 1 of the M27, take the A334 to Lyndhurst (4 miles). The Mailmans Arms occupies a prominent position in the High Street

The 'capital' of the New Forest, Lyndhurst is an attractive little town, noted for its variety of small shops where you can find "anything from fresh food to Ferraris!". The town's most striking building is the Church of St Michael, rebuilt in mid-Victorian times in what John Betjeman described as "the most fanciful, fantastic Gothic style that I have ever seen". The rebuilding coincided with the heyday of the Pre-Raphaelite movement so the church contains some fine stained glass by Burne-Jones as well as a splendidly lush painting by Lord Leighton depicting *The Wise and Foolish Virgins*. In St Michael's churchyard is the grave of Mrs Reginald Hargreaves who, as a young girl named Alice Liddell, was the inspiration for Lewis Carroll's *Alice in Wonderland*.

Standing in the heart of the High Street, **The Mailmans Arms** is an appealing cream and black building, always colourful in summer with an abundance of flower tubs and hanging baskets. Louise Hodgkins and Steve Burridge are your hosts here and they also run the Stag Hotel next door so between these two establishments they offer just about everything you could want in the way of quality food, drink and accommodation. The Mailmans serves food every lunchtime and evening; the Stag offers it throughout the day. There are 3 guest rooms at the Mailmans, while the Stag has 11, - in both hotels all the rooms are en suite but while those in the Mailmans are all doubles, the Stag offers a variety of sizes. The Mailmans also offers a quiet garden at the rear, and a patio area at the front where you can watch the world go by in the busy little town.

Opening Hours: Mon-Fri: Lunchtime & evening. Sat-Sun: Open all day

Food: Every lunchtime & evening

Credit Cards: All major cards accepted

Accommodation: 3 double rooms, all en suite

Facilities: Children welcome; gardens to the rear; benches to the front

Entertainment: Darts

Local Places of Interest/Activities: The New Forest all around; Furzey Gardens, 4 miles; National Motor Museum, Beaulieu, 7 miles

The New Forest Hotel | 211

The New Forest Hotel,
Lyndhurst Road,
Ashurst,
Hampshire SO40 7AA
Tel: 02380 292721
Fax: 02380 292193

Directions:

From Exit 3 of the M27, take the M271 towards South-ampton, After 2 miles, take the A35 towards Lyndhurst. Ashurst is about 5 miles along this road. The New Forest Hotel is at the southwestern end of the town, adjacent to the railway station.

Located on the edge of the New Forest, Ashurst developed in Victorian times around the Lyndhurst Road railway station and it's here you'll find **The New Forest Hotel**. The hotel's name is appropriate since the forest stretches away to the west and south, some 145 square miles of unspoilt woodland which William the Conqueror seized from Saxon farmers and proclaimed a royal hunting ground. Today, wild deer and the famous New Forest ponies roam freely around the most extensive wild area in low-land Britain. The Forest provides ideal walking country and the Forestry Commission has also established a network of waymarked cycle routes which make the most of the scenic attractions.

It was back in 1866 that Henry and James Hine opened their 'Railway Hotel', hav-ing spent the princely sum of £101 in building it. By the time Queen Victoria stayed overnight on her way to Osborne House on the Isle of Wight, the hotel had become the New Forest Hotel. Today's owners, Pete and Cheri Bennett, continue the tradition of offering superb food, drink and accommodation. Food is available for example from noon until 10pm every day, with an outstanding menu listing a wide choice of dishes at affordable prices. You can complement your meal with wine by the bottle or glass, one of the 4 real ales or from the extensive range of other beverages. The hotel makes an ideal base for exploring the New Forest and offers a choice of 3 well-ap-pointed, en suite guest bedrooms.

Opening Hours: All day, every day

Food: Quality food available from noon until 22.00

Credit Cards: All major cards accepted

Accommodation: 3 guest rooms (2 doubles, 1 twin), all en suite

Facilities: Large beer garden with chil-dren's play area, pets corner, bouncy castle; barbecues; ample parking

Entertainment: Darts; large screen Sky TV; Quiz Night, Tuesdays; live band, Saturday evenings

Local Places of Interest/Activities: Walking/Riding in New Forest; Furzey Gardens, Minstead, 5 miles; National Motor Museum, Beaulieu, 7 miles

212 The Old House at Home

Love Lane,
Romsey,
Hampshire SO51 8DE
Tel: 01794 513175

Directions:

From Exit 2 of the M27, take the A36 towards Salisbury. At the first roundabout (0.5 miles) go right on the A3090 to Romsey (3 miles). The Old House at Home is in the centre of the town.

"Music in stone" was one visitor's response to Romsey Abbey, a majestic building containing some of the best 12th and 13th century architecture in England. The Abbey's most spectacular feature is the soaring nave which rises more than 70ft and extends for more than 76ft. Just across from the Abbey stands the town's oldest dwelling, King John's House, built around 1240 for a local merchant. It has served as a royal residence but not, curiously, for King John who died some 14 years before it was built. He may though have had a hunting lodge on the site. Just south of the town is Broadlands, once the home of the flamboyant Victorian Prime Minister, Lord Palmerston, and currently the residence of the Mountbatten family.

Only a minute's walk from Romsey town centre, **The Old House at Home** is a venerable old hostelry with a history going back some 450 years. It's an attractive building with its neat thatched roof and the interior is just as inviting, - wooden floors, old beams and lots of olde worlde character. Mine host, Barrie, has been here since 1971 and his co-tenant, Wendy, joined him in 1976. Barrie is renowned for his cooking, offering a choice of no few than 15 main courses, changed daily, and 10 starters. Food is served either in the separate restaurant, in the lounge, the bar or outside in the pleasant beer garden where barbecues are held when the weather permits. To complement your meal, there's a choice of between 2 and 4 real ales, along with all the popular beers and spirits.

Opening Hours: Open every session

Food: Available every lunchtime & evening except Tues & Sun evenings

Credit Cards: All major cards accepted

Facilities: Beer garden; patio; off road parking

Entertainment: Occasional entertainment in aid of charity

Local Places of Interest/Activities: Romsey Abbey, Guildhall both nearby; Broadlands, 1 mile; New Forest, 6 miles; City of Southampton, 9 miles

The Osborne View | 213

67 Hill Head Road,
Fareham,
Hampshire PO14 3JP
Tel: 01329 664623
Fax: 01329 668732

Directions:

From Exit 11 of the M27 follow the A27 towards Fareham for 3 miles. At Titchfield roundabout turn left on to the B3334 to Stubbington then follow signs for Hill Head Haven. The Osborne View is signposted from the centre of Fareham.

Built in 1852 as a hotel, **The Osborne View** took its name from the superb vista it enjoys across the Solent to Osborne House, Queen Victoria's Italianate mansion on the Isle of Wight which had been completed just a few years earlier. Customers can watch the cruise liners, cargo ships and yachts passing along this busy waterway, either from the spacious garden or from one of the four bars inside. Here, the decor has a strong maritime flavour, with a large scale model of the Queen Mary taking pride of place. Other interesting exhibits include photographs of the 1977 Naval Review and a montage celebrating the exploits of the Special Boat Squadron during World War II. Members of the SBS were billeted nearby and the Osborne View was a favourite watering hole.

Ian and Jenny Readman, and Ian's brother Brian, are your hosts at this welcoming hostelry, one of the family of Woodhouse Inns which rates the Osborne as its 'Top House'. Fresh fish is a speciality here and the menu of wholesome, home made food also presents a good range of snacks and light meals. The extensive choice is supplemented by daily specials listed on the blackboard. There are 5 real ales on tap and the wine list offers wines from around the world along with a selection of Old English Fruit Wines.

Opening Hours: Mon-Sat: 11.00-23.00; Sun: 12.00-22.30

Food: Available lunchtimes and evenings, Mon-Fri; noon until 21.30, Sat-Sun

Credit Cards: All major cards accepted except Diners

Facilities: Children welcome; large car park across the road

Entertainment: The view across the Solent!

Local Places of Interest/Activities: Beach at bottom of garden; riverside and coastal walks nearby; Hill Head Nature Reserve, 1 mile; Gosport Submarine Museum, 7 miles

214   The Peg & Parrot

44 Rumbridge Street,
Totton,
Southampton,
Hampshire SO40 9DS
Tel: 02380 864614

Directions:

From Exit 3 of the M27, take the M271 towards Southampton. At the end of the motorway (2 miles), take the A35 towards Lyndhurst. Totton is about 1.5 miles along this road and The Peg & Parrot is in the centre of the town.

Totton stands at the lowest bridging point of Southampton Water and has been an important crossing place since medieval times. Back in 1852 Totton was described as "picturesque, abounding with river and inland scenery and studded with agreeable residences". Since then the village has expanded enormously but something of that 19th century peace can still be found at Eling Harbour, on the southern edge of the town, and in the heart of the old village. High Street and Rumbridge Street together provide a pleasant shopping area with many personally owned small shops.

Rumbridge Street is also where you'll find **The Peg & Parrot**, a welcoming hostelry owned and run by Ann and Denis Cremin. A warm and likeable couple, they have been in the business since 1979 and at the Peg & Parrot since 1990. The inn itself has had a chequered history since it was built more than 100 years ago. It has served variously as a greengrocer's, a fish shop, a general store, a Co-op outfitter's and a wine bar before finally settling down in 1985 as an inn. An interesting feature of the pub's interior is the display of horseracing pictures and memorabilia which reflect Denis's love of the Turf. The food here is strongly recommended. It's available every lunchtime from noon until around 3pm and on Sunday you can tuck into a hearty roast lunch for a remarkable £3.75 - a price which is guaranteed for the lifetime of this guide. Obviously, it's a good idea to book ahead for this!

Opening Hours: Open all day, every day

Food: Available every lunchtime until around 15.00

Credit Cards: Not accepted

Facilities: Small beer garden; parking at rear

Entertainment: Darts; dominoes; occasional charity quiz

Local Places of Interest/ Activities: New Forest, 3 miles; City of Southampton, 3 miles; National Motor Museum, Beaulieu, 10 miles

The Rising Sun 215

74 Shore Road,
Warsash,
Southampton,
Hampshire
SO31 9FT
Tel: 01489 576898
Fax: 01489 571449

Directions:

From Exit 9 of the M27 turn south on the A27. At the first roundabout turn right onto the A3024. At the third roundabout on this road, turn left onto a minor road signposted to Warsash. Stay on this road to the waterside where you will find The Rising Sun

The busy little village of Warsash with its distinctive knapped flint houses sits on a spit of land at the mouth of the Humble estuary, with the Hamble Marina nearby. **The Rising Sun** occupies a favoured waterside location in this popular village. Warsash has a very active local history society which has traced the inn's origins back to 1784 when "a messuage and malthouse" were rented to a Mr George Parsons for 3d (1.25p) per annum.

The original building was extended in the early 1900s but parts of the old structure survived along with features such as wooden or quarry-tiled floors, and some wood-panelled walls. The upper restaurant (reached by a spiral staircase and non-smoking) has a panoramic window framing a splendid view of the Marina. Here customers are offered an excellent menu in which fish, home made pies and Spanish dishes are the specialities of the house. The downstairs restaurant also serves a good selection of 'Lite Bites' which includes an All Day Breakfast and vegetarian options. The regular menu is supplemented by daily specials and to accompany your meal there's a choice of wine by the bottle, small or large glass, 4 real ales and a wide selection of popular ales and spirits.

Opening Hours: All day, every day

Food: Every lunchtime and evening

Credit Cards: All the major cards

Facilities: Free public hard for boats; parking opposite; showers available

Entertainment: Phone for their newsletter: it provides details of the live music on offer - anything from jazz to Spanish evenings

Local Places of Interest/Activities: Hamble Marina, close by; Hollywell Woodland Park, 1½ miles; Manor Farm Country Park, 5 miles

216 The Robin Hood Inn

Durley Street,
Durley,
nr Southampton,
Hampshire SO32 2AA
Tel: 01489 860229

Directions:

From Exit 7 of the M27, take the A334 east. At the first roundabout (0.5 miles), turn left on the B3342. Stay on this road for about 2 miles to the junction with B3354. At the roundabout here go straight across on a minor road that leads to Durley (1.5 miles). The Robin Hood Inn is on the main street of the village

A few minutes drive from the pleasant little village of Durley stand the impressive ruins of the Bishop's Palace near Bishop's Waltham. It was the country residence of the Bishops of Winchester for centuries and through its portals have passed at least 12 reigning monarchs. Amongst them were Richard the Lionheart returning from the Crusades, Henry V mustering his army before setting off for Agincourt, and Henry VIII entertaining Charles V of Spain to a lavish banquet. The Palace is still a striking building, especially the Great Hall with its 3-storey tower and soaring windows. The ruins are in the care of English Heritage and entrance is free.

Back in Durley, **The Robin Hood Inn** is a charming traditional hostelry which dates back to the 17th century and possibly even further. Formerly, it was a coaching inn serving the stage coaches on the route between Southampton and Alresford. An interesting feature of the inn's lounge bar is the display of vintage artefacts such as longbows and agricultural implements. Your hosts, Euan and Lisa, offer quality home cooked food every lunchtime and evening, except Monday evening. Euan is the chef and his menu is based on fresh, top quality ingredients all cooked to order. There are 3 real ales on tap and if the weather is kind you can enjoy your refreshments in the delightful secluded garden to the rear. The garden also contains a secure children's play area, complete with swings, climbing frame and even a bouncy castle.

Opening Hours: Every session, and all day Sat, Sun

Food: Available every lunchtime and evening, except Monday evening

Credit Cards: All major cards except Amex

Facilities: Large beer garden; patio; children's play area; off road parking

Entertainment: Music once a month on Sunday evening; charity events

Local Places of Interest/Activities: Bishop's Palace, Bishop's Waltham, 3 miles; Itchen Valley Country Park, 5 miles; Manor Farm Country Park, 6 miles

The Royal Oak 217

Fritham, Lyndhurst,
Hampshire SO43 7HJ
Tel: 02380 812606
Fax: 02380 814066

Directions:

From Exit 1 of the M27, take the B3078 towards Fordingbridge. About 3 miles along this road, turn left on a minor road to Fritham. The Royal Oak is in the centre of the village

A tiny hamlet hidden away in the depths of the New Forest, Fritham was once a busy little place with more than one hundred workers producing smokeless gunpowder at Schulze's Gunpowder Factory. Using New Forest charcoal, the factory was in operation from 1865 to 1923 but all that remains are a few buildings and 'Irons Well', an artificial pond created by the factory and now a picturesque lake surrounded by wooded banks. In medieval times there was a holy well here which was reputed to cure leprosy.

This hidden-away hamlet boasts an outstanding hostelry, **The Royal Oak**, a delightful old thatched inn which was voted Pub of the Year in both 1999 and 2000 by the South Hampshire branch of the Campaign for Real Ale. All the ales served here come direct from the casks lined up behind the bar and there's always a choice of three or four real ales. The inn has also been awarded a Cask Marque for the quality of its beers. Back in 1998 there was much concern in Fritham when the inn's then landlords decided to sell up after their family had run it for 90 years. Villagers dreaded that it would be acquired by some brewery chain and 'improved'. Fortunately, local residents Clive and Juliet Bowring bought the property and another local couple, Neil and Pauline McCulloch, took over the running. So the Royal Oak remains wonderfully unspoilt, full of charm and character. Its lovely setting, appetising home made light meals, and quality ales make this a place to seek out. And there really is an oak tree here, a fine specimen shading a corner of the spacious beer garden.

Opening Hours: Mon-Fri: Lunchtime & evenings; Sat-Sun: open all day; also on Bank Holidays & Fridays in summer

Food: Available every lunchtime in summer; lunchtimes & 2 evenings a week in winter

Credit Cards: Not accepted

Facilities: Large beer garden; farmland with animals to the rear; marquee in

season and for special occasions; facilities for 10 horses to be tethered in purpose built pound and more by arrangement

Entertainment: Local musicians, Friday evenings

Local Places of Interest/Activities: New Forest all around; Golf, 2 miles; Rufus Stone, 3 miles; Furzey Gardens, 4 miles

218   The Shoe Inn

Salisbury Road,
Plaitford,
nr Romsey,
Hampshire
SO51 6EE
Tel: 01794 322397

Directions:

From Exit 2 of the M27, take the A36 towards Salisbury. About 5 miles along this road you will come to Plaitford.

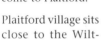

Plaitford village sits close to the Wiltshire border with the New Forest stretching for miles to the south. Its parish church of St Peter is a charming 13th century flint building which was sympathetically restored in the mid-1850s, its handsome gallery of 1800, bench pews and medieval floor tiles decorated with lions and dragons, all carefully preserved. More recently, in the 1980s, a colourful royal coat of arms was installed in the nave.

Even more interesting architecturally is **The Shoe Inn**. Seen from the main road, it's an attractive black-and-white half-timbered structure, built around 1640. But if you step around to the back, the building is even more enchanting. A beautifully-crafted thatched roof protects the original inn which dates back to the early 1400s. Alongside the building runs what used to be main road between Salisbury and Southampton. It's now just a grassy track. The interior of The Shoe Inn is quite as inviting as the outside, as olde-worlde as you could wish with its real fires and many bygones on display. Your hosts here are Jeni and Aart Noordijk. They offer their customers an appetising choice of home made soups and starters, varied main dishes and some irresistible *'Go on, indulge yourself'* home made desserts. In good weather, you can enjoy your meal in the attractive beer garden and at any time you'll find 3 real ales on tap along with an extensive choice of wines, spirits and all the usual popular beverages.

Opening Hours: Mon-Sat, 11.00-15.00, 18.00-23.00; Sun 12.00-15.00, 18.00-22.30. Closed Christmas Day

Food: Available every lunchtime & evening

Credit Cards: All major cards accepted

Facilities: Beer garden; large car park

Entertainment: Pool; darts; Friday evenings, Irish & folk music; Sunday evenings, blues & rock music

Local Places of Interest/Activities: Walking, riding & cycling in the New Forest to the south; Breamore House, 8 miles; Mottisfont Abbey Garden (NT), 10 miles

Uncle Toms Cabin   **219**

48 Havant Road,
Cosham,
Portsmouth,
Hampshire
PO6 2QZ

Tel/Fax:
02392 210145

Directions:
Cosham is on the A3, just north of Portsmouth

Once a small village a few miles from Portsmouth, Cosham has now stands on its northern fringes, conveniently located close to the A27/M27 southern coast road. Also nearby is Portchester Castle which is not only the grandest medieval castle in the county but also stands within the best-preserved site of a Roman fort in northern Europe. As if that were not enough, Portchester also boasts a superb Norman church, built around 1140. Apart from its eastern end the church is entirely Norman and, remarkably, its 12th century font of wondrously carved Caen stone has also survived the years.

In Cosham itself the place to visit is **Uncle Toms Cabin**, an attractive modern building whose picture windows look out onto a spacious beer garden. It has an open plan interior with raised areas and is pleasantly decorated and furnished throughout. Uncle Toms is very much a family run business - licensee Ivan Jones and his mum Pam are local people who have been in the hospitality for some 12 years. Ivan is the chef and his blackboard menu covers the culinary field, - anything from steaks to fish dishes, vegetarian options to filled baguettes. There are always 2 real ales on offer along with all the popular ales and spirits.

Opening Hours: All day, every day

Food: Available every lunchtime & evening

Credit Cards: Not accepted

Facilities: Beer garden; ample parking

Entertainment: Pool; darts; fruit machine; quiz machine; resident DJ, Friday evenings

Local Places of Interest/Activities: Portchester Castle, 4 miles; City of Portsmouth (*HMS Victory*, the *Mary Rose*, Royal Armouries, Charles Dickens Birthplace Museum, etc.) 5 miles

220   The Vintage Inn

Winchester Road,
Shedfield,
nr Wickham,
Hampshire SU32 2HS
Tel: 01329 834685

Directions:
From Exit 10 of the M27, take the A32 towards Alton. After about 5 miles turn left on the A334. Approximately 3 miles along this road, turn right on the B2177 to Shedfield (0.5 miles)

This little village is set beside one of the two streams that meet a few miles to the southwest to form the River Hamble, one of the shortest of England's major rivers, - it flows for barely ten miles from its sources until it spills into Southampton Water. Shedfield is a quiet place which has managed to keep out of the history books but it does have an outstanding hostelry in the form of **The Vintage Inn**. The unusual name is explained by the pub sign which shows a vintage motorcycle and rider, one reason perhaps why the inn is popular with motor cycling clubs.

The older parts of the pub were built in 1880 as two cottages and a farrier's shop. When it was converted into an inn it was named the Black Horse, then for a short while it was the Mad Hatter before finally settling down as The Vintage Inn. Mine hosts here are Jim and Marjorie Willmott, a charming and welcoming couple who have made the pub a popular venue for locals and visitors alike. Jim does the cooking, offering an appetising choice of food every lunchtime and evening. Food is served from noon until 3pm every day and, (another very good reason for the inn's popularity), from 5.30 until midnight Sunday to Thursday, and on Friday and Saturday evenings until 2am. That's what you call service! There are always 3 real ales on tap and if you are lucky with the weather you can enjoy your refreshments in the pleasant beer garden to the rear. Another amenity on offer is the adjacent large field where campers are welcome.

Opening Hours: Every session and all day Sat, Sun

Food: Every lunchtime & evening; at weekends served until 2am

Credit Cards: Not accepted; cash or cheque only

Facilities: Beer garden; children welcome; functions catered for; secure car park; large field for camping

Entertainment: Live music Friday & Saturday from 21.00

Local Places of Interest/Activities: Bishop's Palace, Bishop's Waltham, 5 miles; Manor Farm Country Park, 5 miles; City of Portsmouth, 17 miles

Ye Olde Whyte Harte

221

Hamble,
Hampshire SO31 4JF
Tel: 02380 452108
Fax: 02380 454668

Directions:

From Exit 8 of the M27, take the B3397 signposted Hamble-le-Rice. As you enter the village, Ye Olde Whyte Harte is on the right, past the church

More than 1100 years ago, in 857AD, it was by way of the Hamble Estuary that the Vikings made their first large scale raid on southern England. Thirty-five of their ships sailed in but on this occasion they were beaten off. They tried again three years later and were again repulsed. It wasn't until after the death of Alfred the Great that the Vikings finally captured Southampton, put most of its inhabitants to the sword and went on to pillage Winchester which was then by far the richest city in England. The Hamble Estuary today, by contrast, presents a peaceful scene, busy with colourful pleasure craft.

In the centre of the attractive village of Hamble stands **Ye Olde Whyte Harte**, a traditional village inn built around 1563, although some of its timbers, taken from ships' hulls, date back to 1400. In the bar is one of the oldest existing windows, a feature which is listed with English heritage. The inn has retained its olde worlde ambiance with lots of beams, flagstoned floors and a large central log fire ensuring a warm welcome during the winter months. Mine hosts, Andrea and Stewart, offer their customers a good range of home cooked food in a non-smoking restaurant and also in the bar and garden. Fresh fish is available daily and the regular menu is supplemented by daily specials. There's also a children's menu, a choice of at least 5 real ales and a selection of fine wines. Adults will appreciate the pleasant pub garden and children can have great fun on the swings and swinging boats in the secure play area.

Opening Hours: All day, every day

Food: Available every lunchtime & evening, and all day Fri, Sat, Sun.

Credit Cards: All major cards accepted

Facilities: Beer garden; children's play area; patio; barbecue area; parking at the rear

Local Places of Interest/Activities:
Hamble Marina, 1 mile; Bursledon Windmill, 2 miles; Bursledon Brickworks, 2 miles; Netley Abbey (English Heritage), 3 miles

Internet/Website: www.pubsearch.uk.com

The Hidden Inns of the South of England

This page is intentionally left blank

8 Isle of Wight

Places of Interest:

Pubs and Inns:

The Hidden Inns of the South of England

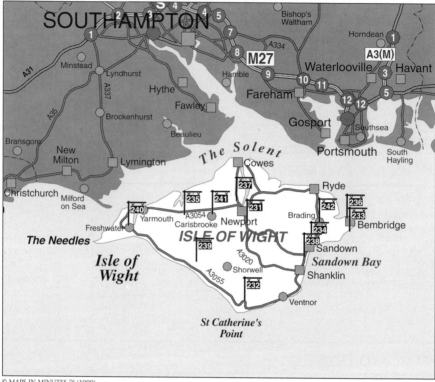

© MAPS IN MINUTES ™ (1999)

Please note all cross references refer to page numbers

The Isle of Wight has adopted a motto which declares: "All this beauty is of God". It echoes the poet John Keats' "A thing of beauty is a joy for ever", the first line of his poem Endymion which he wrote while staying on the island in the hope that its crisp country air would improve his health.

Other distinguished visitors have described Wight as "The Garden Isle", and "England's Madeira" but it was quite late in the day before the island became popular as a resort. This was partly because for centuries, right up until the 1600s, the island was a first port of call for pestiferous French raiders who made the islanders' lives a misery with their constant incursions.

The turning point came in the 1840s when Queen Victoria and Prince Albert bought an estate near East Cowes, demolished an existing house, and Albert designed and built an Italianate mansion he named Osborne House. A few years later, the Poet Laureate, Alfred, Lord Tennyson, bought Farringford on the eastern side of the island. Socially, the Isle of Wight had arrived.

Most of the island's 125,000 residents, (the town of Peterborough outnumbers all of them by about 10,000), live in the northeast quadrant of the island, with its main resort towns of Sandown and Shanklin strung along the east coast. The rest of Wight is wonderfully peaceful with a quiet, unassertive charm all of its own.

PLACES OF INTEREST

BEMBRIDGE

The most easterly point of the island, Bembridge was itself an island until the reclamation of the huge inland harbour of Brading Haven in the 1880s. The story of that major work is one of many aspects of the town's history featured in the **Bembridge Maritime Museum** which also displays ship models, artefacts from shipwrecks, and diving equipment, as well as action videos of underwater footage and lifeboat rescues. A fascinating exhibition of life in Bembridge, past and present, is portrayed in photographs and artefacts at the **Bembridge Roy Baker Heritage Centre** in Church Road. Also well worth a visit is the **Bembridge Windmill** (National Trust). Dating from around 1700, it is the only windmill to have survived on the island, with much of its wooden machinery still intact.

BRADING

For what is little more than a large village, Brading is remarkably well-stocked with visitor attractions, amongst them a diminutive **Town Hall** with whipping post and stocks outside, and a fine church housing some striking tombs of the Oglander family. The most ancient of the village's sights is the **Brading Roman Villa** which in the 3rd century was the centre of a rich and prosperous farming estate. It covers some 300 square feet and has fine mosaic floors with a representation of that master-musician, Orpheus, charming wild animals with his lyre.

The oldest surviving house on the island is now home to the **Isle of Wight Waxworks**, an all-weather family attraction displaying scenes and characters from Island history. Naturally, there's a Chamber of Horrors, as well as a World of Nature Exhibition, Professor Copperthwaites

226

Extraordinary Exhibition of Oddities, some delightful gardens, and a shop. Close by, The **Lilliput Antique Doll & Toy Museum** exhibits more than 2,000 dolls and toys, ranging across the centuries from around 2000 BC to 1945. The collection also includes dolls' houses, tinplate toys, trains, rocking horses, and many unusual and rare playthings.

On the edge of the village stands **Morton Manor**, a lovely old house, dating back to 1249, largely rebuilt in 1680, set amidst one of the finest gardens in England. The landscaped grounds feature rose and Elizabethan sunken gardens, ponds and cascades, and many mature specimen trees including the largest London Plane you're ever likely to see. Other attractions include the Stable Shop, licensed tearooms, a safe children's Play Area with a traditional Elizabethan Turf Maze, and even a Vineyard. In fact, Brading has two vineyards. The other is the well-known Adgestone Vineyard, planted in 1968 and the oldest on the island. Entry is free, as is the wine tasting. There are pony trap rides around the vineyard during the season, a gift shop and café.

A mile or so northwest of the village, **Nunwell House & Gardens** should definitely not be missed. The picturesque house has been a family home since 1522 and is of great historic and architectural interest. It was here that Sir John Oglander, an ancestor of the present owner, was host to Charles I on his last night of freedom and modern day visitors can still see the Parlour Chamber in which they met. The house is beautifully furnished, there are exhibits recalling the family's military connections, and Nunwell is surrounded by 5 acres of tranquil gardens enjoying views across the Solent.

Some of the grandest views on the island can be enjoyed from **Brading Down**, just west of the village on the minor road that leads to Downend. From Downend, it's less than a mile to **Arreton Manor** which claims, with some justification, to be "the most beautiful and intriguing house on the Isle of Wight". There was a house on this site long before Alfred the Great mentioned Arreton in his will of 885 AD and the manor was owned by successive monarchs from Henry VIII to Charles I. The present house was built during the reigns of Elizabeth and James I and it's a superb example of the architecture of that period, with mellow stone walls and Jacobean panelling complemented by furniture from the same era. Perhaps the most appealing aspect of Arreton is that indefinable atmosphere of a house that has been lived in for centuries. Other attractions include a **Museum of Childhood**, **Lace Museum**, **National Wireless Museum**, gift shop, tea-rooms and picnic area.

A mile or so southwest of Arreton Manor stands another grand old house, **Haseley Manor**. In the mid-1970s, it was a deserted and decaying shell but in a heroic work of restoration has been saved by Raymond and Krystyna Young. They have furnished and decorated the rooms in period, adding audio-visual tableaux explaining the different eras. Visitors can also watch a film showing how the mammoth task of restoration was carried out. Inside the house, there's an indoor play area for small children, a working pottery where children can try their hand at the slippery craft, tea-room and gift shop. Outside, the attractions include magnificent herb, flower and water gardens; a Children's Farm and Adventure Playground, and a picnic area.

CARISBROOKE

John Keats wrote: "I do not think I shall ever see a ruin to surpass **Carisbrooke Castle**". The castle is set dramatically on a sweeping ridge and it's quite a steep climb up from the picturesque village to the massive Gatehouse. This was built in 1598 but the oldest parts of the castle date back to Norman times, most notably the mighty Keep which, apart from Windsor, is the most perfect specimen of Norman architecture in Britain. Archaeologists believe that the Castle stands on the site a Roman fort built some thousand years earlier.

During the season costumed guides, or storytellers as English Heritage prefers to call them, conduct visitors around the noble ruins. The most poignant of their stories concern Charles I and his youngest daughter, Elizabeth. Charles was imprisoned here in the months before his trial and the guides will point out the mullioned window through which he unsuccessfully attempted to escape. After the King's execution, Cromwell's Council of State ordered that his daughter Elizabeth, 'for her own safety', should also be incarcerated at Carisbrooke. The 14 year old implored them not to send her to her father's former prison, but they were adamant.

Carisbrooke Castle

Duke's patronage led to amateur gentlemen running their own race and founding a club. The Prince Regent joined in 1817 and on his accession as George IV it was first re-christened the **Royal Yacht Club**, and then the **Royal Yacht Squadron**. Nowadays, **Cowes Week** has become the premier yachting event of the year and also a fixture in the aristocratic social calendar.

Across the River Medina, **East Cowes** is most famous for **Osborne House**, a clean-cut, Italianate mansion designed and built by Prince Albert in 1846. Queen Victoria loved "dear beautiful Osborne" and so did her young children. They had their very own house in its grounds, a full-size Swiss Cottage, where they played at house-keeping, cooking meals for

Osborne House, East Cowes

Elizabeth was a sickly child and less than a week after her arrival at the Castle she 'was stricken by fever and passed away, a broken-hearted child of fourteen'. The story touched the heart of Queen Victoria who set up a monument in Newport church where the Princess was buried. The effigy, in pure white Carrara marble, bears an inscription stating that it had been erected "as a token of respect for her virtues, and of sympathy for her misfortunes by Victoria R 1856".

More cheerful aspects of a visit to the Castle include the Donkey Centre. Donkeys walking a treadmill were once used to turn the huge 16th century wheel in the Wellhouse to draw water from a well 161ft deep. A light at the bottom of the well gives some idea of its depth. Before donkeys were trained to raise the water, the task was performed by prisoners and nowadays visitors are invited to have a go at walking the treadmill themselves.

Also within the Castle grounds are a **Coach House Exhibition** and **Victorian Island Exhibition**, the **Isle of Wight Museum** and a tea room.

COWES

Cowes' origins as the most famous yachting resort in the world go back to the early 1800s. It was then a rather shabby port whose main business was shipbuilding. In 1811, the Duke of Gloucester came to stay and as part of the rather limited entertainment on offer watched sailing matches between local fishermen. The

their parents, and tending its vegetable gardens using scaled-down gardening tools. In the main house itself, visitors can wander through both the State and private apartments which are crammed with paintings, furniture, ornaments, statuary and the random bric-à-brac that provided such an essential element in the decor of any upper-class Victorian home. Osborne House possessed a special place in the Queen's affections. It had been built by the husband she adored with an almost adolescent infatuation: together they had spent many happy family days here. After Albert's premature death from typhoid in 1861, she often returned to Osborne, her staff instructed to lay out the Prince's clothes in his dressing-room each night, and the Queen herself retiring to bed with his nightshirt clasped in her arms. In 1901 she returned to Osborne for the last time, dying here in her 83rd year, her death co-incidentally signalling the beginning of the slow decline of the British Empire over which she had presided as Queen-Empress.

FRESHWATER

Freshwater and the surrounding area are inextricably linked with the memory of Alfred, Lord Tennyson. In 1850, he succeeded Wordsworth as Poet Laureate, married Emily Sellwood, and shortly afterwards moved to **Farringford**, just outside Freshwater. The house, set in 33 acres of parkland, is now a hotel where visitors can relax in the luxuriously appointed drawing room with its delightful terrace and views across the downs. Tennyson was an indefatigable walker and, however foul the weather, would pace along nearby High Down dramatically arrayed in a billowing cloak and a black, broad-brimmed sombrero. After his death, the area was re-named Tennyson Down and a cross erected high on the cliffs in his memory. There are more remembrances of the great poet in the Church of All Saints in Freshwater town where Lady Tennyson is buried in the churchyard and a touching memorial inside commemorates their son Lionel, "an affectionate boy", who died at the age of 32 while returning from India.

As Tennyson grew older, he became increasingly impatient with sightseers flocking to Farringford hoping to catch sight of the now-legendary figure. He moved to his other home at Blackdown in Sussex where he died in 1892.

About a mile south of the town, Freshwater Bay was once an inaccessible inlet, much favoured by smugglers. From the Bay there are regular cruises around the island's most spectacular natural feature, the dreaded **Needles**. The boat trip takes you through the swirling waters around the lighthouse, and past the line of jagged slabs of gleaming chalk towering some 200ft high. The sea has gouged deep caves out of the cliffs. Two of them are known as Lord Holmes' Parlour and Kitchen, named after a 17th century Governor of the Island who once entertained his guests in the "Parlour" and kept his wines cool in the "Kitchen".

The Needles are undoubtedly at their most

The Needles

impressive when viewed from the sea, but they are still a grand sight from the land. There are some particularly striking vistas from the **Needles Old Battery** (National Trust), a Victorian coastal fort standing 250ft above the sea. Visitors pass through a 200ft long tunnel and emerge onto a platform with panoramic views. Alternatively, The **Needles Pleasure Park** at Alum Bay also has good views and offers a wide range of family entertainments, a chairlift from the clifftop to the beach, boat trips to the lighthouse, a glass-making studio and many other attractions.

NEWPORT

Set around the River Medina, Newport has a history going back to Roman times. Excavations in 1926 uncovered the well-preserved remains of a **Roman Villa**, a 3rd century farmhouse in which one side of the building was given over entirely to baths. Visitors can follow the bather's progress through changing room, cold room, warm and hot rooms with underfloor heating systems, and integral cold and hot plunge baths. A Roman style garden has been re-created in the grounds and provides an interesting insight into the wealth of new plants the Romans introduced into Britain.

Newport received its first charter back in 1190 but the growth of the small town received a severe setback in 1377 when it was completely burnt to the ground by the French. Recovery was slow and it wasn't until the 17th century that Newport really prospered again. Indirectly, this was also due to the French since the island was heavily garrisoned during the Anglo-French wars of that period. Supplying the troops with provisions and goods brought great wealth to the town.

Some striking buildings have survived, amongst them **God's Providence House**, built in 1701 and now a tea room; John Nash's elegant Town Hall of 1816; an 18th century brewers warehouse near the harbour which now houses the **Quay Arts Centre**, incorporating a theatre, two galleries, a craft shop, café and bar; and a charming **Tudor Old Grammar School**.

To the northwest of Newport, **Parkhurst Forest** offers miles of woodland walks, while over to the northeast, at **Wootton, Butterfly World and Fountain World** is home to hundreds of exotic butterflies flying free inside a beautifully landscaped indoor garden with ponds, streams, fountains and waterfalls. Other attractions include an Italian water garden, a Japanese water garden with Koi Carp, a restaurant, garden centre and shop.

Sandown

"A village by a sandy shore" was how a guidebook described Sandown in the 1870s. Since then, its superb position on sweeping Sandown Bay has transformed that village into the island's premier resort. Now a lively town, Sandown offers its visitors every kind of seaside attraction. There are miles of flat, safe sands where a Kidzone safety scheme operates during the season, a traditional Pier complete with theatre, colourful gardens, a Sunday market, abundant sporting facilities, and even pleasure flights from the nearby airfield. On the edge of the town, the **Isle of Wight Zoological Gardens** specialises in breeding severely endangered exotic species and is home to the UK's largest variety of Royal Bengal, Siberian and Chinese tigers. The Zoo is also a World Health Organisation centre for venomous snakes, their venom extracted for use in antidotes for snake bites. You may well see TV "Snake Man" Jack Corney handling these lethal reptiles and children who are photographed with a small harmless snake are presented with a handling certificate to prove it! There are all-weather snake and parrot shows, a kiddies' play area and Pets' Corner, a seafront pub and café, the Zoofari Gift Shop, and a snack bar. A Road-Runner Train operates frequent services between the Zoo and the town centre.

In Sandown's High Street, the **Museum of Isle of Wight Geology** is especially popular with children who

229

love its life-sized dinosaurs - the Isle of Wight is renowned for the number and quality of the dinosaur remains that have been discovered here. The museum, "120 million years in the making", has excellent displays on all aspects of the island's geology. As part of its educational programme, museum staff will advise you on the best places to look for fossils and, when you return with your discoveries, will identify them for you.

Shanklin

Like Sandown, Shanklin was just a small village a century or so ago. The old village has survived intact, a charming little complex of thatched houses standing at the head of the **Shanklin Chine**. The famous Chine is a spectacular ravine some 300ft deep, 180ft wide, noted for its waterfalls and rare flora. There's a Nature Trail to follow or you can join a guided tour. The **Heritage Centre** includes an interesting exhibit on PLUTO (the PipeLine Under The Ocean) secretively constructed during World War II to transport fuel from the island to the Continent during the D-Day landings. There's also a memorial to the soldiers of 40 Commando who trained in this area for the disastrous assault on Dieppe in 1942.

The old village stands on a 150ft-high cliff from which the ground slopes gently down to the safe, sheltered beach, with its long, seafront esplanade. With its scenic setting, many public gardens, and healthy climate, Shanklin has appealed to many celebrities. Charles Darwin was particularly fond of the town, the American poet Longfellow fell in love with it, and John Keats was a familiar figure in Sandown throughout the summer of 1818. The grassy open space known as Keats Green commemorates his stay here during which he wrote some of his best-known poems.

Shorwell

Pronounced 'Shorell' by Caulkheads, as Isle of Wight natives are known, the village of Shorwell has no fewer than three venerable manor houses within its boundaries. **West Court**, **Wolverton**, and **North Court** were built respectively during the reigns of Henry VIII, Elizabeth I, and James I. They possess all the charm you would expect from that glorious age of English architecture but sadly none of them is open to the public. However, you can visit St Peter's Church to gaze on its mesmerisingly beautiful 15th century wall-painting and admire its 500-year-old stone pulpit covered by an elaborate wooden canopy of 1620.

This small village has yet another attraction. **Yafford Mill** is an 18th century water mill in full working order. It's surrounded by ponds and streams where you'll find Sophie, the resident seal, and within the grounds there are paddocks which are home to rare cattle, sheep and pigs, a collection of antique farm machinery, a steam engine and narrow-gauge railway. There are also waymarked nature walks, a playground, picnic area, gift shop, tea gardens and licensed bar.

VENTNOR

Along the southeastern corner of the island stretches a 6-mile length of ragged cliffs known as Undercliffe. Clinging to the slopes at its eastern end, Ventnor has been described as "an alpinist's town" and as "a steeply raked auditorium with the sea as the stage". Promoted as a spa town in the 1830s, its distinguished visitors have included a young Winston Churchill and an elderly Karl Marx.

Ventnor Heritage Museum houses a fascinating collection of old prints, photographs and working models relating to the town's history, while **Ventnor Botanical Gardens** shelters some 10,000 plants in 22 acres of grounds, amongst them many rare and exotic trees, shrubs, alpines, perennials, succulents and conifers. There's a picnic area and children's playground, and during August the Gardens host open-air performances of Shakespeare plays. Above the town, **St Boniface Down** (National Trust), at 785ft the highest point on the island, provides some dizzying views across coast and countryside.

A mile or so to the west, in neighbouring St Lawrence, The **Isle of Wight Rare Breeds and Waterfowl Park**, set in 30 acres of coastal farmland, operates as a survival centre for more than 40 breeds of rare farm animals. The Park is also home to over 100 species of waterfowl and poultry, there's a guinea pig "village" and chipmunk "mansion", special children's areas, a unique temperate waterfall house, lakeside cafeteria and gift shop.

About 3 miles inland from Ventnor, **Appuldurcombe House** (English Heritage) is a sad shell of a once-imposing 18th century mansion, but the ornamental grounds landscaped by 'Capability' Brown provide an enchanting setting for walks and picnics.

YARMOUTH

A regular ferry links this picturesque little port to Lymington on the mainland. It was once the principal port on the island which was why Henry VIII ordered the building of **Yarmouth Castle** (English Heritage) in the 1540s. It was garrisoned until 1885 but is now disused, though much remains. The town also boasts a quaint old **Town Hall**, a working Pier, and a 13th century church rather unhappily restored in 1831. It's worth going inside to see the incongruous statue on the tomb of Sir Robert Holmes, Governor of the Island in the mid-17th century. During one of the endless conflicts with the French, Sir Robert had captured a ship on board which was a French sculptor with an unfinished statue of Louis XIV. He was travelling to Versailles to model the King's head from life. Sir Robert decided that the elaborate statue of the King (in full French armour) would do nicely for his own tomb. The sculptor was ordered to replace the Royal head with Sir Robert's. No doubt deliberately, the artist made a poor fist of the job and the head is decidedly inferior to the rest of the statue.

One mile west of this appealing little town, **Fort Victoria Country Park**, owned by the Isle of Wight Council, is one of the major leisure complexes on the island. Set on the Solent coastline, it offers an enormous range of attractions. There are unspoilt sandy beaches, woodland walks, and Ranger-guided tours around the Park highlighting the local and natural history of the area. (These must be booked ahead). Within the Park, you'll also find the largest model railway in Britain, a state-of-the-art Planetarium, a Marine Aquarium with some 80 different species of local and tropical fish, and a Maritime Heritage Exhibition. Speedboat trips are also available from the slipway next to the Boathouse Lunch & Tea Gardens.

Barley Mow

57 Shide Road,
Shide, Newport,
Isle of Wight
PO30 1HS
Tel: 01983 523318

Directions:

From the centre of Newport, take the A3056 towards Sandown. After 1 mile, just past National Tyres on the right, turn right on the B3401. The Barley Mow is on the right.

The little hamlet of Shide on the southern outskirts of Newport shot to public attention in 1926 with the discovery of the well-preserved remains of a Roman villa nearby. Built in the 3rd century, it was a farmhouse in which one wing of the building was given over entirely to baths. Visitors can follow the bather's progress through changing room, cold room, warm and hot rooms with underfloor heating systems, and integral hot and cold water plunge baths. A Roman-style garden has been re-created in the grounds and it provides a fascinating insight into the wealth of new plants the Romans introduced into Britain.

Located about half a mile from the villa, the **Barley Mow** is an attractive building, originally built in the 1830s and redeveloped in the 1950s. There's a spacious beer garden to the rear and, inside, the inn has preserved its old beams, original doors and panelled bar. Gleaming brasses, old pictures of the area and an open fireplace with a wood-burning stove all add to the inn's appeal. Sue and Reg Clements took over here in 1997 after some 15 years experience in the hospitality business. Sue is the cook and her menu offers a good choice of main meals, (curries, stir fries and steaks, for example), along with jacket potatoes, basket meals, filled baguettes and sandwiches. There's also a selection of vegetarian dishes, a children's menu and a choice of daily specials. To complement your meal, choose between one of the two real ales on tap, a short but well-selected wine list or a whole range of popular beverages.

Opening Hours: Mon-Sat: 10.30-23.00. Sun: 12.00-22.30

Food: Main meals and bar snacks, lunchtimes and evenings

Credit Cards: Not accepted

Facilities: Large beer garden; family room

also available as function room accommodating 30; parking to front and side

Local Places of Interest/Activities: Riverside walks and cycle path opposite; Roman Villa, 0.5 miles; Newport town, 1 mile; Carisbrooke Castle, 2 miles

232 The Buddle Inn

St Catherine's Road,
Niton,
Isle of Wight
PO38 2NE
Tel: 01983 730243

Directions:

From Ventnor, take the A3055 towards Freshwater. As you enter Niton village, turn left (the Buddle Inn is signposted) and the pub is on the right, overlooking the sea

Niton is the most southerly town on the island, close to St Catherine's Point and the remarkable natural feature known as Blackgang Chine. This giant fissure was created by a massive landslip in 1799 and since mid-Victorian times a pathway through the awesome scenery has been open to the public. Also well worth visiting is the Isle of Wight Rare Breeds and Waterfowl Park at St Lawrence. Set in 30 acres of coastal farmland, the Park operates as a survival centre for more than 40 breeds of rare farm animals and is also home to more than 100 species of waterfowl and poultry.

The Buddle Inn has the distinction of being the most southerly pub on the island and enjoys a superb position overlooking the English Channel. A former farmhouse, dating back to the 16th century, the inn has retained its flagstoned floor and heavily beamed ceilings. There are 2 bars, one of them - a converted barn - is used as a non-smoking, family room. In good weather there are gardens to the front and rear to enjoy. The inn is renowned for the quality of the food and drink it serves. John and Pat Bourne's menu offers an excellent choice of home-cooked food, - pub favourites such as gammon steak, a seafood selection, basket meals, and options for vegetarians and children. Complement your meal with one of the 6 real ales on tap, sample the local cider, or choose from the extensive wine list which also includes Isle of Wight wines.

Opening Hours: Mon-Sat: 11.00-23.00; Sun: 12.00-22.30

Food: Main meals, lunchtimes and evenings. Also bar snacks at lunchtime

Credit Cards: Most major cards accepted

Facilities: Children & dogs on leads welcome; beer gardens; family room; function room for 50 seated, 120 buffet style; large car park

Entertainment: Pool; occasional traditional entertainment and Morris dancing

Local Places of Interest/Activities: Coastal Path close by; Blacking Chine, Tropical Bird Park, both 2.5 miles; Rare Breeds Park, St Lawrence, 4 miles

Internet/Website: www.buddleinn@aol.com

The Crab & Lobster Inn | 233

*32 Foreland Field
Road,
Bembridge,
Isle of Wight
PO35 5TR
Tel: 01983 872244
Fax: 01983 875349*

Directions:

From Bembridge town centre follow the signs for the Lifeboat Station. You will then pick up the brown and white signs for the Crab & Lobster

Living up to its name, the **Crab & Lobster** inn specialises in seafood dishes. The waters off Bembridge Ledge provide rich catches for local fishermen and within a few hours of being landed, some of their succulently-fresh fish will be on offer at the Crab & Lobster. As you tuck into your lobster on the pub's patio, you can enjoy panoramic views across the waters in which, not very long ago, it was still swimming.

Bembridge itself used to be an island until the reclamation of huge inland harbour of Brading Haven in the 1880s. The story of that major work is one of the many aspects of the town's history featured in the Bembridge Maritime Museum. Life in Bembridge is also portrayed, in old photographs and artefacts at the Bembridge Roy Baker Heritage Centre. Also well worth a visit is the Bembridge Windmill (NT). Dating from around 1700, it is the only windmill to have survived on the island and much of its wooden machinery is still intact.

Back at the Crab & Lobster, pride of place on the menu is naturally given to local seafood dishes but there's also a good choice of meat, poultry and vegetarian options. Three real ales are on offer along with an extensive wine list.

Opening Hours: Summer: Mon-Sat: 11.00-23.00; Sun: 12.00-22.30. Winter: Mon-Sat: 11.00-1500; 18.00-23.00. Sun: 12.00-15.00; 18.00-22.30

Food: Seafood is the speciality; other dishes and bar snacks also served

Credit Cards: All major cards accepted except Amex

Facilities: Extensive patio seating enjoying views across the Solent; large car park; à la carte restaurant seating 32 guests; steps to beach

Entertainment: Quiz Nights during the winter

Local Places of Interest/Activities: Coastal walks start a few steps away; Lifeboat Station, 0.5 miles; Bembridge Windmill (NT), 1.5 miles; Bembridge Harbour and Maritime Museum, 2 miles

234 | The Fountain Inn

2 Carter Street,
Sandown,
Isle of Wight
PO36 8BP
Tel: 01983 401492
Fax: 01983 403757

Directions:

The Fountain Inn is located close to the centre of the town

Enjoying a superb position on sweeping Sandown Bay, this "village by a sandy shore" (as it was described in the 1870s) has become the island's premier resort, offering visitors a wide range of attractions. One of the most popular is the Isle of Wight Zoological Gardens which specialises in breeding severely endangered exotic species. It's also home to the UK's largest variety of Royal Bengal, Siberian and Chinese tigers. You may well see TV's "Snake Man" Jack Corney handling lethal reptiles and children who are photographed with a small harmless snake are presented with a handling certificate to prove their bravery!

Located close to the town centre, **The Fountain Inn** is an impressive Victorian building with spacious rooms and lots of style, character and charm. One of its major attractions is the extensive garden and patio at the rear. This eye-catching area full of colour is lovingly tended by Will Pressey who, together with his wife Pam, has been running the Fountain Inn since the early 1980s. Pam is the cook and her menu offers a wide range of main meals, ploughman's, panini, sandwiches, baguettes and jacket potatoes. In good weather, barbecues are held in the garden and to complement your meal, real ales, a selection of wines and a wide range of other beverages are available. This lively inn offers a good choice of entertainment, - pool and petanque, live music 3 evenings each week, and karaoke twice weekly in summer, once a week in winter.

Opening Hours: Open all day, every day

Food: Available every lunchtime & evening

Credit Cards: All major cards accepted

Facilities: Award-winning beer garden & patio area; barbecue area; ample parking

Entertainment: Darts; pool; petanque; Sky TV; live music Tue, Fri, Sat; karaoke twice weekly in summer, once a week in winter

Local Places of Interest/Activities: Isle of Wight Zoo, 1.5 miles; Shanklin Chine, 2 miles; Nunwell House, Brading, 3 miles

Horse and Groom 235

Main Road,
Ningwood, Newport,
Isle of Wight
PO30 4NW
Tel: 01983 760672

Directions:

From Newport, take the A3054 towards Yarmouth. Stay on this road for about 6 miles. As you enter Ningwood, you will see the Horse and Groom on your right

From the car park of the **Horse and Groom** you can step onto the Hamstead Trail, a 5.5 mile circular ramble that takes you through some surprisingly remote countryside and also skirts the National Trust-owned Western Haven of the Newtown River. An alternative excursion is to another National Trust property, Newtown's Old Town Hall, a quaint 18th century building which houses some interesting old documents and the town's mayoral mace.

Or you could simply settle down at the Horse and Groom, Craig and Gabrielle Knowles' inviting old hostelry located on the edge of Ningwood village. There has been an inn on this site since 1542 but the present building dates back to stage-coach days when it provided a convenient refreshment stop along the Newport to Yarmouth toll road. Ancient beams and a flagstone floor evoke that era and they co-exist happily with the more modern open-plan fireplace and an elegant, detached conservatory. Outside, the spacious beer garden has a well-equipped children's play area and children are also welcome in the Horse and Groom's dining area. Here, the menu offers a good choice of home-made main meals, (steaks, pies, traditional dishes), as well as freshly-cooked filled baguettes, ploughman's, jacket potatoes and basket meals. Vegetarian options, daily specials and desserts are listed on the blackboard. Beverages on offer include 2 real ales, (one of them brewed on the island), and a limited selection of wines available by the bottle or in a 125ml glass.

Opening Hours: Mon-Sat: 11.30-15.00; 18.00-23.00. Sun: 12.00-15.00; 19.00-22.30

Food: Main meals, lunchtimes and evenings

Credit Cards: All major cards except Amex and Diners

Facilities: Spacious beer garden; conservatory restaurant also available as a function room for up to 40 guests; large car park; children welcome

Entertainment: Pool room; karaoke evening once a month

Local Places of Interest/Activities: The Hamstead Trail passes the car park; Calbourne Mill and Newtown Old Hall, both 3 miles

236 | The Pilot Boat Inn

Station Road,
Bembridge,
Isle of Wight
PO35 5NN
Tel: 01983 872077

Directions:

From Ryde, take the B3330 to Bembridge (6 miles)

Bembridge is a popular coastal town with a spectacular coastal path that stretches for miles around this northeastern corner of the island. Just south of Bembridge, the path crosses the great Culver Cliff, a natural sanctuary for wild sea birds and now in the care of the National Trust. Within the National Trust land rises Bembridge Down, the site of an Iron Age hill fort and a location which offers some stunning views. From this vantage point you can see where the name Bembridge comes from. In Old English the word denoted "the land within the bridge" because until the 1880s the town became an island at high tide.

Located on the corner of Station Road, overlooking Bembridge Harbour, **The Pilot Boat Inn** is a striking building designed to resemble a boat with portholes as windows on the ground floor and an upper deck. Inside, the maritime theme continues in the furnishings and the pictures and prints on display. Naturally, the menu here is strong on seafood but the Pilot Boat's galley is also noted for its tasty curries and home made steak & kidney puddings. Customers can enjoy their meal in the restaurant area, lounge bar, walled patio, or on the picnic tables at the front of the inn. Devotees of real ales will find a choice of between 2 and 4 brews always on tap.

Opening Hours: Every lunchtime & evening, and all day during July & August

Food: Available every lunchtime & evening

Credit Cards: All major cards accepted

Facilities: Patio area to the front; off road parking; Walled patio area to the rear

Entertainment: Fun Quiz, Wednesday evenings; live music, Sunday evenings

Local Places of Interest/Activities: Adjacent to Bembridge Harbour and 200 yds to Maritime Museum; Bembridge Windmill (NT), ¼ mile; Lifeboat Station, ½ mile; Coastal walks nearby

Internet/Website:
e-mail: info@pilotboatinn.co.uk

The Old Stag

2 Cowes Road,
Newport,
Isle of Wight
PO30 5TW
Tel: 01983 522709
Fax: 01983 821340

Directions:

From the centre of Newport, take the A3020 towards Cowes. After about 1.5 miles you will pass the Hospital on your right. The Old Stag is a little further on, also on the right

Set around the River Medina, Newport has a history going back to Roman times. Excavations in 1926 uncovered the well-preserved remains of a 3rd century farmhouse one side of which was given over entirely to baths. A Roman style garden has been recreated in the grounds and provides an interesting insight into the wealth of new plants the Romans introduced into Britain. Just outside the town, Carisbrooke Castle is one of the island's major attractions, a superb example of massive Norman architecture.

A former coaching inn, **The Old Stag** was originally known as The Stag, was later renamed The Cask & Custard Pot and became The Old Stag in October 1999. The spacious interior is attractively furnished, and decorated with many old prints, bygones and local memorabilia. Your hosts here are Emma and Steve Perry both of whom are very experienced in the catering business. Steve is in charge of the kitchen and the range of appetising fare on offer includes tasty home made pies and Cornish pasties while the blackboard lists at least half a dozen daily specials. Meals can be enjoyed in the conservatory overlooking the garden or in the bar area. Complement your meal with one of the 3 real ales on offer along with a wide selection of other beverages. The Old Stag welcomes children and if you're planning to eat here, booking ahead is advisable.

Opening Hours: Easter-October: open all day. November-Easter: every lunchtime & evening

Food: Available every lunchtime & evening except Sunday evenings

Credit Cards: All major cards accepted

Facilities: Beer garden; patio; children's play area; conservatory restaurant; barbecues weather permitting

Entertainment: Darts; pool; card games; chess; live music on Friday evenings

Local Places of Interest/Activities: Parkhurst Forest, 1 mile; Roman Villa, Newport, 2 miles; Carisbrooke Castle, 2 miles

238 The Stag Inn

The Stag Inn,
45 Sandown Road,
Lake,
Isle of Wight
PO36 9JL
Tel: 01983 403149

Directions:

From the centre of Sandown, take the A3055 towards Shanklin. After about 1 mile, at Lake, you will come to the junction with the A3056 which is where you will find The Stag Inn

Lake is located about halfway between the two popular resorts of Sandown and Shanklin. Both towns share the 5-mile long sandy beach and grand seascapes over Sandown Bay to the English Channel. Attractions in Sandown include the Isle of Wight Zoological Gardens and the Museum of Isle of Wight Geology, - very popular with children because of its life-sized models of dinosaurs. Shanklin is famous for its Chine, - a spectacular ravine some 300ft deep and 180ft wide noted for its waterfalls and rare flora. Charles Darwin, Henry Longfellow and John Keats all fell in love with Shanklin village, a charming little complex of thatched houses standing near the head of the Chine.

The Stag Inn has been a hostelry since the 1830s but the building itself is quite a bit older and was originally two houses. The interior looks very welcoming with its low ceilings, gleaming brasses, bygones and local memorabilia, dried flower arrangements and real fires in winter. This free house is owned and run by Lesley Bullen and her son Mark, two charming people for whom nothing seems to be too much trouble. Lesley is the chef and her menu of wholesome and appetising home cooked food is supplemented by daily specials listed on the blackboard. Children are welcome and the dining room is non-smoking. Evenings at the Stag are lively affairs with karaoke four times a week and live musicians performing twice a week from Spring to the end of October. The inn also offers bed & breakfast with a double and a twin room available all year round.

Opening Hours: All day, every day

Food: In summer, from noon until 22.00; rest of the year, every lunchtime & evening

Credit Cards: All the major cards

Accommodation: 2 guest rooms (1 double, 1 twin)

Facilities: Patio; parking

Entertainment: Pool; darts; dominoes; crib; rings; Sky TV; karaoke 4 times weekly, all year; live musicians twice-weekly from Spring to October

Local Places of Interest/Activities: Lake train station, 2 mins; Lake beach 5 mins

The Three Bishops 239

Main Road,
Brighstone,
Isle of Wight
PO30 4AH
Tel: 01983 740226

Directions:

From the centre of Newport, take the B3323 to Shorwell (5 miles). In Shorwell, turn right on the B3399 to Brighstone (2 miles).

Located just a mile from the coast and at the foot of Brighstone Down (the highest point on the island, 700 ft high), Brighstone village is an appealing place with picturesque thatched cottages and an ancient church with a beautiful interior. Remarkably, three of St Mary's rectors rose through the church hierarchy to become bishops. The first was Dr Thomas Ken, rector of Brighstone from 1667-69 and author of the two famous hymns *Awake my soul and with the sun,* and *Glory to Thee, my God, this night.* Charles II appointed him bishop of Bath & Wells in 1684. Next came Samuel Wilberforce, son of the 'Great Emancipator', William. Samuel was a favourite at the Court of Queen Victoria and in 1845 she appointed him Bishop of Oxford. Then in 1866, Dr George Moberley was installed as Rector of Brighstone: just three years later he was appointed Bishop of Salisbury.

Back in 1973, **The Three Bishops Inn** was renamed in honour of these luminaries of the church. (Until then it had been known as the New Inn). As long ago as 1797 this inviting old hostelry was recorded as "providing an appetising and satisfying breakfast". Today, the inn offers a lot more than breakfast, - there's a full restaurant menu of delicious home made food, bar snacks and daily specials, complemented by superb traditional ales, including a choice of 4 real ales. The spacious restaurant, (with a no-smoking area), can cater for up to 134 people and outside there's a very extensive beer garden. This welcoming free house is run by partners Keith & Maureen Overton, Adrian Lane and Sandra Sutton. They reckon that "there's definitely something special in the air at Brighstone" and they've definitely created something special at The Three Bishops.

Opening Hours: Open every session

Food: Available every lunchtime & evening

Credit Cards: All major cards accepted except Amex

Facilities: Large beer garden; function room; barbecue area; ample parking

Entertainment: Live music most Saturday evenings

Local Places of Interest/Activities: Coastal Path, 1 mile; Brighstone Down, 1 mile; Yafford Mill, Shorwell, 2 miles

240   The Vine Inn

School Green Road/
Avenue Road,
Freshwater,
Isle of Wight
PO40 9UP
Tel: 01983 752959

Directions:

Freshwater is at the western tip of the island, on the A3054/ A3055.

Freshwater and the surrounding area are inextricably linked with the memory of Alfred, Lord Tennyson who moved to Farringford, just outside Freshwater in 1850. An indefatigable walker, he would pace along the nearby High Down, dramatically arrayed in a billowing cloak and a black, broad-brimmed sombrero. After his death, the area was re-named Tennyson Down and a cross erected high on the cliffs in his memory.

It's not known if the celebrated poet ever called in at **The Vine Inn** for a pint, but this former coaching inn which still has its stables was certainly there and had been for more than half a century. The Vine makes a pleasing picture with its whitewashed walls and masses of flower baskets, window boxes and tubs, - a display which has won a Highly Commended award for floral and garden display from Wight in Bloom Year 2000. The interior is just as inviting, - olde worlde and with lots of atmosphere. Mac and Paulette Herbert are your hosts at this lively pub where there always seems to be something going on - a quiz on Monday evenings, a Theme Night on Wednesdays, live entertainment on Fridays and also twice a month on Sunday evenings. The kitchen serves a wide selection of 'Good Old British Grub' along with vegetarian choices, salads, pasta dishes, jacket potatoes, baguettes, sandwiches and children's meals. Once a month there's a special Curry Night. Beverages available include 3 real ales and at the time of writing a beer garden to the side of the inn is being landscaped.

Opening Hours: All day, every day

Food: Available every lunchtime & evening except Sunday evening

Credit Cards: Not accepted

Accommodation: B&B available from late 2000

Facilities: Beer garden; parking

Entertainment: Darts; pool; quiz & fruit machines; Sky TV; Quiz Night, Mondays; Theme Night, Wednesdays; live entertainment, Fridays; entertainment twice a month on Sunday evenings

Local Places of Interest/Activities: Dimbola Lodge, 1 mile; Tennyson's Monument, 2 miles; The Needles, 4 miles

The Waverley

2 Clatterford Road,
Carisbrooke,
Newport,
Isle of Wight
PO30 1PA
Tel: 01983 522338

Directions:

From the centre of Newport take the B3401 towards Carisbrooke & Freshwater. The Waverley is located about 1½ miles along this road, at its junction with the B3323

The picturesque village of Carisbrooke is dominated by the dramatic ruins of its ancient castle. The massive Gatehouse was built in 1598 but the oldest parts of the castle date back to Norman times. The mighty Keep is regarded as second only to Windsor as the finest Norman architecture in Britain. During the season costumed guides, or storytellers as English Heritage prefers to call them, conduct visitors around the noble ruins. Within the castle grounds there's also a Donkey Centre, Coach House Exhibition and Victorian Island Exhibition, and the Isle of Wight Museum.

Just a short walk from the castle, **The Waverley** is a substantial Victorian building with spacious room, highly decorative ceilings and an original fireplace. On display is the fascinating range of ornamental teapots collected by your hosts, Peter and Terrie Potter. Terrie is the cook and offers both a regular menu and at least 3 daily specials, all home made and very appetising. Traditional Sunday lunch is served and for this it is definitely advisable to book ahead. The Waverley provides a wide choice of brews, amongst which there are always 3 real ales on tap, two of them guest ales with Wadsworth 6X as a permanent resident. Outside, there's a pleasant beer garden although it is not suitable for young children since it is close to the road.

Opening Hours: Every session and all day on Saturdays

Food: Available every lunchtime & evening except Sunday evening

Credit Cards: All major cards accepted

Facilities: Beer garden; ample parking

Entertainment: Darts, pool; dominoes; crib; big screen TV; live music on Friday evenings

Local Places of Interest/Activities: Carisbrooke Castle nearby; Roman Villa, Newport, 2 miles; Parkhurst Forest, 2 miles

242 The Wheatsheaf Inn

High Street, Brading,
Sandown, Isle of Wight
PO36 0DQ
Tel: 01983 408824

Directions:

From Sandown, take the A3055 towards Ryde. Brading village is
about 2 miles along this road. The
Wheatsheaf is on the left just before a sharp left turn.

In addition to the welcoming
Wheatsheaf Inn, the old inland
port of Brading offers a remarkable cluster of visitor attractions.
There's a 3rd century Roman Villa with some very fine mosaic floors; the Isle of Wight
Waxworks, which occupies the oldest surviving house on the island and, close by, the
Lilliput Antique Toy and Doll Museum with more than 2000 dolls and toys. The oldest of them dates back to 2000 BC, the most recent to 1945. Just outside the town are
two lovely old houses, both with superb gardens: Morton Manor, originally built in
1249 and remodelled in 1680, and Nunwell House & Gardens which has been a family home since 1522 and was where Charles I spent his last night of freedom.

Back in Brading High Street, the Wheatsheaf has been trading continuously ever
since it was built in 1768. One of its landlords, Harry Garland Duffett, ran the inn for
38 years from 1915 to 1953. The present landlords, Helen and Trevor Cleaver, have a
long way to go before they match that record. Their inn has two bars, with a pool
room attached to the public bar, and the Cleavers offer a wholesome menu of traditional pub food (Ploughman's, sandwiches, toasts, and so on) as well as daily home
made specials. Devotees of real ales will be pleased to find a choice of 2 authentic
brews and there's also a limited wine list. In good weather, you can enjoy your refreshments in the beer garden or on the patio. Brading is a pleasant and interesting place to
stay and the inn has a completely self-contained en suite twin room, fully equipped
for self-catering holidaymakers.

Opening Hours: Mon-Fri: 12.00-15.00;
19.00-23.00. Sat: 12.00-23.00. Sun: 12.00-
22.30

Food: Traditional pub fayre plus daily
specials

Credit Cards: Not accepted

Accommodation: Self-contained en suite
twin room with separate entrance

Facilities: Patio; beer garden; large car park
at rear; parties catered for by arrangement

Entertainment: Pool room; darts; occasional live music

Local Places of Interest/Activities: Isle of
Wight Waxworks; Lilliput Antique Doll &
Toy Museum (both 0.5 miles); Morton
Manor, 1 mile; Nunwell House; Roman
Villa (both 1.5 miles)

ALPHABETIC LIST OF INNS 243

ALPHABETIC LIST OF INNS

ALPHABETIC LIST OF INNS

ACCOMMODATION

BUCKINGHAMSHIRE

The George Inn	Little Brickhill, nr Milton Keynes, Buckinghamshire	24
Green Man	Church End, nr Eversholt, Buckinghamshire	25
The Old Bell	Wooburn Green, Buckinghamshire	29
The Royal Oak Inn	Aston Abbotts, nr Aylesbury, Buckinghamshire	33
The Swan	Great Kimble, nr Aylesbury, Buckinghamshire	36

OXFORDSHIRE

The Barley Mow	Blewbury, Oxfordshire	84
The Bird Cage	Thame, Oxfordshire	85
The Black Boy Inn	Milton, nr Banbury, Oxfordshire	86
Court Inn Hotel	Witney, Oxfordshire	91
The Crown Inn	Benson, nr Wallingford, Oxfordshire	92
The Elephant & Castle	Bampton, Oxfordshire	93
The Lampet Arms	Tadmarton, nr Banbury, Oxfordshire	96
Merrymouth Inn	Fifield, nr Burford, Oxfordshire	97
The Red Horse Inn	Shipton-under-Wychwood, Oxfordshire	99
The Red Lion	Islip, Oxfordshire	102
The Red Lion	Woodcote, Oxfordshire	104
The Swan	Bicester, Oxfordshire	105

NORTH WILTSHIRE

The Bell Inn	Broad Hinton, nr Swindon, Wiltshire	118
Crown Hotel	Wootton Bassett, Wiltshire	121
The Lord Nelson Inn	Marshfield, nr Chippenham, Wiltshire	126
The Neeld Arms	Grittleton, nr Chippenham, Wiltshire	128
The Patriot's Arms	Chisledon, nr Swindon, Wiltshire	129
The Plough Inn	Crudwell, nr Malmesbury, Wiltshire	130
The Star Inn	Hullavington, nr Chippenham, Wiltshire	132
The Wheatsheaf at Oaksey	Oaksey, nr Malmesbury, Wiltshire	134

SOUTH WILTSHIRE

Crown Inn	Alvediston, nr Salisbury, Wiltshire	150
The Crown Inn	Tisbury, Wiltshire	152
The Grosvenor Arms	Hindon, nr Salisbury, Wiltshire	154
The South Western Hotel	Tisbury, Wiltshire	158
The Stonehenge Inn	Durrington, Wiltshire	159
The Tipsy Miller	Marten, nr Marlborough, Wiltshire	161

NORTH HAMPSHIRE

The French Horn	Alton, Hampshire	176
George & Dragon	Townsend, nr Wolverton, Hampshire	177
The George Inn	Ash Vale, nr Aldershot, Hampshire	178
The Holly Bush	Headley, nr Bordon, Hampshire	180
The Lion Brewery	Ash, nr Aldershot, Hampshire	183
The White Hart	Petersfield, Hampshire	188

ALL DAY OPENING

BUCKINGHAMSHIRE

The Bell	North Marston, Buckinghamshire	16
Green Man	Church End, nr Eversholt, Buckinghamshire	25
Milton's Head	Chalfont St Giles, Buckinghamshire	27
The New Inn	Buckingham, Buckinghamshire	28
The Red Cow	Wooburn Green, Buckinghamshire	30

BERKSHIRE

The Red Lion	Mortimer West End, nr Reading, Berkshire	57
Oxfordshire		
The Angel	Witney, Oxfordshire	83
The Bird Cage	Thame, Oxfordshire	85
The Kings Arms	Chipping Norton, Oxfordshire	95
The Red Cow	Chesterton, nr Bicester, Oxfordshire	98
The Red Lion	Islip, Oxfordshire	102
The Swan	Bicester, Oxfordshire	105

NORTH WILTSHIRE

The Blue Boar	Aldbourne, Wiltshire	119
The Elm Tree	Chiseldon, nr Swindon, Wiltshire	122
The Horse & Jockey	Ashton Keynes, Wiltshire	125
The Mallard	Lyneham, Wiltshire	127
The Wellington Arms	Marlborough, Wiltshire	133

SOUTH WILTSHIRE

The Cavalier	Devizes, Wiltshire	149
The Crown Inn	Cholderton, nr Salisbury, Wiltshire	151
The Crown Inn	Tisbury, Wiltshire	152
The Dog & Gun Inn	Netheravon, Wiltshire	153
The Grosvenor Arms	Hindon, nr Salisbury, Wiltshire	154

NORTH HAMPSHIRE

The George Inn	Ash Vale, nr Aldershot, Hampshire	178
The Hen & Chicken Inn	Upper Froyle, nr Alton, Hampshire	179
The Lion Brewery	Ash, nr Aldershot, Hampshire	183

SOUTH HAMPSHIRE

The Compass Inn	Winsor, nr Cadnam, Hampshire	201
Gleneagles	Butts Ash, nr Hythe, Hampshire	203
The Gordon Arms	Fareham, Hampshire	204
The Jolly Sailor	Old Bursledon, nr Southampton, Hampshire	207
The Ketch Rigger	Hamble, Hampshire	208
The Langley Tavern	Blackfield, nr Southampton, Hampshire	209
The New Forest Hotel	Ashurst, Hampshire	211
The Osborne View	Fareham, Hampshire	213

250

ALL DAY OPENING

CHILDRENS FACILITIES

BUCKINGHAMSHIRE

The Brickmakers Arms	Wheeler End Common, nr High Wycombe, Buckinghamshire	18
The Crown	Radnage, Buckinghamshire	20
The George Inn	Little Brickhill, nr Milton Keynes, Buckinghamshire	24
Green Man	Church End, nr Eversholt, Buckinghamshire	25
The New Inn	Buckingham, Buckinghamshire	28
The Rose & Crown	Hawridge Common, nr Chesham, Buckinghamshire	32
The Royal Oak Inn	Aston Abbotts, nr Aylesbury, Buckinghamshire	33
The Stag Inn	Flackwell Heath, nr High Wycombe, Buckinghamshire	35
The Waggon & Horses	Stone, nr Aylesbury, Buckinghamshire	37

BERKSHIRE

The Duke of Wellington	Twyford, Berkshire	53
The Red Lion	Mortimer West End, nr Reading, Berkshire	57
The Rising Sun	Woolhampton, nr Reading, Berkshire	58
Royal Oak	Ruscombe, Berkshire	59
The Stag & Hounds	Pinkneys Green, nr Maidenhead, Berkshire	61

OXFORDSHIRE

The Black Boy Inn	Milton, nr Banbury, Oxfordshire	86
The Bricklayers Arms	Old Marston, Oxfordshire	87
The Red Cow	Chesterton, nr Bicester, Oxfordshire	98
The Red Horse Inn	Shipton-under-Wychwood, Oxfordshire	99
The White Hart	Harwell, Oxfordshire	106

NORTH WILTSHIRE

The Bell Inn	Broad Hinton, nr Swindon, Wiltshire	118
The Bug & Spider	Calne, Wiltshire	120
Crown Hotel	Wootton Bassett, Wiltshire	121
The Freke Arms	Swanborough, nr Highworth, Wiltshire	124
The Mallard	Lyneham, Wiltshire	127
The Patriot's Arms	Chisledon, nr Swindon, Wiltshire	129
The Shepherd's Rest	Foxhill, nr Swindon, Wiltshire	131
The Star Inn	Hullavington, nr Chippenham, Wiltshire	132

SOUTH WILTSHIRE

Crown Inn	Alvediston, nr Salisbury, Wiltshire	150
The Crown Inn	Cholderton, nr Salisbury, Wiltshire	151
The Crown Inn	Tisbury, Wiltshire	152
The Dog & Gun Inn	Netheravon, Wiltshire	153
The New Inn	Amesbury, Wiltshire	156
The Rose & Crown	Worton, nr Devizes, Wiltshire	157

NORTH HAMPSHIRE

SOUTH HAMPSHIRE

ISLE OF WIGHT

CREDIT CARDS ACCEPTED 253

BUCKINGHAMSHIRE

The Bell	North Marston, Buckinghamshire	16
The Black Lion	Well End, nr Bourne End, Buckinghamshire	17
The Brickmakers Arms	Wheeler End Common, nr High Wycombe, Buckinghamshire	18
The Cock & Rabbit Inn	The Lee, nr Great Missenden, Buckinghamshire	19
The Crown	Radnage, Buckinghamshire	20
The Derehams Inn	Loudwater, nr High Wycombe, Buckinghamshire	22
The Garibaldi	Bourne End, Buckinghamshire	23
The George Inn	Little Brickhill, nr Milton Keynes, Buckinghamshire	24
The Hit or Miss	Penn Street, nr Amersham, Buckinghamshire	26
The Old Bell	Wooburn Green, Buckinghamshire	29
The Red Cow	Wooburn Green, Buckinghamshire	30
The Robin Hood Inn	Bufflers Holt, nr Buckingham, Buckinghamshire	31
The Rose & Crown	Hawridge Common, nr Chesham, Buckinghamshire	32
The Royal Oak Inn	Aston Abbotts, nr Aylesbury, Buckinghamshire	33
The Seven Stars	Dinton, nr Aylesbury, Buckinghamshire	34
The Stag Inn	Flackwell Heath, nr High Wycombe, Buckinghamshire	35
The Swan	Great Kimble, nr Aylesbury, Buckinghamshire	36
The Waggon & Horses	Stone, nr Aylesbury, Buckinghamshire	37

BERKSHIRE

The Fox & Hounds	Theale, Berkshire	54
Horse & Groom	Mortimer, nr Reading, Berkshire	55
Lamb Inn	Hermitage, nr Newbury, Berkshire	56
The Red Lion	Mortimer West End, nr Reading, Berkshire	57
The Rising Sun	Woolhampton, nr Reading, Berkshire	58
Royal Oak	Ruscombe, Berkshire	59
The Spotted Dog	Cold Ash, nr Newbury, Berkshire	60
The Stag & Hounds	Pinkneys Green, nr Maidenhead, Berkshire	61
Ye Olde Red Lion	Chieveley, nr Newbury, Berkshire	62

OXFORDSHIRE

The Barley Mow	Blewbury, Oxfordshire	84
The Bird Cage	Thame, Oxfordshire	85
The Black Boy Inn	Milton, nr Banbury, Oxfordshire	86
The Bricklayers Arms	Old Marston, Oxfordshire	87
The Butchers Arms	Kings Sutton, nr Banbury, Oxfordshire	89
The Chequers Inn	Aston Tirrold, Oxfordshire	90
Court Inn Hotel	Witney, Oxfordshire	91
The Crown Inn	Benson, nr Wallingford, Oxfordshire	92
The Elephant & Castle	Bampton, Oxfordshire	93
The Kings Arms	Chipping Norton, Oxfordshire	95
The Lampet Arms	Tadmarton, nr Banbury, Oxfordshire	96
Merrymouth Inn	Fifield, nr Burford, Oxfordshire	97
The Red Cow	Chesterton, nr Bicester, Oxfordshire	98
The Red Horse Inn	Shipton-under-Wychwood, Oxfordshire	99
The Red Lion	Chalgrove, Oxfordshire	100

254 | *CREDIT CARDS ACCEPTED*

CREDIT CARDS ACCEPTED | **255**

256 GARDEN, PATIO OR TERRACE

GARDEN, PATIO OR TERRACE | 257

The Red Lion	Islip, Oxfordshire	102
The Red Lion	Woodcote, Oxfordshire	104
The White Hart	Harwell, Oxfordshire	106

NORTH WILTSHIRE

The Bell @ Ramsbury	Ramsbury, nr Marlborough, Wiltshire	117
The Bell Inn	Broad Hinton, nr Swindon, Wiltshire	118
The Blue Boar	Aldbourne, Wiltshire	119
The Bug & Spider	Calne, Wiltshire	120
Crown Hotel	Wootton Bassett, Wiltshire	121
The Elm Tree	Chiseldon, nr Swindon, Wiltshire	122
The Foxham Inn	Foxham, nr Chippenham, Wiltshire	123
The Freke Arms	Swanborough, nr Highworth, Wiltshire	124
The Horse & Jockey	Ashton Keynes, Wiltshire	125
The Lord Nelson Inn	Marshfield, nr Chippenham, Wiltshire	126
The Mallard	Lyneham, Wiltshire	127
The Patriot's Arms	Chisledon, nr Swindon, Wiltshire	129
The Plough Inn	Crudwell, nr Malmesbury, Wiltshire	130
The Shepherd's Rest	Foxhill, nr Swindon, Wiltshire	131
The Star Inn	Hullavington, nr Chippenham, Wiltshire	132
The Wellington Arms	Marlborough, Wiltshire	133
The Wheatsheaf at Oaksey	Oaksey, nr Malmesbury, Wiltshire	134
The White Horse Inn	Winterbourne Bassett, nr Swindon, Wiltshire	135

SOUTH WILTSHIRE

The Bruce Arms	Easton Royal, nr Pewsey, Wiltshire	148
The Cavalier	Devizes, Wiltshire	149
Crown Inn	Alvediston, nr Salisbury, Wiltshire	150
The Crown Inn	Cholderton, nr Salisbury, Wiltshire	151
The Crown Inn	Tisbury, Wiltshire	152
The Dog & Gun Inn	Netheravon, Wiltshire	153
The Grosvenor Arms	Hindon, nr Salisbury, Wiltshire	154
The New Inn	Amesbury, Wiltshire	156
The Rose & Crown	Worton, nr Devizes, Wiltshire	157
The South Western Hotel	Tisbury, Wiltshire	158
The Swan at Enford	Enford, nr Pewsey, Wiltshire	160
The Tipsy Miller	Marten, nr Marlborough, Wiltshire	161

NORTH HAMPSHIRE

The Anchor Inn	Lower Froyle, nr Alton, Hampshire	171
Carpenters Arms	Burghclere, nr Newbury, Hampshire	173
The Chequers Inn	Well, nr Long Sutton, Hampshire	174
The Five Bells	Buriton, nr Petersfield, Hampshire	175
The French Horn	Alton, Hampshire	176
George & Dragon	Townsend, nr Wolverton, Hampshire	177
The George Inn	Ash Vale, nr Aldershot, Hampshire	178
The Hen & Chicken Inn	Upper Froyle, nr Alton, Hampshire	179
The Holly Bush	Headley, nr Bordon, Hampshire	180

258 GARDEN, PATIO OR TERRACE

LIVE ENTERTAINMENT

BUCKINGHAMSHIRE

The Brickmakers Arms	Wheeler End Common, nr High Wycombe, Buckinghamshire	18
The Crown Inn	Tingewick, nr Buckingham, Buckinghamshire	21
The Garibaldi	Bourne End, Buckinghamshire	23
The New Inn	Buckingham, Buckinghamshire	28
The Old Bell	Wooburn Green, Buckinghamshire	29
The Red Cow	Wooburn Green, Buckinghamshire	30
The Royal Oak Inn	Aston Abbotts, nr Aylesbury, Buckinghamshire	33
The Waggon & Horses	Stone, nr Aylesbury, Buckinghamshire	37

BERKSHIRE

The Fox & Hounds	Theale, Berkshire	54
Lamb Inn	Hermitage, nr Newbury, Berkshire	56
The Rising Sun	Woolhampton, nr Reading, Berkshire	58
Royal Oak	Ruscombe, Berkshire	59
The Spotted Dog	Cold Ash, nr Newbury, Berkshire	60
Ye Olde Red Lion	Chieveley, nr Newbury, Berkshire	62

Oxfordshire

The Bricklayers Arms	Old Marston, Oxfordshire	87
The Butchers Arms	Fringford, nr Bicester, Oxfordshire	88
Court Inn Hotel	Witney, Oxfordshire	91
The Elephant & Castle	Bampton, Oxfordshire	93
The Red Lion	Northmoor, Oxfordshire	103
The Swan	Bicester, Oxfordshire	105
The White Hart	Harwell, Oxfordshire	106
The White Hart	Minster Lovell, nr Witney, Oxfordshire	107

NORTH WILTSHIRE

The Bug & Spider	Calne, Wiltshire	120
The Mallard	Lyneham, Wiltshire	127
The Star Inn	Hullavington, nr Chippenham, Wiltshire	132

South Wiltshire

The Crown Inn	Tisbury, Wiltshire	152
The Dog & Gun Inn	Netheravon, Wiltshire	153
The New Inn	Amesbury, Wiltshire	156
The Rose & Crown	Worton, nr Devizes, Wiltshire	157
The South Western Hotel	Tisbury, Wiltshire	158
The Stonehenge Inn	Durrington, Wiltshire	159

NORTH HAMPSHIRE

Blues Tavern II	Sleaford, nr Bordon, Hampshire	172
The Chequers Inn	Well, nr Long Sutton, Hampshire	174
The Five Bells	Buriton, nr Petersfield, Hampshire	175
The George Inn	Ash Vale, nr Aldershot, Hampshire	178
The Lamb Inn	Andover, Hampshire	182
The Lion Brewery	Ash, nr Aldershot, Hampshire	183

260 LIVE ENTERTAINMENT

RESTAURANT/DINING AREA 261

BUCKINGHAMSHIRE

The Brickmakers Arms	Wheeler End Common, nr High Wycombe, Buckinghamshire	18
The Cock & Rabbit Inn	The Lee, nr Great Missenden, Buckinghamshire	19
The George Inn	Little Brickhill, nr Milton Keynes, Buckinghamshire	24
The Hit or Miss	Penn Street, nr Amersham, Buckinghamshire	26
The Robin Hood Inn	Bufflers Holt, nr Buckingham, Buckinghamshire	31
The Rose & Crown	Hawridge Common, nr Chesham, Buckinghamshire	32
The Stag Inn	Flackwell Heath, nr High Wycombe, Buckinghamshire	35

BERKSHIRE

The Red Lion	Mortimer West End, nr Reading, Berkshire	57
The Rising Sun	Woolhampton, nr Reading, Berkshire	58
Royal Oak	Ruscombe, Berkshire	59
The Spotted Dog	Cold Ash, nr Newbury, Berkshire	60
Ye Olde Red Lion	Chieveley, nr Newbury, Berkshire	62
Oxfordshire		
The Barley Mow	Blewbury, Oxfordshire	84
The Black Boy Inn	Milton, nr Banbury, Oxfordshire	86
Court Inn Hotel	Witney, Oxfordshire	91
The Red Cow	Chesterton, nr Bicester, Oxfordshire	98
The Red Horse Inn	Shipton-under-Wychwood, Oxfordshire	99
The Red Lion	Northmoor, Oxfordshire	103
The Red Lion	Woodcote, Oxfordshire	104

NORTH WILTSHIRE

The Bug & Spider	Calne, Wiltshire	120
Crown Hotel	Wootton Bassett, Wiltshire	121
The Foxham Inn	Foxham, nr Chippenham, Wiltshire	123
The Freke Arms	Swanborough, nr Highworth, Wiltshire	124
The Horse & Jockey	Ashton Keynes, Wiltshire	125
The Lord Nelson Inn	Marshfield, nr Chippenham, Wiltshire	126
The Neeld Arms	Grittleton, nr Chippenham, Wiltshire	128
The Plough Inn	Crudwell, nr Malmesbury, Wiltshire	130
The Shepherd's Rest	Foxhill, nr Swindon, Wiltshire	131
The Wellington Arms	Marlborough, Wiltshire	133
The Wheatsheaf at Oaksey	Oaksey, nr Malmesbury, Wiltshire	134
The White Horse Inn	Winterbourne Bassett, nr Swindon, Wiltshire	135

SOUTH WILTSHIRE

The Black Dog	Chilmark, Wiltshire	147
Crown Inn	Alvediston, nr Salisbury, Wiltshire	150
The Crown Inn	Cholderton, nr Salisbury, Wiltshire	151
The Grosvenor Arms	Hindon, nr Salisbury, Wiltshire	154
The New Inn	Amesbury, Wiltshire	156

262 RESTAURANT/DINING AREA

INDEX OF PLACES OF INTEREST 263

264 INDEX OF PLACES OF INTEREST

HIDDEN INNS ORDER FORM

To order any of our publications just fill in the payment details below and complete the order form *overleaf*. For orders of less than 4 copies please add £1 per book for postage and packing. Orders over 4 copies are P & P free.

Please Complete Either:

I enclose a cheque for £ .... made payable to Travel Publishing Ltd

Or:

Card No:

Expiry Date:

Signature: ....

NAME: ....

ADDRESS: ....

....

....

POSTCODE: ....

TEL NO: ....

Please either send or telephone your order to:

Travel Publishing Ltd   Tel : 0118 981 7777
7a Apollo House   Fax: 0118 982 0077
Calleva Park
Aldermaston
Berks, RG7 8TN

The Hidden Inns of the South of England

	Price	Quantity	Value
Hidden Places Regional Titles			
Cambridgeshire & Lincolnshire	£7.99	....	....
Channel Islands	£6.99	....	....
Cheshire	£7.99	....	....
Chilterns	£7.99	....	....
Cornwall	£7.99	....	....
Derbyshire	£7.99	....	....
Devon	£7.99	....	....
Dorset, Hants & Isle of Wight	£7.99	....	....
Essex	£7.99	....	....
Gloucestershire & Wiltshire	£7.99	....	....
Heart of England	£7.99	....	....
Hereford, Worcs & Shropshire	£7.99	....	....
Highlands & Islands	£7.99	....	....
Kent	£7.99	....	....
Lake District & Cumbria	£7.99	....	....
Lancashire	£7.99	....	....
Norfolk	£7.99	....	....
Northeast Yorkshire	£6.99	....	....
Northumberland & Durham	£6.99	....	....
North Wales	£7.99	....	....
Nottinghamshire	£6.99	....	....
Potteries	£6.99	....	....
Somerset	£7.99	....	....
South Wales	£7.99	....	....
Suffolk	£7.99	....	....
Surrey	£6.99	....	....
Sussex	£7.99	....	....
Thames Valley	£7.99	....	....
Warwickshire & West Midlands	£6.99	....	....
Yorkshire	£7.99	....	....
Hidden Places National Titles			
England	£9.99	....	....
Ireland	£9.99	....	....
Scotland	£9.99	....	....
Wales	£8.99	....	....
Hidden Inns Titles			
West Country	£5.99	....	....
South East	£5.99	....	....
South	£5.99	....	....
Wales	£5.99	....	....
		_____	_____
		_____	_____

For orders of less than 4 copies please add £1 per book for postage &
packing. Orders over 4 copies P & P free.